POLAND

• Blechhammer   • Mielec

• Oswiecim   • Lvov

CZECHOSLOVAKIA

Bratislava

NGARY   • Budapest

Danube R.

Balaton

RUMANIA

Danube R.

Brasov
•

Danube R.

Ploesti
•

Turnul Severin   Bucharest
•   Craiova   •

UGOSLAVIA   • Belgrade

Danube R.

• Kraljevo

Danube R.

olit

• Nis

BULGARIA

BLACK
SEA

Dubrovnik
•   • Sofia

DRIATIC
SEA

Bari

ALBANIA

GREECE   AEGEAN SEA

D0709543

MUSTANG ACE

Memoirs of a
P-51 Fighter Pilot

BY

Robert J. Goebel

Pacifica Press

Copyright 1991 by Robert J. Goebel

All rights reserved. No part of this publication may be reproduced or transmitted in any form or by any means, electronic or mechanical, including photocopy, recording, or any information storage and retrieval system, without permission in writing from the publisher.

Requests for permission to make copies of any part of the work should be mailed to: Permissions, Pacifica Press, 1149 Grand Teton Drive, Pacifica, California 94044.

Designed by Toni Murray and Elizabeth von Radics

Printed in the United States of America

First edition

Library of Congress Cataloging-in-Publication Data

Goebel, Robert J., 1923-
Mustang ace : memoirs of a P-51 fighter pilot / Robert J. Goebel.
p. 220.
ISBN 0-935553-03-7 : $24.95
1. Goebel, Robert J., 1923-   . 2. World War, 1939-1945—Aerial operations, American. 3. Fighter pilots—United States—Biography. 4. World War, 1939-1945—Campaigns—Mediterranean Region. 5. World War, 1939-1945—Personal narratives, American. 6. United States. Army Air Forces—Biography. I. Title.
D790.G63 1991
940.54'4973—dc20   91-13477
CIP

To my one and only wife,
June,
who bore us nine fine children.
"They also serve who only stand and wait."
And wait, and wait, and wait.

To Neil Brodway
With best wishes
Bob Goerbel
08/15/01

Contents

Glossary
&
Guide to Abbreviations

Abort: A return to base without completing a mission; caused by mechanical, electrical, or some other problem.

Ack-ack: Antiaircraft fire.

A/D: An airdrome, a military airfield.

Airdrome: Airfield.

Aldis lamp: A signal light used in the control tower. Rotating the handle caused a red, yellow, or green lens to fall in front of the light source. An open sight on the top helped the operator aim the light at an aircraft.

Ammo: Ammunition.

Angle-off: The relative angle between the direction of flight of the attacking and the target aircraft. When the attacker is dead astern, the angle-off is zero.

API: Armor-piercing incendiary. A type of ammunition whose projectile, when striking a target, ignited a small pellet in the base, causing a flash.

Balls out: Maximum speed; at full throttle.

Bandit: An aircraft identified in the air as enemy.

Batman: A personal orderly for officers in the British Army.

Big friend: Heavy bomber. Rarely used by fighter pilots.

Black out: To lose vision because of excessive positive g's. Consciousness is usually retained, although increased or prolonged g's can cause loss of consciousness; the blackout point is about 4 g's but varies with the individual. At 4 g's, all parts of the body, including the blood, are forced downward toward the seat by a force equal to four times normal. The heart is unable to push the blood upward against this force. The eyeball itself is probably distorted.

Blitz cloth: A packaged cloth impregnated with chemicals and sold in the PX. Blitz cloth was used for polishing metal items of the uniform, especially brass.

Bogey: Unidentified aircraft.

BOQ: Bachelor officers' quarters.

Bought it: Killed in an accident or shot down.

Bought the farm: Killed in an accident or shot down.

Bounce: To attack from above with the advantage of speed and altitude.

Break: A violent sudden turn called by any member of a formation if attacked without warning. Calling a break triggers an emergency defensive maneuver; it is not used to call out enemy aircraft that have not actually begun an attack.

Call out: To give the first warning that unidentified aircraft have been spotted flying nearby. Transmitted by any member of a formation, the call out consists of the other aircraft's relative bearing in terms of clock position; twelve o'clock is straight ahead and six o'clock is dead astern. The call out also includes a relative measure of the enemy's elevation by stating low, very high, level, or the like.

CG: Center of gravity; fore and aft balance point.

Chocks: Wooden blocks wedged in front of and behind the main wheels of an aircraft to prevent movement while the plane is parked.

Chow: Food. Mealtime.

Clobber: To attack aggressively, shoot down. To crash (He clobbered in). To get drunk (He got clobbered).

CO: Commanding officer.

Court-martial: Military trial.

Cuban eight: A figure-eight maneuver performed in the vertical plane. It begins like a loop but after the halfway point, as the aircraft dives inverted, the airplane is half-rolled to a right-side-up position. The dive continues to gain speed, then the pilot pulls up to repeat the maneuver to complete the second half of the eight.

Deck: The surface of the ground. Zero altitude.

Deflection shot: A shot wherein an attacker must aim in front of the target when the angle-off is greater than zero. This overaiming allows for the distance the target travels while the projectiles are in transit.

D/F Station: Direction finding station. By rotating an antenna during an aircraft radio transmission, a D/F station operator could determine the relative bearing and provide the pilot with a course to steer.

E/A: An enemy aircraft.

Echelon: A formation of several aircraft in which all are on the same side of the leader, stepped back and down. Echelon formation is not used for air-to-air combat; it is used only when each aircraft must peel off in succession, as when attacking a ground target or when entering a landing pattern.

Empennage: The tail assembly of an aircraft.

Ess: While taxiing, to make a continuous series of turns resembling the letter *S*. By allowing a pilot to alternately look out each side of the aircraft as it turns back and forth, essing allows the pilot to see if the taxiway ahead is clear. For a fighter with a tail wheel and a long nose, essing is necessary because visibility directly forward is zero.

ETA: Estimated time of arrival.

External tanks: Fuel tanks carried under the wings; could be jettisoned by the pilot.

Feather: In a multiengine aircraft, reducing the drag of a failed engine by rotating the propeller blades until they are edge-on to the slipstream.

Flak: German antiaircraft fire. (From *Fl*ieger *A*bwehr *K*anone.)

Form 1: In each aircraft, a standard form on which was recorded the maintenance status of the plane. After a flight the pilot used the Form 1 to record the time flown and to list any defects discovered during the flight.

Form 5: A monthly flight record for each individual pilot; maintained by a clerk in squadron operations.

Fuselage: The body of an aircraft.

g: The force exerted on the pilot downward through the seat of the aircraft when turning at high speed. Measured as a multiple of the force of gravity. A pilot ordinarily begins to lose his vision at 4 g's.

Glycol: A chemical additive used as a coolant in liquid-cooled engines.

GSAP camera: Gunsight aiming-point camera. A 16mm camera in the wing root on the Mustang; filmed action while the gun trigger was depressed. The GSAP camera recorded the results of the machine-gun fire.

Had it: *See* Bought it.

Hardstand: A designated aircraft parking area with a concrete pad or PSP.

Harmonization: Alignment of the line of sight to the long axis of the aircraft, and the machine guns to the line of sight.

Harmonization Point: The point or range at which the guns and line-of-sight point converge.

Highball: A hand salute.

Initial: That part of a fighter landing pattern in which the pilot lines up with the runway. The initial begins one or two miles from the field.

Jink: To make quick, uncoordinated maneuvers to throw off the aim of a pursuing pilot.

Lead: When aiming an aircraft, an allowance made by an attacking pilot for the distance traveled by the target during the time it took for projectiles to travel from the guns to the target. The lead is always in front of the target on a line projected along its direction of flight. Actual lead distance is determined only by the speed of the target and the bullet transit time; however, the apparent lead is foreshortened by the angle made between the long axis of the attacking aircraft and the target. Lead was estimated by the pilot in multiples or fractions of the sight radius.

Little friend: A fighter plane. The term was used facetiously by fighter pilots when referring to themselves.

Lufbery circle: Originally conceived by World War I flying ace Raoul Lufbery as a defensive maneuver, any tight circle in which the formation flies single file behind the leader.

Mag check: Magneto check. Aircraft engines were equipped with two complete and independent ignition systems. Each consisted of a magneto, wire harness, and spark plugs. Just prior to takeoff the pilot switched off each of the systems in turn. Any drop in engine output indicated that one ignition set was not functioning properly.

MIA: Missing in action.

Mil: A measure of angle that subtends an arc of 1 foot at 1,000 feet. The ring of a gunsight with a 100-mil reticle depicts 100 feet at a range of 1,000 feet.

Milk run: An easy mission.

MPC: Military Payment Certificate. U.S. dollars were not used in foreign theaters of operation; troops were paid in MPCs, which were accepted in PXs and by local merchants.

Ops: An abbreviation for *Operations.*

Perch: The position above and to the side of a bomber; the position from which a fighter usually begins his attack.

Pipper: The dot in the center of the optical-sight picture denoting the aiming point.

POW: Prisoner of war.

Prang: An RAF expression for crash or accident.

Prop wash: The wind created by the propeller. In the air, the area of turbulence immediately behind an aircraft.

PSP: Pierced steel planking. Metal strips that lock together to form a temporary runway or taxiway.

Pursuit squadron: An archaic Army Air Corps designation for a fighter squadron.

PX: Post Exchange. A retail store on a military base.

RAF: Royal Air Force. The British air arm.

R and R: Rest and recuperation. A vacation from combat operations.

Reciprocal: The exact opposite direction. For example, the reciprocal of a heading of 010 degrees is 190 degrees.

Red line: A red line on the airspeed indicator. Marked the maximum safe airspeed limit.

Reef in: To turn an aircraft as hard as possible without inducing a high-speed stall. Reefing in requires much arm strength as well as a fine touch.

Reticle: Within an optical sight, the mask that forms the sight image on the reflector glass, which is used to aim the aircraft. The image itself is referred to as the sight reticle.

RPM: Revolutions per minute. An engine characteristic indicated on the instrument panel by the tachometer.

R/T: Radiotelephone. Radio communication. Saying the abbreviation was easier than saying the word.

Sear: A metal slide in the machine-gun mechanism; controls firing by holding or releasing the firing pin.

Shavetail: A brand-new second lieutenant.

Snap roll: A maneuver induced by jerking the stick back and kicking in rudder, causing the aircraft to rotate around its long axis in a stalled condition. A snap roll is never done in high-performance aircraft because it causes excessive stress on the structure. Certain aircraft snap unexpectedly as the result of a high-speed stall.

Split S: A manuever in which the plane half-rolls onto its back then dives vertically and ends up traveling in the opposite direction at a lower altitude and much higher speed.

Stand down: To go off duty. The term is probably a carryover from World War I trench warfare, when British soldiers were allowed to stand down from the firing step.

Taxi: To move the aircraft under its own power on the ground.

TDY: Temporary duty away from one's home station.

TO: Technical order. A publication containing aircraft maintenance, operation, and technical information.

T/O: A takeoff; to take off.

Tracer: A projectile whose end contains a pellet that glows in flight. Tracers allow the path of the projectile to be followed visually.

Vee formation: A formation in which equal numbers of aircaft fly on both sides of the leader, forming a *V* shape. An unwieldy formation of little tactical value.

Walkover: A contest or mission with no opposition.

Wingover: A maneuver to begin a dive by rolling past the vertical while dropping the nose.

Wrack in: To turn suddenly and steeply.

Wring out: To fly an aircraft at the limits of its manueverability.

Foreword

This work stems from my early attempts at researching the genealogy of my family and the realization that I had done no better than my forebears in leaving a testament for my present and future offspring. I remember myself as a lad sitting in the attic, poring over what few pictures we had of our ancestors, wondering who my great grandparents were and what they looked like. Perhaps this book will help some yet unborn child to better understand from whence he came.

I had always intended to set down my wartime experiences, but somehow the years slipped away. Now, as I approach the far side of middle age, I am warned that I had best make a start, while my recollections are still clear and my memory is more or less intact. We are a dying breed, the World War II aviator, and soon we will all be gone. I suppose there are those who will say, "Good riddance," not referring to us as individuals but to us as symbols of a barbaric and destructive way of settling disputes. War is destructive and frequently barbaric. But, on the whole, I think the fighter combatants in Europe on both sides fought a gentlemen's war, respecting each other and the unwritten conventions of individual mortal combat that had been observed since medieval times. World War II was a time when airmen could still boast, like St. Paul, that we had fought "the good fight."

In this narrative, I merely try to describe things as they were or as I perceived them to be. If my story has little literary merit, so be it; I am not a writer but a teller of things seen, felt, and done. Nor is this story an apologia for times over and past. I do not recollect, with maudlin breast-beating, the killing of my fellow pilots in other uniforms. Like the rest of my generation, in combat I did what I had to do, the best way I knew how. There was no hating, no anguish, no sense of guilt. Only an attitude of getting the job done.

Since those days I have met many ex-Luftwaffe pilots, men who were worthy adversaries. I listened as they dispassionately described the downing of an American bomber or fighter. I have concluded that their attitude, then and now, was very much like my own.

Bob Goebel

Robert J. Goebel
Torrance, California
1991

Prologue

When Hitler's armies marched into Poland in 1939, I was sixteen years old. It was a well-established tradition that one or another of the Goebel boys delivered the *Racine Journal Times* on North Main Street. Of us, my oldest brother, Norb, originally had the paper route. It was successively passed down to Larry, Roman, Dick, and Matt, until now it was mine. The extra edition was a moribund institution by this time, but it was not dead yet. So one morning the circulation manager summoned me from my bed in the early hours to sell the extras.

It was a balmy, late-summer morning, and the grass and trees were wet with dew as I hurried through the empty streets. I shouted, "Extra! Extra paper! Read all about it!"

Occasionally an upstairs window would shoot up and a head would appear, demanding to know what had happened. The daily paper cost three cents and the extra edition sold at a premium—a dime, I think—so of course I didn't sell many papers; it was too easy to turn on the radio and find out everything that was in the paper, and more. For my part, I realized that something important had happened, but, try as I might, I just couldn't see how it had anything to do with me; or Racine, Wisconsin; or the U.S.A., for that matter. Poland was so very far away. I would never have believed then that, during the next five years, the events of that day were to touch every house that I passed that morning—especially mine.

In the summer of 1940, as the clouds of war began to gather over the United States, I decided that I would like to visit my brother Matt, who had joined the Coast Guard and was stationed at Galveston, Texas. Maybe I would also visit Romie, who was in the Air Corps and based at Kelly Field, near San Antonio. I talked it over with one of my neighborhood buddies, Glen Nelson, and we agreed that hitchhiking from Wisconsin to Texas would pose no problem at all. Even if it took ten days or two weeks, we had plenty of time—no money, but plenty of time. The lack of funds did not concern us because it was warm enough to sleep outside. As for food, well, we could always eat stale bakery or hit a backdoor if we got real hungry, a not uncommon practice in those days for travelers down on their luck.

Parental approval posed some difficulty for both of us, but eventually we wore down the opposition. On the day of departure, I made a bundle of a light jacket rolled up with a few odds and ends and tied it with a short length of clothesline. My mother asked Glen how much money he had; she knew I didn't have a nickel. "Two eighty-six," he told her, and so she counted out a like sum, exactly $2.86, for me, admonishing us to keep it in a safe place and not to tell anyone we had money. I put the coins in my pocket and slipped the bills in my shoe, an action I was to regret later, when I took them out in Galveston.

Things went well the first day, and we made it to Springfield, Illinois, where we put up for the night on a loading dock at the railroad freight station. The next morning, early, we were making our way through the city streets toward the edge of town and breakfasting on a cantaloupe that had fallen into our hands from off a farmer's truck. As we walked along, I spied what looked to be folded paper money. On picking it up, I discovered that it was a five-dollar bill. Such good fortune could hardly be imagined. As we stood there relishing the moment, a lad rounded the corner and came scuttling along the sidewalk toward us, head down, scanning the ground right and left. Glen and I exchanged glances as we recognized, at the same instant, what had happened. As he came up, breathing hard, I asked him what he was looking for. He was near panic and his voice shook a little as he replied, "I lost five dollars."

For an instant, I was tempted, but only for an instant. "Here it is," I told him, holding the now-straightened bill out to him. "We found it here on the sidewalk."

With a great sigh of relief he accepted the money, thanked us several times, and was off. Glen gave me an approving nod and we walked on in silence, each thinking wistfully about what could have been bought with such a princely sum. We joked about it later, but it was hard to laugh then at the good and bad hands that the Fates had dealt us in such quick succession.

We accepted some rides that got us off the main highway, a serious mistake that found us in Malden, Missouri, with little or no chance to catch a ride. After several futile hours by the side of the deserted road, we decided to follow the advice of a local fellow who had stopped to chat. He had told us to catch the freight train at the neighboring town of Dexter and head for Poplar Bluff. At dusk, just as he had predicted, the engine came chuffing up the grade, slowly enough for us to swing aboard. I had learned from listening to my older brothers that you always caught the head end of the car so that, if you missed, you would be thrown clear. Catching the tail end involved the risk of falling between the cars and under the wheels. Once safely aboard what turned out to be an open gondola, we relaxed. I lay on my back, arms cushioned beneath my head, and watched the faint early stars swing back and forth in the sky as the train wound its way through the countryside.

Poplar Bluff was a division yard for the Missouri Pacific, so there were a fair number of hoboes in the jungle there. The jungle was a spot, usually near the yard, where the tramps congregated to exchange information; sleep; or just lie about, waiting for the next train to somewhere. There always seemed to be someone around who knew what trains were making up on which tracks and when and to where they were bound. By making a few discreet inquiries, we found out that a freight train was leaving about 11:00 that night for Little Rock. Since Little Rock was in our direction, we scouted out the track on which the 11:00 train would be made up.

We took to riding the rails quite naturally, as if we'd been doing it all our lives. When the train slowed to stop for water on the outskirts of town, it was our practice to get off. We'd walk through town and catch a car on the other side as the train pulled out. This was the best way to avoid the special agents, or railroad dicks. After a while, getting off and on seemed like an awful lot of trouble for nothing, so we began staying on the train, waiting quietly until it got under way again.

We worked our way down through Little Rock, Texarkana, Dallas, and were on our way to Houston when we came a cropper. Eight to ten of us were riding in an open car loaded with steel I beams when we stopped at Teague, Texas. As we lounged about, waiting to get going again, the silence was broken by a stern voice commanding, "All right, everybody out."

I looked up to see the face of a very mean-looking special agent peering over the edge of the car. It happened so suddenly that for a second or two, everyone was paralyzed.

"Damn it, I said everybody *out*," he shouted, banging his night-stick on the side of the steel car with all his might. It sounded like a cannon shot. In two seconds that car was empty. He lined us up alongside the train and asked each of us what we had been doing on the railroad. One fellow had the good sense to say he was going home to see his sick mother; he was told to get the hell out of there—tacit permission to get back on the train. The rest of us were unceremoni-ously marched down to the main street crossing.

"That there is the way outa town," said our captor, pointing with his nightstick. "If'n I catch any of you bastids on railroad propity agin, it'll be seventeen days on the road gang. Now git."

We got. After a hundred yards I looked back. He was still standing there, glaring after us. I tugged on Glen's sleeve, motioned with my head, and we began moving up through the crowd to the front of the column so that the others effectively screened us from his view. We ducked into the next cross street and then started running in the direction the train would take when it pulled out. We went at a good pace for five or six blocks to the edge of town, and then we turned and doubled back to the tracks. Within half a block of the rails, we slowed cautiously—just in time to see the headlights of an auto, which had been moving alongside the tracks, stop. The driver got out. We could guess who that was. As the train began to move slowly, he played his flashlight beam over each car that moved past him. We had no choice but to retreat, go another block out, and then get back to the tracks again. As we came panting up to the train, it was already moving at an alarming rate and gathering speed. With my last burst of energy, I raced alongside and grabbed at the first head-end ladder that came by. The jerk almost tore my arms out of their sockets, and I went flying head over heels into the weeds. I was momentarily stunned and couldn't figure out why Glen was looking down at me anxiously.

"You okay?" he shouted above the clattering and clanking.

"I guess so," I answered uncertainly as I struggled to my feet.

We searched around in the weeds for my bundle and then went off to find a place to sleep, giving up on that train as a bad job. We laid low and caught one out the next afternoon, gladly shaking the dust of Teague from our shoes.

In due time we arrived in Galveston, where Matt put us up for a few days and fattened us up. But we soon tired of lying on the rocks in the sun or riding the toll-free Bolivar ferry across Galveston Bay. We decided to go over to San Antonio to visit Romie. We thumbed our way to Kelly Field all right, but we had trouble finding Romie's tent because he had recently moved. However, everyone was quite helpful and eventually we located him. He was surprised and seemed genuinely glad to see us. We were outfitted with too-big fatigues, a kind of khaki coverall; shown how to salute if we met anyone with insignia on his shoulders; and off we went to the mess hall to stuff up. We heard a lot of grumbling around us about "lousy Army chow," but the portions were huge and we thought it all was absolutely delicious. The mess sergeant took one look at us and remarked with a shake of his head that the Army Air Force was really robbing the cradle these days. We must have been the youngest-looking GIs on Kelly, with the worst-fitting fatigues.

In the evening the three of us sat on the grass in front of the hangar and watched the military planes taking off and landing. Little did I suspect that in two years' time I would be starting my Aviation Cadet Pre-flight training a scant two miles away, at the San Antonio Aviation Cadet Center.

After saying good-bye to Romie, we headed straight for the freight yards. This proved to be a serious mistake. A city policeman rounded up five or six of us and took us downtown to the courthouse. Our guard ushered us to a row of wooden benches, where we awaited our fate with growing apprehension. We were advised that we were charged with vagrancy and would have to enter a plea of guilty or not guilty. A guilty plea would land us in jail. A not-guilty plea would land us in jail until they got around to trying us, finding us guilty, and then landing us in jail. It didn't seem like much of a choice.

After several hours of waiting on those steadily hardening benches, the time of reckoning arrived. We were led into a smallish courtroom, and the proceedings began. I leaned over to Glen and asked him if I could do the talking for both of us. He readily agreed. I had made up my mind that I didn't want to plead either way but wanted a chance to talk to the judge, who seemed to be a reasonable and decent man. When our turn came I tried, at one and the same time, to strike a humble pose but to speak up firmly.

"I'm not exactly sure what vagrancy is, Your Honor. We have got some money," and I showed him the clean dollar bills Matt had exchanged for the dirty, smelly ones I had kept in my shoe. Glen did the same.

"Well now, you boys wouldn't have that money very long if you rode the freight trains. You know that, don't you?" He peered over the top of his glasses at us.

"No, sir, we sure didn't know that, 'cause we never rode trains before. We hitchhiked down from Wisconsin to visit my brother in the Air Corps, and now we're on our way home," I replied innocently. I couldn't quite bring myself to try the "sick mother" bit.

"If I let you boys off, you promise to stay away from the trains?"

"Yes sir, Your Honor, we sure do," I promised, and Glen nodded his head vigorously in assent.

The judge motioned with his head toward the door, and we needed no second invitation. We left promptly. Not until we were on the street did we feel really safe enough to rejoice at our deliverance. We swore to stay on the highways until we got home, a resolution we kept all the way to southern Illinois, where we went back on the rails.

When we finally saw the "Racine City Limit" sign again, we had been gone almost a month. We had covered over 3,000 miles and still had a few cents left. But more important, I, for one, had found a self-confidence born of the realization that somehow I could get by in the world, no matter what. In retrospect, I truly believe that this trip prepared me for my later role as a single-seat fighter pilot. It had forced me to make my own decisions, to solve my own problems. In the process I had learned that I didn't have to rely on anyone anymore. Only myself.

PART I

Cadet

With eager shout, they march about,
And learn the many things
To climb and dive,
And keep alive
The hope for silver wings.

1

Although by mid 1940 the United States had come down openly on the side of the Allies in the war in Europe, my personal involvement was limited to a mild passing interest. Many Americans shared my attitude. Though the war in Europe was reported thoroughly in the United States and followed closely, few felt an emotional impact. I remember puzzling over a remark my father made about the British ambition for empire, and I suspect that his opinion about leaving Europe's troubles in Europe was shared by a sizable portion of Midwesterners. Our emotional detachment was blown away with the first bomb that was dropped at Pearl Harbor on December 7, 1941. My own interest in the war flared like a skyrocket.

There are a handful of times in one's experience when an event occurs of such import that, forever afterward, the exact circumstances are etched indelibly in the memory. I will never forget that day in 1941 or the sensation of the moment when I heard the news of the bombing. It was early on a Sunday afternoon, and I had just arrived at our high-school hangout, a soda fountain in the interurban train terminal downtown. After the initial shock, the feeling of outrage gave way to the giddy elation of being in on a great national adventure. The consensus among us teenage strategists was that it would take no more than a few months to clean up the Japanese Army and Navy. Then we would turn our attention to Europe and do the same to Germany and Italy. We were unanimous in bemoaning the fact that it would be over before we could get into the fighting. Only Tom Navratil seemed to be plagued by any doubt. In the midst of all our brave talk, he turned to me and said earnestly, "We *can* wipe them up in a couple of months, can't we?" Tom was killed in Europe three years later.

Through the rest of December and the first months of 1942, the war news was all bad. It produced a sobering effect on everyone. Bataan fell and then Corregidor, and finally we were ingloriously kicked out of the Philippines. It was considered unpatriotic to ask the question on everyone's mind: Where is the Navy? For those whose frustration drove them to ask, there was always someone to answer with the accepted cliché: "Join the Navy and find out." The man on the street had no idea how badly we had been hurt at Pearl Harbor.

Three of my brothers were already in the military service—Dick had joined the Coast Guard even before Romie and Matt had enlisted. This boded no good for my chances of getting parental approval to do the same. At nineteen, I needed their written consent.

My father was a gentle, God-fearing man who believed in the old-time ethics of hard work and scrupulous honesty. He was a devout man, faithful to all the teachings of the church. Never did I hear him use profanity, although on the occasion of a minor accident he used some German words I suspect came close enough. He never had much to say, deferring to my mother for most decisions that affected the household or the children.

She was cut from different cloth, an aggressive and strict disciplinarian. What I remember most about her was her indomitable courage. One of her favorite sayings was "Where there's a will, there's a way," and she believed every word of it. Even in small matters she absolutely refused to give up, trying anything and everything until the problem yielded under her relentless pursuit. How else could she have fed, clothed, and educated seven children during the Great Depression?

I can understand now a great deal better than I could then what a difficult thing it must have been for them to see their youngest go off to war. As it turned out, their objections were modest and easily overcome once they saw that I was determined to go. Then the question of which service to join became the biggest problem for me to solve. My first inclination was to become a Marine. I liked the idea of getting into the fighting with a minimum of time spent in training. Besides, the Marine dress uniform looked awfully good on those boys who had joined earlier and had come home on furlough. I spent many hours of reflection, trying to weigh one choice against another.

I had always been a great fan of the Army Air Corps pilots of the '30s, with their Sam Browne belts and silver wings, but I knew that this heady stuff was beyond my reach. I knew that, to qualify for membership in this elite band, one had to be a perfect physical specimen, be more than twenty years of age, and have a college degree or equivalent. What I did not know was that events in Washington were going to change all that.

In 1939 the Army Air Corps had a total of 2,000 pilots and was adding about 300 newly graduated pilots per year. Under these conditions the Air Corps could be extremely selective in setting criteria for the chosen few. But with the fall of France, President Roosevelt, the Congress, and the entire country became painfully aware that the air arm had been sadly neglected. The Air Corps needed an immediate expansion in terms of aircraft and trained manpower.

What was planned was a force of 13,000 planes by mid 1942. By August 1941, even this was considered inadequate; a study concluded that the air arm would ultimately need 63,000 planes of all types to fight the coming war. Obviously the pilot training program had to undergo some drastic changes if there were to be pilots available to fly this air armada.

The two most significant changes were implemented by General Hap Arnold. He decided to use civilian schools for Primary training and save the limited flight-training resources of the Army for Basic and Advanced. In addition, Arnold decided to reduce the original stringent requirements for air service. By the end of 1941, the cadet program was open to anyone between the ages of eighteen and twenty-seven who could pass the flight physical and a battery of written tests. Previously, all applications had gone to Washington; now, local examination boards had the authority to approve candidates, streamlining the procedure.

The word went through the young men of Racine like wildfire. On the basis of a successful preliminary physical in Milwaukee and passing the written test, candidates were sworn in to the Army as privates and thereafter sent to Kelly Field, where the *real* flight physical was administered. If the aspiring airman could not pass or if he subsequently washed out of flight training, he promptly reverted to his enlisted status and was sent to the infantry.

An incident a few years earlier made the risk of failing the physical very real to me. My Boy Scout troop was going to summer camp, and one of the requirements was to be pronounced healthy by a doctor. Several of us scouts went for the examination together. On coming out of the doctor's office, we compared the slips of paper that each of us had been given. Mine was the only one that had any extra writing on it. The typically illegible scrawl said: "Heart sound accentuated probably due to nervousness." I chose to punctuate the statement myself, putting the tiniest of dots after the second word, before turning it in to the scoutmaster. When the day of departure arrived and I had heard no news of my being disqualified, I congratulated myself on being prudent in the ways of the world. This sounded a whole lot better than being a common cheat. The second day at camp, after I had demonstrated my proficiency in the water, I asked the swimming counselor if I could go out to the raft, which was anchored some 50 yards from shore. He looked down at me and said, "Let's see, you're the lad with the bum ticker. I'll get someone to go out there with you." I hadn't fooled anyone.

This incident now loomed large in my memory. I wanted to be a flying officer, but if that was not to be I certainly had preferences other than the infantry. I finally decided to have a go at being an aviator. I passed the qualifying tests at Milwaukee with flying colors and on April 4, 1942, was sworn in and sent home as a private with a ninety-day furlough in my pocket. The Pre-flight schools were so glutted with candidates that thousands of aspirants, like me, had to wait at home until called. The monthly twenty-one-dollar check representing my private's pay was welcomed each month, but time passed with no orders.

I had married my high-school sweetheart, June Meany, in a quiet ceremony earlier. I was torn between wanting to get started on my great adventure and staying home with her. The furlough was extended twice. Finally, in August, the long-awaited summons arrived. I was to report at Milwaukee, join a group there, and then travel to the San Antonio Aviation Cadet Center to start on the long road toward the coveted silver wings.

I bade farewell to June at her parents' house, where she would be staying during my absence. There were copious tears, but we were young and confident of the future—perhaps a bit more so than the circumstances warranted. Then I went over to the old homestead, the house in which I was born and where I had grown up. It was the only home I had ever known.

The parental blessing was an institution at our house. As a young lad I had knelt with the rest of the family on the occasion of one of the older boys leaving the hearth or setting off on a long journey. The principal knelt before our parents and, with the rest of us grouped around, Mother would say an extemporaneous prayer and conclude with a blessing.

Now it was my turn. Since I was the last, I knelt alone on the worn linoleum in the kitchen. I don't remember what was said, but I do remember being shaken by the realization that I was really going this time and not coming back in a couple of weeks. I shook my father's hand, kissed my mother, and made my way down the long porch, down the uneven stairs, and onto Yout Street. My vision was blurred by the tears that welled up. I walked up La Salle Street with a heavy heart. But by the time I got to cousin Gil Gorski's house, I was on the mend. Gil and I were going in together. I waited for him outside and understood perfectly when he finally came out, silent and red eyed. We walked to the interurban train stop at High Street and Douglas Avenue in silence.

2

The train trip from Milwaukee to San Antonio was pleasant enough. There were perhaps 200 of us from all over Wisconsin and, for most, I believe, it was the first time they had been out of the state. We traveled in our own section of the train, which was a good thing because our deportment was the typical boisterous behavior of young men. There were interminable waits for buses, for orders, for officers, for more buses, for who knows what. Once under way the waits were for coal, for a green light, for water, for another train, or maybe just because the engine was tired and had to rest.

To while away the hours, I took to observing my fellow travelers, trying to figure out from what part of the state each came. I divided them into two groups: City Boys and Outlanders. The Outlanders, from places like Ladysmith and Rice Lake and Hartland, were inclined to be reticent, as if overwhelmed by being thrust into such close contact with so many strangers and being subjected to sights, sounds, and smells so different from the song of the meadowlark and the pungency of the barnyard. Outlanders were burned by the summer sun. Their red necks bulged above tight collars; indeed, all their clothing seemed to be too tight. Either their well-muscled frames could not easily be fitted into ready-made sizes or the clothing they wore "for good" was used so infrequently that it was outgrown before it was worn out. Most big mouths and know-it-alls were City Boys, but not all City Boys were loud. A goodly number, though unawed by the crowd and the clamor, were nevertheless sobered by the realization that they were going away to the Army. I suppose Gil Gorski and myself came by our membership in the City Boys honestly; Racine, with 68,000 souls, was the second largest city in Wisconsin. But I think that our shyness and insecurity made us feel more like Outlanders.

Invariably, talk turned to how things were done in the Army Air Corps. "Facts" were always put forward by someone with the straight poop from a brother, cousin, or friend who had gone in a few months earlier. Such information was devoured and then chewed again and again. The information was of little value and frequently wrong, but our curiosity had created a vacuum that demanded to be filled. Among us were those who had a few hours of flying time in Piper Cubs. These intrepid airmen were continuously surrounded by avid listeners as they spouted such esoterica as *chandelle, lazy eight, base leg*, and so on, with no fear of contradiction.

★

The San Antonio Aviation Cadet Center (SAACC) was commonly called Sack, or the Hill, no doubt because of the fact that it was on high ground overlooking Kelly Field. Much construction was still in progress at the Hill, so our group was installed in Tent City, out in the mud. As we struggled with our baggage down between the rows of tents, those who had arrived a few days earlier serenaded us with cries of "You'll be sorry!" By the time we had weathered several days on the Hill, we joined in so welcoming yet newer arrivals as they walked sheepishly past our tents.

Before moving into the barracks and getting honest-to-goodness cadet uniforms, it was necessary to be classified as Pilot. To get the classification, a recruit had to pass the flight physical and psychological and psychomotor tests. I suppose the purpose was to try to identify and weed out those individuals who had little chance of getting through flight training before spending too much time and effort on them. The rumor mill had it that, whenever a test asked the candidate to list job choices—pilot, navigator, or bombardier—in order of preference, he should insist on pilot, even to the point of listing the preference as "pilot, pilot, and pilot." That was the only rumor I can remember that appeared to have been true.

My biggest concern was the physical examination. Any feeling of well-being that I had gained from passing in Milwaukee was quickly dispelled as I listened to returnees from Kelly exclaiming about the thoroughness of all aspects of the physical, especially the eye and heart portions. My vision had always been excellent; I didn't give the depth-perception test, which everyone else seemed to fear, a second thought. But my Boy Scout experience regarding my "heart condition" still lurked in my memory. As I lay on my cot, sleepless, the night before I was scheduled to go down to Kelly, I could think of nothing else.

The next day was a blur. We were a herd of nude, two-legged cattle who followed signs, arrows, lines on the floor, and pointed fingers that directed us from place to place to be struck, stuck, pinched, and peered at. Only two verbal orders were addressed to each of us that day; both will live in infamy: "Bend over and spread your cheeks" and "Turn your head and cough." (To this day when I hear the latter, I rise up on my toes in anticipation of that dreadful stabbing finger in the groin.) Then I was in the truck on my way back up to the Hill, remembering how my heart pounded uncontrollably when the stethoscope was placed on my chest.

The worst part of the whole business was waiting for the results. Although compiling and posting them took several days, I began to haunt the bulletin board the very next day. I pored over the lists of names, searching out the G's, even though my name couldn't be there yet and I knew it. The days thereafter consisted of countless trips to the PX, the movie theater, and the mess hall. Gradually, the names of our group began to appear. Some were classified as navigators or bombardiers, and a few busted out completely, but most were tabbed to be pilots.

My cousin Gil was found to have a slight eye defect, which disqualified him from pilot training. He was told that it could be corrected by surgery to allow him to enter navigation training. He moved out to a different part of the base. He must have been keenly disappointed, but he never let it show. He remained cheerful and, what's more, he remained true to himself. Whenever a knot of pilot-hopefuls gathered, we joined in the general conversation. I laughed at ethnic jokes or leered in feigned appreciation at some especially salacious account, even though all my upbringing told me that such things were not very nice—certainly not funny. But in my zeal to be accepted, to not be marked as an oddball, I went along. Not Gil. He was made of better stuff and would speak up when he thought someone had crossed the bounds of decency. I was embarrassed for him when I should have been embarrassed for myself and the rest of us. I don't believe I appreciated Gil, probably because those manly qualities he possessed are not readily identified and valued by young men. But I see them now; he was one of the finest men I ever met. I saw him only once or twice more and then our paths diverged permanently. He died in a B-26 over France in 1944.

Finally my name appeared on the bulletin board. To my great relief, I was classified as pilot, moved into barracks on the main base, and issued a cadet uniform. The business of making me and thousands of other young civilians into members of the military establishment could now begin in earnest. For those who had previous National Guard or ROTC training, the transition was relatively easy; most of them were made cadet officers. The rest of us were ushered into a whole new world in which individuality was nonexistent. All of us were given the same short haircut. All were taught how and exactly where to attach the insignia to the uniform. The hat had to be worn square on the head and low in front, so that two fingers of the right hand would just slide between the nose and the underside of the cap visor. The belts that we were issued were very long—long enough to girdle the largest of waists and then some.

"I don't want to see any more than two inches of the end protruding beyond the buckle," the sergeant said. "Mark it and cut it off. And don't be coming to me afterward like some stupid cadets in the last class and asking me how to get the metal end back on."

I inspected the end of the belt. A brass clip had been permanently clamped onto it. I finally decided that I, too, was stupid; I couldn't figure out how to get the clip off and reinstalled. I swallowed my pride and asked an older cadet how to cut the belt down to my 28-inch waistline. He looked at me with a faintly bemused, I-must-be-tolerant expression and said, "Take the buckle off, cut off the belt and throw the piece away, and then snap the buckle back on the bare end. Don't touch the end with the brass clip."

"Oh yeah, sure. Thanks," I shot back lightly. To myself I said, "Robert, you really *are* stupid. You better wise up."

Our days were filled with approximately equal portions of ground school, close-order drill, calisthenics, and athletics. Of course, we marched in formation everywhere—to the mess hall, to school, to the theater for lectures, and to any other place where we had to go en masse—counting cadence at the top of our lungs when commanded to do so. Sometimes we sang as we marched, most often to a song appropriated from the RAF:

> I've got sixpence, jolly jolly sixpence,
> I've got sixpence, to last me all my life.
> I've got sixpence to spend and sixpence to lend
> And sixpence to send home to my wife (dear wife).
>
> No cares have I to grieve me,
> No pretty little girls to deceive me.

I'm happy as a king believe me
As we go rolling, rolling home.

Rolling home (dead drunk)
Rolling home (dead drunk)
By the light of the silvery moon,
Happy as the day that the Air Corps gets its pay
As we go rolling, rolling home.

Two other songs, almost as popular, were the Army Air Corps Song and our version of an old cavalry ballad:

Around her neck she wore a yellow ribbon,
She wore it in the springtime and the merry month of May.
And when they asked her why the hell she wore it,
She wore it for a cay-det who was far, far away.
Far away, far away,
She wore it for a cay-det who was far, far away.

The Air Corps introduced us to the mysteries and dangers of venereal disease. Most of the lecture went over my head. But the Army was dead serious, as I soon found out. Early one morning, everyone was awakened and ordered to stand at attention at the foot of his bunk, naked, while medical personnel passed down the aisle between the two lines, inspecting the root cause of all this trouble and occasionally ordering some hapless cadet to "Milk it down." I don't think they caught anyone with VD, but the "short-arm" inspections, as these visits were known, continued at odd times through the rest of Preflight. We had surrendered the right of privacy long ago, when we were first sworn in, and so this indignity was added to an already lengthening list. We looked upon this humiliation as just one more to be endured on our long quest for those magical silver wings.

I brought out my picture of June, of which I was very proud, on those occasions when the talk turned to home and girls. Most of my newfound friends inspected it with a halfhearted show of interest and made some passing comment about "pretty" or "nice"—nothing at all measuring up to my feeling about it. I thought the girl in the picture was an example of rare beauty, but I hid my disappointment in my comrades' judgment and said nothing. The picture was the black-and-white kind that had been tinted by the photographer. When I look at it now, almost half a century later, with its too-red lips and yellowing edges, I see no reason to change my mind about the beauty of the subject. Showing my fellow cadets the picture had been a mistake under the circumstances. I myself had noticed, after looking at ten or twelve such photos, that they all began to look alike. Another reason contributed to most viewers' disinterest. After being confined to the post for several weeks, most everyone—but especially the older southern boys—were focused on limited portions of the female anatomy, none including the face. All the cadets were beginning to take on a common personality, and even those individuals from puritanical backgrounds had started using the speech and manner-isms of the Hordes of the Horny. I'm sure I was no exception.

The language of the man in the ranks was not deliberately ob-scene, although it was liberally sprinkled with obscenities. It was not taught or learned; it invaded the consciousness gradually by some osmotic process, without the cadet realizing it. The idiom was not intended to be disrespectful or blasphemous or crude, but the words flowed out naturally in much the same manner, I suppose, as the equivalent four-letter words flowed from the grumbling lips of the Roman legionnaires as they tramped through the forests of Gaul.

During the next two months, our existence was conditioned by the phrase, " . . . or you'll be washed out." It was used by anyone in authority, as in "If you can't keep up in the cross-country run, you'll be washed out" or "If you faint or drop out of parade formation, you'll be washed out." This must have had the desired effect; I've never seen a more eager bunch of young men before or since.

During this period I struck up an acquaintance with Claude Greene, a rather worldly, handsome fellow several years my senior. Little did I know then that we would be constant companions for the next two years. He was one of a group that had attended a southern college—Clemson, I think—and all had entered the Aviation Cadet program together. Their manner of speaking and general attitude were so different from anything I had been exposed to that I was completely fascinated with them. Although I was married, I realized what a bumpkin I was when listening to tales of the amorous esca-pades of these fellows, even though I suspected that the tales had been embellished a little in the telling.

Brown Forbes was the other member of the Clemson ROTC group to whom I became attached. He was short, so short that I suspected he had used some ruse to get past the minimum height requirement. After I got to know him better, I was sure of it. Where most of the rest of us were timid or even scared of doing anything that would involve a risk of elimination from the program, Brown took a far more casual approach. He'd bend each rule just to the breaking point but never beyond. His speech sounded as I thought someone's from Rock Hill,

South Carolina, should sound, and there was no mistaking that high-pitched nasal laugh as it rose distinctively and often above the barrack's hum. He was a good guy and fun to be around. He and Claude and I spent much of our free time together, off post and on.

Claude bought an officer's blouse, which wasn't a blouse at all but more like a dark green, single-breasted coat finished with a belt and brass buttons. The cadet issue was not bad looking—I thought it was a dandy bit of military apparel—but Claude preferred something finer for his forays off post. One Saturday night, when we met at the Gunter Hotel to catch the bus back to base, I noticed that Claude was in a black mood, probably because of a hole the size of a half-dollar in the shoulder of his fine new blouse. When I asked him about it, he let out a string of language that started with the blouse, went through the Air Corps, the city of San Antonio, and wound up with me. I left him alone. Halfway back to the Hill, he had cooled down enough to tell me what had happened. He had succeeded in inviting a guest into his hotel room. After a while, when it began to get warm in the room, he took off his blouse. He was in such a hurry to get on with entertaining his guest that he didn't even take the time to hang the blouse in the closet; he threw it over a floor lamp. Claude said he thought he smelled something burning but was so wrapped up with his guest that he didn't take time to investigate. Later, when he did, he found that his pride and joy had a neat hole where it had rested on the light bulb. He had the blouse repaired at the tailor shop, but it never looked the same.

Another of the friendships that I formed in Pre-flight was to last through the war and beyond. Wally Goehausen was a Midwesterner, like myself; his home was Webster Grove, Missouri, so we had much in common. Since we were about the same height and because of the similarity of our surnames, it was inevitable that our paths would intertwine. He vaguely resembled a cartoon character popular at that time, and so he became Little Henry, a moniker that was to enjoy such universal appeal that not many people remembered his real name.

Wally had done a good bit of flying before signing up for Aviation Cadet training. Though he didn't put his experience on display for all to admire, as others had done, it did give him an extra measure of confidence. It never entered his head that he would not make it through to graduation; in fact, he was one of the few I picked in Pre-flight who couldn't possibly wash out of the flying training program. We were both right. He became one of the best pilots that ever strapped on a fighter plane.

I wasn't that sure of myself. I no longer felt the fear of coming in second in aerial combat that I had hidden so carefully as a lad. That was gone, discarded unconsciously somewhere along the way. My concern was more immediate and had to do with fitting in, with learning quickly enough everything I had to know to be a second lieutenant and an Air Force pilot. One day I was down on Kelly Field for some reason. As I was walking the couple of miles back up to the Cadet Center, I came upon an AT-6 Advanced Trainer that was standing temporarily on a hardstand next to the street. The airplane looked awfully big and massive. Nobody seemed to be around, so I boosted myself up hurriedly onto the wheel and then onto the wing for a peek into the cockpit. With hands cupped against the closed canopy, I peered inside. I could see the pistol grip on the stick. Down beneath the instrument panel, which was absolutely covered with dials and gauges, I made out the large square rudder pedals. Every inch of space was taken up with knobs, switches, levers, and more dials—all unfamiliar to me. I jumped down quickly and was on my way. Walking up the street, I struggled with the idea of mastering such a complicated machine.

"Let's see," I figured, "one more month in Pre-flight, two months in Primary, and two months in Basic. In five months' time, I'm going to have to *fly* that thing." I fought the sinking feeling in the pit of my stomach. Hell, it was being done every day; if some guys I had met could do it, then I could do it. But my resolve lacked conviction.

Finally the day came when we were to leave the purgatory of calisthenics, marching, and countermarching. Our class, 43-E, was to be distributed through eight or ten Primary flight schools in the Gulf Coast Training Area. I was part of the contingent that included Claude, Brown, and Little Henry Goehausen, and we were going to Corsicana, Texas, to begin our flight training. Finally.

3

The atmosphere at Corsicana was completely different from that at Pre-flight. We were attending a contract school operated by a civilian who provided the instructors, maintenance personnel, and base support. The business here was flying instruction rather than endless marching, rifle cleaning, brass shining, and the like. Not that the lessons of Pre-flight were to be forgotten—we still drilled and carried on in the military manner. But the day-to-day activities were slanted toward flying and classroom subjects associated with flying. The civilians who taught us treated us, if not as equals, at least with a modicum of respect. There was purported to be a commandant, a major, in charge. I would have thought he was a myth—some sort of Air Force trick—except that someone actually saw him once during our two-month stay. Much more in evidence were a handful of lieutenant pilots, whose job it was to perform the flight evaluation check rides.

The PT-19 Primary Trainer, the aircraft we would be flying, was a wood-and-fabric, low-wing monoplane with two open cockpits in tandem. It had no radio, so one-way communication between the cockpits was provided by a gosport, a long flexible tube that ran from the instructor's cockpit to the student's, where it branched. Each end was pushed onto a fitting over the ears of the student's helmet. In terms of audio fidelity, this device left something to be desired, especially with a nervous student who was uncertain what the instructor wanted and unfamiliar with the terminology. Short-tempered instructors were known to vent their frustration by sticking the mouthpiece of the gosport out into the slipstream. What happened inside the helmet of the poor student had to be experienced to be fully appreciated.

Our upper class had been there for a month and was almost halfway through its stint at Corsicana. From them we learned that another rumor from Pre-flight was true: More than half our class would be washed out in Primary. Even from such unimpeachable sources, it seemed incredible that this cream of the crop, which had already passed through so many wickets, would be reduced so drastically before leaving here.

I fell to observing my classmates, trying to pick out the half who would make it. They were all such smart, well-coordinated specimens that I found myself measuring them with growing dismay. I felt a cold chill of self-doubt. Did I belong here? What chance did I have, with no college and no flying experience? All I had going for me was a dogged determination, but that I had aplenty; my mother had seen to that. I had been taught early on that anything could be accomplished if only one would press forward without limit. Then too, I was driven by the terrible fear of failing after I had announced to friends and relatives back home that I was going to be an Air Corps pilot.

Five cadets were assigned to each instructor. Little Henry Goehausen and I were fortunate in drawing Mr. Pine, a soft-spoken man in his late twenties. He had infinite patience.

Most of the flying training was done at a satellite field about 20 miles from the home base. One student would fly over to the auxiliary field with the instructor, and all the others would crowd onto buses for the trip over. Then each student took his turn in the cockpit, the last one returning with the instructor at the end of the period.

Flight instrumentation in the front cockpit was limited to an altimeter. An airspeed indicator was installed, but the cover glass was painted over, rendering it unusable. Without an airspeed indicator, the early air work consisted of establishing climbs and glides by the feel of the controls and the aircraft attitude with respect to the horizon. Next came turns in which the stick and rudder had to be coordinated to produce a smooth turn without skidding or slipping.

The stick was connected to elevators on the horizontal tail and to the ailerons, the movable surfaces out on the wings. The stick controlled the airplane in two axes: pitch (that is, nose up or down) and roll (that is, wingtips up or down). The ailerons controlled roll. The rudder pedals pushed the nose right or left, a movement called yaw. When making a level turn, the pilot had to move the stick and rudder together—coordination, it was called—to produce a constant-rate turn, all the while applying back or forward pressure on the stick to stay at the same altitude. Too much aileron produced a slip; too much rudder, a yaw. When both were used in just the right amounts, the pilot felt as if he was held firmly in his seat, the same as when flying straight and level. There was no sensation of leaning, even though the pilot looked down along the lowered wing and saw the ground instead of the sky.

When the instructor called for a 90-degree turn to the left, he expected a coordinated roll-in to a fixed angle of bank; a constant rate of turn and angle of bank throughout the turn; and then a roll-out begun so that, as the wings came level on the new heading, the aircraft had turned exactly 90 degrees and was at the same altitude at which the turn was started. This way of flying was characteristic of all the maneuvers taught in Primary—a style the Army Air Force was fond of calling precision flying. If a cadet couldn't learn it or couldn't learn it quickly enough, he was not long for the program.

Learning about stalls and spins followed. Everything was demonstrated once or twice, and then the student was expected to do it. The first time Mr. Pine performed a spin and spin recovery, I was in shock as the aircraft whipped over and the green fields began to rotate around the nose. He did it again, and then the words in the gosport sounded very much like he wanted me to do a two-turn spin to the right.

I tried to remember everything he had said and done. The section lines in that part of Texas provided a ready-made grid that served nicely as north-south and east-west reference lines. I turned the aircraft to put the nose in line with the nearest one, pulled the throttle back to idle, and raised the nose well above the horizon. Then, as aileron control was lost and the plane began to shake at the onset of a stall, I snatched the stick right back and banged the right rudder all the way home. She stalled cleanly and broke over to the right, with the rudder, into a spin. One half, one, one and a half. . . . Now! I applied full opposite rudder. As the rotation slowed, I banged the stick forward to break the stall. Then, as she began to fly again, I eased the stick back, returning the aircraft to the starting altitude. I had overshot by a quarter turn, but that couldn't dim my elation; I had done it! I was going to make it! I *could* learn to fly. Mr. Pine was a little more reserved. On the ground, afterward, he gave me the usual critique in general terms and, even though I tried to draw him into giving me some kind of reassuring pat on the back, he refused the opening and strode off without further comment.

The first two weeks were pretty carefree. In every idle moment the talk was of flying and more flying. This was especially true after the evening meal, when we sat around on our bunks exchanging tidbits of information and describing our adventures of the day. I had found that I became a little nauseated in the air when the horizon flashed past the nose at odd angles, as happened while practicing spins. But I wouldn't admit this to anyone, not even Little Henry. I reasoned that the less liquid I had in my stomach, the harder it would be to vomit. So, before I was scheduled to fly, I took to eating solids only. I'm sure there was no medical basis for what I prescribed for myself, but it worked. The ropy saliva, headaches, and that awful feeling in the stomach gradually disappeared.

After a few more hours of dual flying, I felt I was getting the hang of landing the PT-19, but I couldn't really tell how much the instructor was on the controls when I thought I was doing the flying. Then, one day after shooting a couple of landings at the auxiliary field, Mr. Pine told me to taxi over to the wind tee, where several other instructors were standing. I knew that The Day had arrived. He was going to get out. Although it wasn't unexpected, I felt exhilaration and apprehension simultaneously. He climbed out of the rear cockpit, secured the lap belt, and then crouched on the wing beside me to give me some last-minute instructions. I tried to concentrate on what he was saying, but I didn't hear a thing. Then he was gone, and I was bumping along the open grass field to my takeoff position. I checked for landing traffic, swung into the wind, cast one backward glance at the empty cockpit, and opened the throttle.

As the PT-19 gathered speed, I started to think aloud. "Keep it straight. *Keep it straight!* Tail up. Now a little back pressure on the stick. I'm up. Climbing nicely. Throttle back a little, clear right. Nobody there; start a turn. That was a helluva sloppy turn. Hurry up, start another ninety right or you'll be way the hell out of the pattern. Now I'm on the downwind leg. Correct to the left a little to parallel the landing direction. Just time to wipe my sweaty palms on my pants before turning onto the base leg. Throttle back, turn, flaps down. Well, here we go. That ground is coming up awfully fast. Hold it off. Hold it off." *Bump.* A little skip. "Now I'm rolling. Not too bad."

I slowed down, turned, and taxied back. As I passed the knot of instructors, I raised my arm in a half salute. The next few circuits were easier, and I was able to relax somewhat and enjoy the pleasure of solo flight. Then it was time to come in. I taxied over to pick up Mr. Pine. Before he climbed in, he reached over and shook my hand. It was a mighty proud moment for me, and I wished that my family and friends back in Wisconsin had been there to share it with me.

Close on the heels of my first solo, the check rides began. Civilian check pilots gave periodic check rides to all students but also gave elimination rides to those who were making unsatisfactory progress. The former was routine, but the latter was the first step out the door. Of course, no one ever told the students anything, so it was always a matter of concern whenever a check ride was scheduled. If the civilian check pilot turned thumbs down, the condemned man was scheduled to ride with an Air Corps officer, who would administer the coup de grace. The aircraft used by the military pilots was sardonically dubbed the Maytag because it was the machine in which the ultimate washing out was done. Rare indeed was the cadet who survived a ride in the Maytag.

Since I was one of the first to solo, I was scheduled for a check almost immediately. Considering the state of my nerves, I thought that I did rather well. The only complaint the check rider had was that I was using too much rudder in the turns. I counted my blessings. The attrition began in earnest now, and the long faces and red eyes at chow in the evening told the story of the fledgling pilots who had had their wings clipped permanently that day. Some wanted to be left alone in their misery, others sought companionship, but the talk was always awkward. One fellow spoke loudly about how his father was going to get him reinstated through some congressman friend of the family. But, as far as I could see, it didn't do any good; he shipped out along with the other washouts.

The buses to the auxiliary field, which initially had standing room only, now had sitting room for everyone. As the days went by, the number of empty seats increased until, eventually, lucky survivors lounged across several or stretched out and slept. Just when it seemed that our class was to be exterminated, the attrition slowed and then stopped. The last ten days were relatively peaceful, and the final check rides were little more than a formality. The word came down that we were going to Majors Field at Greenville, Texas, for our Basic Flight Training. On the appointed day we were all packed and waiting for the bus convoy to take us to the railroad station. Someone counted noses and did some mental arithmetic. We had lost more than 60 percent of our class during our stay at Corsicana. The prediction that I had found so incredible two months before had turned out to be quite accurate.

4

Majors Field at Greenville, Texas, was a true Army airfield, recently hacked out of the east Texas countryside. The living accommodations were strictly GI: typical World War II temporary buildings, long and narrow, with unfinished raw wood interior and tarpaper nailed to the outside. The tarpaper was for insulation, I suppose, since it did nothing for appearance. The inside of the barracks smelled of newly sawn lumber. The boards oozed and dripped resinous sap, testifying to a recent life enjoyed as trees in the sun and rain. Metal cots were arranged down the sides of the building in two rows, allowing for a wide aisle between them. Into this space was installed the heating system: three pot-bellied stoves spaced down the length of the aisle. When the winter wind whistled across the Texas plains, those coal stoves developed an insatiable appetite that had to be fed from coal scuttles filled from bins behind the barracks. Humidity was supplied by a large can of water set on each of the stoves. One of the more memorable malfunctions of our central heating system had nothing to do with equipment failure. One weekend, a cadet, overly full of good cheer, woke up during the night with a distended bladder. He decided the water can made as good a urinal as those out in the latrine. Perhaps the facts that the latrine was a hundred feet from the barracks and it was bitter cold outside had something to do with his decision. As luck would have it, the stove was very hot and boiled the contents of the can to dryness in short order. A very distinctive smell pervaded the room and remained for several days, in spite of our efforts to air it out. There was a lot of finger pointing and some muttered threats about how things were going to be if it ever happened again, but the culprit was never found out for sure.

The BT-13 Basic Trainer, or Vultee Vibrator, as it was called by the cadets, was a sizable step up from the primary trainer. It was still a low-wing monoplane with two cockpits in tandem, but the similarity to the PT-19 ended there. The BT-13 was all metal with a Plexiglas greenhouse and sliding canopies over each cockpit. The engine had over 400 horsepower and drove a two-position propeller, either pitch being selectable from the cockpit. A coffee-grinder radio had to be cranked to the desired frequency and was used for communication with the control tower. The radio also had an intercom mode for communication between student and instructor, so the gosport mouthpiece held out into the slipstream was one weapon removed from the instructor's arsenal.

After gaining a measure of familiarity and confidence in the primary trainer, the BT-13 seemed terribly big and complicated. The first few flights felt awkward, as if I were starting all over again. I had trouble landing the BT-13, and almost everyone soloed before I did. My instructor didn't help any, either. He was a first lieutenant, a cocky little bugger who had the unnerving habit of complaining in a high-pitched whining voice about everything I did in the air. When it was time to come in from my first dual ride, I pulled the throttle back and began making gliding turns down to traffic-pattern altitude, as I had been taught in Primary.

"What the hell are you doing?" he yelled. "You're not in Primary now. We *fly* the airplane in Basic."

I wasn't at all sure what he meant, but I figured I better do something different. The entry to the pattern was almost directly beneath me, so I rolled it over and did a near split S, pulling out right at the traffic-pattern altitude and on the right heading—except I was going about twice as fast as I wanted to.

All he said was, "That's better. Next time make a clearing turn first."

He left the distinct impression that he was not at all keen on instructing. When he received orders assigning him to heavy-bomber training a few weeks later, his joy was easily matched by that of his students. I got on much better with his replacement.

In a short time we had all recovered the proficiency we had achieved in the PT-19 and, while flying the BT-13, were able to duplicate the maneuvers we had learned in Primary. But some new lessons were waiting for us, too. We were to be initiated into the rudiments of formation flying. Heretofore we had never been allowed to come anywhere near another plane while practicing our air work. Now we were to be taught to fly a wing position of a two-ship formation, the basic unit of all operational flying.

The objective was to maintain a fixed position with respect to the leader, a position stepped down and away and far enough aft to provide clearance to avoid a collision. This was hard work and required total concentration. For one thing, the throttle had to be moved continuously to hold station. Since there was a time lag between the application or reduction of power and the response of the aircraft, the throttle movement had to be made at the first sign of divergence. If this was not done promptly and positively, the result was a constant cycle of overrunning followed by excessive lagging. All the while, the airplane had to be flown with stick and rudder to maintain the up-and-down and in-and-out position.

After we mastered straight-and-level formation flight, we started turning in formation. Our turns gradually increased in steepness. There seemed to be something weird and unnatural about being above the lead airplane in a steep turn, looking down at it with the earth in the background. The first few times, I tensed up, half expecting to fall down into the leader. But I didn't—for the same reason that I didn't fall against the low side of the cockpit: centrifugal force. After doing steep turns on several flights, I took all the sensations in stride, as if formation flying was the most natural thing in the world.

About halfway through our stay at Majors Field, we were introduced to night flying. The rumormongers who made it their business to pass along every bit of gossip picked up while sitting in the latrine made the usual dire predictions. After listening to some of them, you had to conclude that it was suicidal to fly at night. At night we were all going to:

    a. Land 50 feet in the air
    b. Get lost on the cross-country flight
    c. Get vertigo and spin in
    d. All of the above

We soon discovered that, so long as we observed the minimum precautions and followed instructions, we could learn night flying in relative safety. Once the initial mystery and fear were gone, we were as much at home in the air at night as in daylight.

While we were at Primary, the cross talk about flying gave each of us some kind of feel for what the other students were doing in the air. But even listening closely to the more articulate, I couldn't figure out where I fitted among them as a pilot. True, we had all run the gauntlet and survived, so we had to be somewhat on the same level of accomplishment, but I was still curious and wanted to fly with my peers and see for myself. Now, in Basic, it was going to happen. Cadets were scheduled to fly dual, practicing together and observing for each other. And I discovered what the instructors had known all along; some of us were a little rougher on the controls, some a bit slower and more methodical, but essentially we all flew alike. I thought it was great fun to fly with another cadet. I think we all did.

Our tactical officers—administrative supervisors—were young lieutenants fresh out of Officer Candidate School. Having completed just three months of training, they were commonly referred to as Ninety-day Wonders. Because they were not flying officers and did not wear wings, we cadets treated them correctly but with a slight air of disdain, which did not go unnoticed and was deeply resented. To a man, the lieutenants considered it a sacred duty to bring the cadets to heel, and they missed no opportunity to make life miserable for us. The standard unit of punishment was the tour—one hour of marching back and forth in a designated area, with a parachute strapped to the culprit's back, during what would normally have been free time. With sadistic pleasure the tac officers handed out tours for the smallest of transgressions. One officer, a tall gangly fellow called Lazy Eight behind his back, had occasion to test the resourcefulness of his charges and found them equal to the task. Standing orders required that anyone going from the barracks to the latrine to take a shower had to wear his GI raincoat as an outer garment. Whether this was in deference to the few female secretaries who worked in the area or just another device for making life hard, no one seemed to know or care. It was just one more rule we had to live with. Even though it was pretty chilly outside, there was always a gambler who would wrap a towel around his waist and make a dash for it. One morning Lazy Eight spotted a naked body streaking across the forbidden space and decided to make an example of the man. When Lazy Eight went into the latrine, he found the shower crammed with cadets. He decided to sit down and wait, reasoning that eventually there would be one body left in the shower when all the raincoats were gone from the hooks. As he waited, there was a steady stream of men coming and going. He missed the knowing glances exchanged between them and the bulges beneath some of the raincoats. When he finally decided to make his move, he found to his chagrin that there was one more coat on the hooks than people in the shower. The cadets had defeated him by applying their motto: "Cooperate and Graduate."

It wasn't all sweetness and light, though. We lost a few more to washouts, one of them a very good pilot. Eric had been one of the cadet officers at Pre-flight. He made the mistake of flying down to Corsicana from Greenville in a BT-13—he wanted to demonstrate his flying proficiency for the new Primary students and old instructors. Unfortunately, one of the military pilots was in the air at the time, and he did not share the civilian instructors' amused tolerance of Eric's stunt. To make matters worse, Eric stayed long enough to fly rings around the lieutenant in the PT-19, who was desperately trying to get close enough to read Eric's number. After a brief investigation, Eric was summoned to the commandant's office. We all thought Eric's stunt was great, if imprudent—even if he was going to have to walk tours every weekend for the rest of his stay at Majors Field. One look at his face when he came out told us that his punishment was a lot worse than anyone expected. He was finished as a cadet. I thought that, after a period of appropriate contrition, he would be reinstated. I didn't know the Army. It may have happened that way to Tyrone Powers or Errol Flynn in the movies, but this was the real world; Eric had used up his one and only chance. Flying was everything to him, and he had worked toward becoming a pilot since enlisting in the Army Air Corps as a private years before. Eric was a broken young man as he said good-bye.

The next and last phase of our flying education was the Advanced Flying School. There were two kinds of Advanced schools: those equipped with twin-engine aircraft, presumably preparing students for transition into bombardment or transport aviation, and those with the single-engine AT-6 for prospective pursuit pilots. Almost to a man, everyone wanted to go to a single-engine school. It was a certainty that someone was going to be disappointed. Each cadet had his own rational basis on which the division was to be made. Those of us of medium height or shorter were convinced that physical size was to be the determining factor, since the pursuit-ship cockpit was bound to be a tight fit. The taller people assured us that they would fit comfortably in any size cockpit. Anyway, they said, the assignments would really be made on the basis of the élan exhibited in the air, which of course they had amply demonstrated.

Finally, the list of the chosen was posted. I discovered, with some relief and a great deal of satisfaction, that I was one of the fortunate who were going to Moore Field at McAllen, Texas, to fly the AT-6. So was Claude, Brown, and Little Henry. We never did figure out how the choice was made, but I for one had no quarrel with the method, whatever it was.

The last weekend before shipping out, Brown, Claude, and I headed for Dallas. Our trip started inauspiciously when we couldn't even manage a ride to the train station. The local cab company, whose limited resources were sufficient for the Greenville citizenry, were woefully inadequate for the added burden of cadets and weekends. But Brown was not to be put off. He picked up the phone, dialed the cab number, and announced into the mouthpiece, "This is Captain [mumble]. I need a cab at the main gate out at the field immediately."

He must have seen my concerned frown, because he laughed his unique laugh and waved his hand as if to say, "No sweat." When the cabbie pulled up asking for a captain, Brown was right there.

"He was held up, but he told us to go ahead and he'd catch up later. Take us to the train station," he said, all the while opening the rear door and climbing into the backseat. The rest of us needed no urging. We leaped in also, a half step behind. As the cab moved off, Brown smirked and gave the raised-finger salute to the milling cadets staring in disbelief after us.

When we got to Dallas, I let the two BTOs (big-time operators) operate; I just tagged along. The Adolphus was the best hotel in town, so up to the front desk we marched and got a room big enough for the three of us. It was a nice room, and we started off there drinking Canadian Club. I don't remember leaving the room, but we must have, because I dimly remember other places where our drinking continued unabated. We switched to beer briefly in a rathskeller when one of the college girls at the next table proclaimed that something called Michelob "was the fahnest thang ah ever did taste." I took her word for it; I had never heard of Michelob. Having recently come from the beer capital of the country, I had just gotten used to Lone Star and Pearl. But the girls didn't last long and neither did the beer. In a basement dive somewhere, a sergeant, puzzling over our uniforms and insignia, asked if we were officers.

"No," we answered in unison, and Claude added, "Just dumb-assed cadets."

For some reason I thought that was hilarious and laughed uproariously. Somehow we drank and flirted our way through the evening, finally making it back to the Adolphus. So it went for the rest of the weekend. Small wonder we missed the last train and spent the late night and early-morning hours hitchhiking back to Greenville. As we straggled up the barracks street, some of the more eager cadets were already coming out, bags packed, ready for the trip to the train station. Our packing consisted of one of us tipping a footlocker up until the contents spilled into a barracks bag held by another of us. A pull of the drawstring, a quick check around for any forgotten items, and we were out the door—finished with Basic for good.

5

The time spent at Moore Field was to be one of the more enjoyable assignments that I ever spent anywhere. The city of McAllen is in the extreme south of Texas, a scant few miles from the Rio Grande River and Mexico, and the clear spring air was balmy and pregnant with the sweet scent of citrus blossoms. The constant fear of elimination from the program had receded, since washing out of Advanced was almost unheard of; curiously, everyone seemed to fly better. I believe that I finally began to fly instinctively, as if the aircraft were part of me, that it responded to my intentions almost without my pushing consciously on the stick and rudder. In addition, I noticed that the base personnel treated us differently that before. Before we had been barely tolerated as rough equivalents to recruits. We were now looked upon as officers to be, which in fact we were.

The North American AT-6 was an all-metal, low-wing monoplane, but a much more powerful and sophisticated machine than the BT-13. I remembered well my first peek inside the cockpit of an AT-6 at Kelly, but the situation was different now. Now I was a pilot—only a student pilot to be sure, but a pilot nonetheless and a pretty good one at that. I knew that I could fly the AT-6. Most of the instruments and controls were familiar to me; I could understand and manage the differences.

The AT-6 had a constant-speed prop; retractable landing gear; and was fully equipped for instrument flying, such as it was in those days. With a fixed-pitch propeller, the throttle controlled the power of the engine and was set by reference to the tachometer. In a dive the engine speeded up, in a climb it slowed down. In the AT-6, the pilot used a lever on the throttle quadrant to set engine RPM and the pitch of the prop changed automatically to keep the engine at that RPM regardless of the attitude of the aircraft. The power of the engine was still controlled by the throttle but now—since engine RPM was separately controlled—the throttle was used in conjunction with the manifold pressure gauge. The BT-13 had no need for hydraulic power, since the landing gear was not retractable and the flaps had to be cranked down manually—it took something like twenty turns to get full flap, as I recall. On the AT-6, an engine-driven hydraulic pump provided the muscle to move the landing gear to the retracted or extended position. Hydraulic pressure moved the wing flaps, also. And most impressive of all, the AT-6 sported a gunsight and provision for two real, honest-to-goodness .30-caliber machine guns, one mounted on the cowl and one in the right wing root.

After everyone was checked out in the AT-6, we practiced four-ship formation flying, instrument flying, night flying, and air tactics, with some navigational cross-country flights thrown in. I liked the afternoon flights the best, especially when I had the airplane to myself. By mid afternoon, the puffy cumulus clouds had usually built into massive snowy white billows with dales and valleys between. No matter what the scheduled practice flight, I could not resist their siren song. Down I'd plunge between them, gathering speed; then up in a climbing turn, spiraling upward, skirting the edges, searching the pillowy forms for a passage through; then, as I lost air speed, sliding the nose over gently at the last second to start downward again. This celebration was my version of what a ballet dancer or figure skater does if unfettered by routine, and I rejoiced in the sheer fun of it.

Not nearly as much fun was the introduction to instrument flying. On a practice instrument flight, the cadet would go under the hood—pull a cloth canopy over himself so he could not see out—and control the airplane with reference to the flight instruments only. The instrumentation and methods were extremely primitive and would enable a pilot to climb up through an overcast but little else.

The method of instruction, too, was uncomplicated and unsophisticated. The instructor simply repeated "Needle, ball, and airspeed; needle, ball, and airspeed," over and over again. The cadet was supposed to control the needle, which deflected right or left while the plane was turning, by using the rudder. He was supposed to keep the ball centered by using the ailerons. Since, at a fixed throttle setting, the airspeed increased in a nose-down attitude and decreased when climbing, the pilot controlled the pitch by fore and aft stick pressure and used the airspeed indicator as a reference. After mastering straight-and-level flight under the hood, the next challenges were single–needle–width turns and then double–needle–width, or steep, turns. If the nose was allowed to drop in a steep turn, pulling back on the stick made matters worse; instead of causing the plane to climb, as it did when straight and level, it merely tightened the turn, resulting in a downward spiral. The correct action to get the nose back up was to shallow the bank as back pressure was applied to the stick. The crowning achievement was to do a steep, 360-degree turn under the hood and feel the gentle turbulence of prop wash, signaling that the altitude had been maintained throughout the turn. As primitive as this instrument flying was, it did teach us one thing: The physical senses were absolutely useless in trying to fly the aircraft blind; the pilot had to trust the instruments implicitly.

One of the highlights of Advanced training was aerial gunnery. Since there were no gunnery ranges near McAllen, the entire student squadron—including instructors and ground personnel—went for two weeks on temporary duty to Matagorda Island in the Gulf of Mexico. The ground gunnery range had a series of large square targets placed side by side, each with its own identifying number. When the flight scheduled to fire ground gunnery arrived at the range, the instructor put the students in line astern and set up a rectangular pattern so that each made a firing pass at his own target in a slightly diving attitude. Each student stopped firing in time to pass over the target and then began a climbing turn to put him in behind his predecessor at pattern altitude.

The scores on ground gunnery were not too bad; at least we could see where the rounds were going from the spurts in the sand and could manage a few hits by hosing the target. But air-to-air gunnery was something else. The target was a large sleeve, a sort of overgrown wind sock dragged behind a tow plane. Before the belts of ammunition were loaded into the aircraft guns, they were rolled up and dipped in pans of different-colored paint so that each round had a half inch of color on the tip of the projectile. Since the whole flight fired at the same target, the different colors were to provide the means of scoring. The armament personnel could have saved themselves a lot of trouble. After each mission the sleeve would be retrieved and stretched out for the scoring. And each time it was the same; the target was almost as virginal as the proverbial driven snow. The results were embarrassingly universal for student and instructor alike. One cadet, Al Hayes, managed to get a few hits on every flight, but in spite of our detailed and repeated questioning, he was unable to communicate to us how he worked his magic. The unmarked targets remained largely unscathed right up to the end.

None of the instructors were combat veterans and apparently were as ignorant as their students on the proper way to make a firing pass and how to pull the correct amount of lead for a deflection shot. Just before our return to Moore Field, the aerial gunnery ratings were published on the bulletin board. I was dumbfounded to learn that I had qualified as a sharpshooter, as had a goodly number of other cadets who were equally inept. How we had achieved this astonishing feat will remain a mystery. I suppose the responsible officers were not about to admit the true state of affairs to higher headquarters; the truth certainly reflected poorly on the capability to teach a most important subject. So almost all the cadets were awarded a sharpshooter's badge with a small aerial gunnery bar hanging beneath it. We weren't a bit bashful about wearing it proudly on our blouses, either.

There were a handful of Curtiss P-40s at the base, and the word hot off the third stool in the latrine was that everyone was going to get a crack at them before graduation. We had gained a modest amount of proficiency in training aircraft, but the P-40 was a real honest-to-goodness fighting machine, exactly like those scattered around the world, keeping the enemy at bay. It had six .50-caliber machine guns and, although its size and wing were approximately the same as the AT-6, it weighed more than twice as much. It looked to me like a great brick sitting out there on the ramp. I'm sure that others besides myself wondered how it could possibly stay in the air, even with 1,300 horsepower.

Since there were no two-place P-40s, the first flight had to be a solo, a sporty proposition indeed. The instructor could warn about certain flying characteristics and give advice, but when the moment of truth arrived about all he could do before jumping down off the wing was to monitor the engine start and give a reassuring shoulder pat to the perspiring pilot.

I felt awfully alone as I inched up the throttle and that great block started to move. My first problem was to get out of the ramp area without wiping out any of the AT-6s parked nearby. This was no small feat, because the P-40's long nose stuck out so far in front of the cockpit that the forward visibility while taxiing was zero. So the pilot could clear himself forward by looking out first one side and then the other, the aircraft had to be essed continuously while on the ground.

My problems began even before I reached the end of the runway. The liquid-cooled engine could not stand much ground operation in warm weather. Just as I got to the end of the taxi strip, the coolant temperature hit the red line and the little warning light came on. I knew that, if I didn't dawdle, I could get off the ground before it boiled over and that it would cool down once I was airborne. A quick magneto check, a call to the control tower, and I was on the active runway opening the throttle. I had been thoroughly warned about the torque, so I added the power slowly and steadily until I was at full throttle. Still, it took all the strength in my right leg to keep that hurtling machine on the runway. After that, flying the P-40 was pretty much a matter of reflexes. I remember getting the landing gear up and continuing in a shallow, straight climb for a long way, trying to get up enough nerve to make the aircraft do something different. I had the distinct impression that I was only along for the ride and that the machine just barely tolerated me. It obeyed my commands belatedly and reluctantly. When it was time to go in, I made a terribly large pattern so I wouldn't have to make any steep turns at low altitude and airspeed. This put me on a long, low final approach, exactly what I didn't want. As I lined up with the runway and that long nose started to come up as I lost airspeed, I simply couldn't see where I was going. No chance now to do any essing, only to look out to the side and hope for the best. Heaven knows how I got that thing on the ground without breaking it. It was actually a good landing.

By the time I had ten hours in the P-40—the time allotted to each cadet—I felt ready to help keep the world safe for democracy, etc. Of course this was complete nonsense, but sagacity was not easily found in young pilots. We were elated when told we were going overseas.

The day of graduation finally arrived. My wife, June; my parents; and my brother Larry all braved the railroad system and were on hand to see the youngest member of the clan get his silver wings and become an officer and a gentleman. Officer training, however, was one topic the Army Air Forces had neglected in its haste to turn out pilots. We'd had only the most meager training about an officer's duties, responsibilities, and privileges. Those officers with whom we came in contact were not much better off. The flight instructors had come by their commissions via the Aviation Cadet route, too, and the tactical officers—the Ninety-day Wonders—were even less prepared for their leadership roles than we were. But in the wartime environment of the 1940s, no one seemed to worry about such details except perhaps some of the older Regular officers, who must have wondered more than once what the Army was coming to.

The pleasure of finally graduating and being sworn in as second lieutenants was dimmed for all of us by a switch pulled by the Army

Air Corps, or rather the Army Air Forces, as the Air Corps was now known. When we had signed up for the Aviation Cadet program, we were told that, upon successful completion of the training, we would be commissioned as Reserve officers. Reserve officers serving on active duty were paid a bonus of $500 for each year served. In those days, when a new car cost $1,000, the bonus was a considerable sum, and more than a few of us were making plans on how to spend it. A couple of days before graduation, we were told that we were to be commissioned not in the Army Reserve but in the AUS, the Army of the United States. What the hell was the AUS? Well, it was kind of like the Reserve, except you didn't get the $500 bonus. We felt like the rube when he discovers that the pea is not under any of the three shells. We'd been had. But the disappointment didn't last. We had our silver wings, and we were lieutenants of one kind or another, and that was good enough.

There was much good-natured bantering among us shavetails as preparations were made for the class to disband. Those few poor souls who were being posted to multiengine assignments came in for the most verbal abuse. Even those going to fly the twin-engine P-38 did not escape the slings and arrows of those who considered themselves the *real* pilots. I was as haughty as any in the single-engine bunch. I recall ending one exchange with the observation that "If Wilbur and Orville had meant for an airplane to have more than one engine, they would have built it that way."

We were losing Brown, but Claude and Little Henry were part of the group I was in. Our orders ceremoniously proclaimed that we were to be given a ten-day leave of absence and then were to report back to Kelly Field for shipment overseas. I looked forward to my trip to Racine with great relish. I had spent the entire clothing allowance provided to newly commissioned officers on a variety of outfits that were authorized by the Air Force but frowned on by the rest of the Army. "Pinks" were trousers—sort of tan but with a pinkish cast to them. It wasn't a baby pink or hot pink, just a slight hint of color, and the trousers looked great with the forest-green blouse. I had pink trousers with the dark-green blouse, pink trousers with the pink shirt—in fact, I had everything but olive drab and khaki. I planned to cut quite a swath at home with such fine feathers, which were topped off with the silver pilot's wings over the left breast pocket and my aerial gunnery sharpshooter's badge.

Alas, it wasn't to be. I soon found out that all my friends and acquaintances had also gone off to the military services. Impressing relatives just wasn't much fun, so I did the only thing I could think of;

I went back to the high school I had so recently left. Admiring glances from the faculty and students weren't exactly the rewards I had been thinking about since my first solo, but this was wartime and one had to make do. I don't know precisely what I had expected, but what I got was a polite but distant deference from everyone. Where I had been on close, even friendly, terms with the nuns and other teachers during my years of attendance, I was now one of the hardly recognizable legion of the graduated and gone. I walked down the steps that I had trod so often as a student and felt a little like yesterday's newspaper. The rest of the leave was pleasant enough. My infant son, Gary, who had been born while I was at Majors Field, provided June and me with hours of amusement.

Before I'd gotten accustomed to sleeping late in the morning, it was time to pack up.

6

Overseas turned out to be neither Europe nor the Pacific, as we had hoped, but Panama. Our transport landed at Albrook Field, in the Canal Zone, and disgorged us disappointed new pilots onto the ramp. There was no mistaking us as neophytes. Not only did we look alike, even our baggage looked identical. Each name and serial number was stenciled neatly on the sides of the new B-4 bags. Aguadulce, whence we were bound, was a kind of pursuit school for the squadrons scattered throughout the Isthmus and the Canal Zone.

On our arrival at Aguadulce we met quite a few pilots who had been in our upper class at Moore Field and were just finishing. A surprising number had dropped out of the program and were headed back to the States to the Training Command. Their stories were nearly all the same: "They're not telling you now, but wait until they get you up in the air. They even do lazy eights past the vertical and loops in formation." This was such an outlandish idea that I put it down as an alibi and filed it in the latrine.

We were all quite adept at formation flying with the AT-6. But with only ten hours in the P-40, none of which was in formation, we were all a little shaky, feeling our way. To be sure, we could get the P-40 off the ground and back down again without breaking it, but that was a long way from feeling that it and you belonged together in the air. To have to stay in formation 15 feet away from your leader during acrobatics with an airplane that felt like a lead sled made me feel uneasy.

But the rumors were right and I was wrong. Within a week we were doing those things and more in two- and four-ship formation flights. It was hard work keeping a P-40 tucked in close to the lead aircraft. If I had not been so totally consumed with forcing myself and the aircraft to perform, I would have been terror stricken when the shadow of the wing moved across the cockpit and out of the corner of my eye I could see the horizon 90 degrees away from where it was supposed to be or, worse still, when the ground was where the sky was supposed to be. But no one else said anything and I was determined that, if the others could do it, so could I. They were probably thinking the same thing. After the initial shock we just got on with P-40 training and took it in stride like everything else that was new. At least none of us quit.

By the time we finished our training, we were a pretty cocky bunch. We were convinced that our destiny was to clear the skies of enemy fighters in aerial combat and fearful that it would all be over before we got the chance. At parting we agreed that it would be "Off the Isthmus by Christmas or through the Locks in a box."

Units equipped with single-engine aircraft had been known as pursuit squadrons. A year before we finished P-40 training, they had been officially redesignated as fighter squadrons. Although the aircraft were now known as fighters, the aircraft model designations were left unchanged and were still identified with the letter *P*, as in P-40.

Five of us, including Claude Greene and Little Henry Goehausen, went to the 43d Fighter Squadron, at La Jolla, a temporary strip hacked out of the jungle near Pecora, about 50 miles east of Panama City, toward Columbia. The squadron was equipped with the P-39K, which meant that we had to start all over again in a new type of aircraft. The Airacobra, as it was called, was radically different from the P-40 though it was surprisingly similar in terms of speed and altitude. The Airacobra and the P-40 had the same Allison V-12 engine, but in the Airacobra it was mounted *behind* the cockpit. The drive shaft passed beneath the pilot's seat to the propeller gearbox in the nose. It was probably this long shaft that caused the P-39's distinctive whistling sound in the air. Instead of a sliding canopy, it had doors very much like those of the family sedan. In addition, the P-39 had a tricycle gear, which allowed the pilot to motor about on the ground with perfect visibility. Rumor had it that, with so much weight aft, it would tumble if stalled in a nose-high attitude, a charge vehemently denied by the manufacturer and the Army Air Forces. I'm not sure whether it actually went end over end or not, but I am willing to swear that it could be made to go through some very strange convolutions that no other aircraft did.

The armament was a mixed bag. A 37mm cannon fired through the hub of the propeller and two .50-caliber machine guns were mounted on the cowling, forward of the cockpit. Also, four .30-caliber machine guns were in the wings, two on each side. All three types of weapons had different muzzle velocities, the cannon being the slowest and the .30-caliber the fastest. This made no difference against ground targets, but I often wondered how we were supposed to hit an enemy aircraft if we had to take a deflection shot. If the correct amount of lead was used for the .50-caliber guns, the .30s would be out in front of the enemy and the cannon fire would miss behind him. Mine was only a theoretical question. Our experience at Matagorda had made it abundantly clear that, when it came to deflection shooting, we probably wouldn't hit anything with the .50-caliber machine guns or the other guns, either.

They did have one nice feature though, the guns; they could be charged individually from the cockpit. If one of them jammed or had a stoppage, the bolt could be manually cycled and the gun would be ready to go again. Handles for this purpose connected to the .50s and protruded into the cockpit. For the .30s out in the wings, cables attached to the bolts ran through a series of pulleys and into the cockpit, terminating in stirrup-type handgrips on the floor beside the seat, two on the right and two on the left.

Sighting was done by reference to a fixed-reticle optical sight mounted just inside the windscreen. The sight consisted of a light bulb, a series of lenses, a reticle arranged in a vertical column, and a reflector that turned the light image 90 degrees toward the pilot's eye. The reflector was clear glass, so, although the pilot could see the orange sight reticle on the reflector when it was turned on, he could also look through it and see the target. The reticle in most of the planes was a 70-mil ring with a dot in the center, representing the aiming point. When a pilot looked through a sight with a 70-mil ring, the diameter of the ring covered a distance of 70 feet at a range of 1,000 feet.

Some older sights had a Christmas-tree reticle. This type consisted of a long vertical line with a horizontal one forming a cross, plus a shorter third line above it—sort of like the Christmas Seal emblem. The crosshairs were the aiming point and the shorter, higher line was used to estimate range. It was a step up from the iron ring and bead used in World War I but a short step, to be sure.

The squadron aircraft were dispersed in camouflaged revetments connected by a maze of taxiways leading through the jungle to the runway. The revetments sloped down toward the back so that all a pilot had to do when returning from a flight was pivot the aircraft around on the hardstand in front of the revetment and then let it roll backward to the chocks. The taxiways were quite narrow and the brakes of the P-39 were notoriously bad, so this maneuver was not as easy as it sounds. Thus, on my very first flight I succeeded in doing something I had avoided during my entire training period. I bent a flying machine.

The check-out flight went well enough and the landing was the easiest part of all because of the wide-set tricycle gear. A light rain was falling. As I moved to the edge of the taxi strip to get around a fuel truck, I felt a sickening lurch. The left wing dropped almost to the ground. I shut down and climbed out as the ground crew came running up with long faces. My left wheel had dropped into a three-foot ditch that had been dug right up to the edge of the taxiway, and the wing had some nasty-looking wrinkles in it. By the time the squadron operations officer and my flight commander finished with me, I had some wrinkles, too, but not in my wings. I was a glum young man and was not looking forward to the comments I was going to get from my fellow second lieutenants. My misery must have shown on my face as I walked into the BOQ, because I was let off with a few remarks about how long it took to pay for a P-39 on a lieutenant's salary. I was grounded for several days and then, without explanation, returned to flight status. I found out from one of the crew chiefs that the ditch was supposed to be marked with a yellow flag, and that may have accounted for the ease with which I escaped the wrath of officialdom.

Since the Japanese forces were several thousand miles away, our air-defense role consisted of interminable periods of standing alert and then scrambling pell-mell to intercept some commercial airliner that had missed its estimated time of arrival (ETA). After we had read every tech order and regulation several times, whiling away the hours in the alert shack became something of a problem. One pastime was to strip down and reassemble a .50-caliber machine gun, which had been left there for instructional purposes. After the millionth time, that also lost its fascination. One day, when no one else was around, I was fiddling with a couple of live rounds and decided to try an experiment. I managed to get one projectile out of its casing. I emptied the powder and ran the casing into the chamber of the gun. With a pencil I pushed the projectile into the end of the barrel. I reasoned that, when the primer went off, the small pop would cause the projectile to dribble out the barrel and fall on the floor. When I pushed the sear over and the firing pin snapped forward, that infernal contraption let out a thunderclap that really shocked me. There was no bullet on the floor—only a nice round hole in the screen on the opposite side of the room. I spent the next fifteen terrifying minutes waiting for someone to burst in with the news that someone had been shot. When enough time had gone by to convince me that it wasn't going to happen, I breathed a little easier—not a sadder but certainly a wiser man.

Local formation flights were always flown with very tight spacing—wingmen were expected to get their wingtip inside that of the leader but back a little and stacked down. This positioning allowed the flight leader to maneuver the four-plane flight almost as if it were one. Flying that way wasn't too hard on us peons who flew the wing positions, once we caught onto it, except that it left precious little time to tend to our own housekeeping. I didn't dare take my eyes off the leader for more than a fraction of a second. This was the only excuse I had when, on a routine patrol flight up near the San Blas Islands, I stole a quick glance at the panel and thought I saw a needle out of place, well below the red line. Another quick flick back a second later told me that my oil pressure was down. I was in trouble. The engine was still running smoothly, but I knew that I didn't have much time—a couple of minutes at the most after it hit zero. I keyed the mike button on the throttle and tried to keep my voice down as I informed the flight leader of my problem.

"Stay in formation," he said. "There's a strip just over near the coast. I'll get you there, and then you go ahead and take it in."

He made a slight turn and started a rapid descent while I moved out a little so I could continue to check my engine gauges. I was pretty tensed up, but then I let out a nervous laugh at a mental picture that popped into my head unbidden. In pilot jargon, if you were scared, you had a puckered asshole. I could see myself wreaking havoc on the parachute I was sitting on as I waited anxiously for the first sputter. I hoped I didn't have to use the chute!

"There's the strip, about eleven o'clock," the flight leader called. "Good luck."

Sure enough, right where he said it was, I could make out a temporary strip parting the carpet of green jungle that stretched below. It looked to be about 3,500 feet long—long enough, if I played it right. Hell, I could make it now even if the plane did quit. I made a straight-in, descending approach. At the end of the runway I pitched up into a 360-degree turn to the left, closing the throttle; as I got halfway around, I dropped gear and full flaps. Then I was on the ground and hard on the brakes. No other aircraft were on the field and no one was about, so I just pulled off on a small ramp and shut it down. Above me, the guys made a low pass and left.

In a couple of minutes I heard a vehicle coming. Suddenly a jeep driven by a second lieutenant materialized out of the jungle. I told him my troubles and he told me his. He and a captain were the only military people stationed there, and it required no great feat of perception to figure out that he was a very unhappy second lieutenant. When he spoke of the captain, his talk was guarded, as if he didn't want to be quoted; in fact, I felt as if we were in a room bugged with listening devices rather than standing in a clearing in the Panamanian jungle.

I clambered into the jeep. We drove down a rutted dirt track for a mile or two. There the road widened slightly, exposing a half dozen dilapidated wooden buildings scattered about. It must have been a native village of sorts—the few people to be seen here and there were dark skinned with straight black hair and short, squat physiques. I was ushered in to see the captain, but where he was holding forth didn't seem to be an office; it was a native dwelling. Two Indians, a man and a woman, were in the room with us. Odd, I thought.

The captain was an older man, at least forty, and though he wore a khaki uniform, it was badly wrinkled and sweat-stained. He looked more like a tugboat captain than a military officer. He tried to put me at ease with his unctuous manner, but he had the unnerving habit of looking two feet above my head when he spoke to me. I was more than a little relieved when he finally turned to my escort, the lieutenant, and curtly instructed him to put me up for the night. As we walked up the road together, a feeling of foreboding overtook me and I couldn't shake my uneasiness. What was it? The sunless gloom from the high, leafy canopy overhead? The damp smell of rotting vegetation? The quiet? Or was the tense apprehension of the lieutenant reaching into me?

He showed me a cot and then we drank a little, talked a little, ate, talked a little more, drank a little more, and went to bed. The next morning, I saw the captain again briefly. He asked, in that condescending way of his, how I had slept, but I don't think he really wanted to know. He was still accompanied by his retinue. I think it was then that I realized they were a threesome. The dusky man was the local chief and the woman was his wife. And the captain? Well, he fitted into the relationship somewhere, but exactly what manner of accommodation they had come to, I could only guess. Apparently it was all quite civil, but hardly civilized.

The lieutenant gave me a lift down to the field and, as we pulled up to my P-39, an L-4—a kind of overgrown Piper Cub—landed and taxied over. One of the squadron pilots had brought a mechanic. He hauled out his toolbox, had the engine panels off in short order, and tore expertly into the guts of my ailing machine. How he knew what the problem was, I couldn't figure out, but he was a crackerjack. He "pulled the screens" (whatever that meant), found them clogged, and worked his magic in some way or other so that by noon he had run up the engine and pronounced it fit for a one-time flight back to La Jolla. The wizard got his tools together and loaded them and the other bits and pieces he had brought along, flipped the L-4's prop for the pilot, and then they were gone. As I shook hands with the lieutenant, he managed a weak smile and said something about "a couple more months to go." I wished him good luck as I opened the door and slid into the cockpit. The engine fired up promptly, and the oil pressure was right where it belonged. I released the brakes; gave the lieutenant one more perfunctory wave; and left him standing there beside the jeep, looking after me.

The return flight was uneventful, and my thoughts kept turning back to that eerie, sinister place and those strange people. The captain, I was convinced, had gone native. Or worse, he was mad as a hatter. I had not yet read Conrad's "Heart of Darkness" or I would have recognized the captain as the classic Mr. Kurtz.

Soon after going on operational flying, I witnessed my first fatal accident. A practice dive-bombing mission had been laid on for our morning flight, though a layer of broken clouds had formed between 4,000 and 10,000 feet. The bombing range was just off the edge of the field, however, so there would be no problem getting back if we had to abort the mission because of worsening weather. After takeoff we formed up in the normal four-ship flight. I, as the junior man, was flying number 2, or wingman, on the flight leader. Bill Knight, flying number 3, or element lead, was on the other side and slightly farther out with his wingman. We leveled off at 12,000 feet, just above the clouds; went into echelon formation; and began searching for an opening to start a dive-bombing run. Suddenly, the flight leader gave a hurried hand signal and immediately whipped into a wingover. The next thing I saw was the underside of his P-39 rapidly disappearing into a gap in the clouds. Almost by reflex I peeled off after him, going straight down, trying to keep him in sight while looking to pick up the big bull's-eye of whitewashed stones on the ground. I rolled around one more puff of cloud and caught a glimpse of the target slightly to my left. It was coming awfully fast. No thought now of trying to hit anything; get the bomb off and pull out. I horsed the stick back and went into the stomach-tightening crouch, fighting the blackout as best I could, treading on the edge of a high-speed stall. As soon as I was sure I had it made, I eased the stick back pressure, and the lessening g's allowed my full vision to return. The nose came up through the horizon and, as I turned to rejoin, I glanced back at the target to see where my bomb had fallen. At the instant I looked back, a great orange ball of fire engulfed the target.

Those ordnance dummies, I thought, they must have put a *live* bomb on instead of a practice one with a small spotting charge.

I cut inside the flight leader and joined on him. Even from 50 feet away, I could tell that something was very wrong indeed. He was white as a ghost and kept shaking his head. Pretty soon Bill's wingman joined up and we started back. And then, suddenly, I understood. That was Bill that went into the target.

I made the approach, landing, and taxi to the revetment by instinct. I struggled with the idea that the fellow with whom I had talked a few minutes before was dead. Dead, hell. He didn't even exist anymore.

With only twenty-five pilots in the squadron it was a personal thing when one "augered in." Some of us had known Bill from Moore Field, where he was in our upper class, so we were shaken for a couple of days. The older heads were either more philosophical about the accident or were able to give the impression they were. It turned out that the squadron had been losing about one pilot every two months, either to weather or to structural failure. "Weather flying" was still quite primitive. We had no instrument-landing systems or ground-controlled approaches, no omni ranges, not even a low-frequency range; we had only needle, ball, and airspeed. And hope, which wasn't much in mountainous country.

My next brush with the Grim Reaper involved a structural failure that was a good bit closer to home. Al Hayes, one of my friends from flight school, got pretty sick from his series of annual vaccinations and went to bed. I wasn't scheduled to be vaccinated until the following day, so I took Al's place on the flight schedule. We were about the same size, so I didn't bother to switch parachutes. I went ahead and used his; the harness just fit. The next day, I got my shots. Soon my head ached and I felt plain lousy. I asked the flight leader to scratch me from flying that afternoon, and as I headed back to the quarters I met Al going the other way. He said he felt a lot better and thought he'd give the mission a go. I went on back, dropped into the sack, and slept the fitful sleep that comes with nausea and afternoon slumber. I was dimly conscious of a high level of activity, of shouts and running footsteps. Slowly I regained my senses and found out the cause of the frantic action. Al had crashed on the bombing range. As I dressed, a fellow in the next room told me what happened.

Al had taken my place on the afternoon flight, which was a mission to drop two loads of bombs. After the first drop, the flight landed. While the armorers attached the second load of bombs, the flight leader assembled the other pilots for a critique. He told Al that he had released too low and made too sharp a pullout off the target. He cautioned Al that pulling out too sharply could overstress the tail. Maybe the flight leader was a little gun-shy because he had been leading the day Knight was killed. Al nodded and smiled, probably because his bomb had gone squarely into the target. On the second run, Al had gotten partway through his pullout when he lost half his horizontal stabilizer. He fought the airplane as best he could and had gotten the nose up almost level before the plane fell off on a wing and crashed on a riverbank a scant mile from the field. Al had jettisoned the door, but that was as close as he'd come to getting out before impact. At the crash site, however, almost everything was accounted for except Al. Griswold, another classmate and friend of Al's, figured he was in the river and began working his way downstream through the underbrush. About a mile downstream, he spotted Al's body. He waded in, hoisted it onto his shoulder, and brought it ashore. I don't believe I could have done that.

Al's death always bothered me, I suppose because he was flying my airplane and wearing my parachute. I could never make up my mind whether he had overstressed the tail or if it would have failed on that flight regardless of who was in the cockpit. For sure, his death was a rotten waste of talent. Al was potentially a brilliant fighter pilot, the only one in the cadet class who ever consistently hit the air-to-air training target at Matagorda.

The summer of '43 went fast. The subtropical climate of Panama meant that every morning the cumulus started building, until, by early afternoon, the sky had darkened and a thundershower pelted down. Then the sun reappeared and, by late afternoon, the dust was flying again. Between showers we managed to sleep, play softball, or go swimming in the river. When we had breaks from flying for a few days, we would head for Panama City and the bright lights, more for a change of scenery than anything else. The BOQ and Officers' Club at Albrook Field were the rendezvous points for transient pilots from the outlying bases. It provided a meeting place for renewing old acquaintances and catching up on the goings-on in the other squadrons.

Mail service at the outlying fields was not the greatest, but we did manage to collect our letters eventually. Besides those from June and my parents, I occasionally received one from a pal back in Racine, who kept me abreast of all the happenings. One letter from him mentioned that a mutual acquaintance, Frank Deschler, was stationed at Howard Field, just west of Panama City. I got permission to take the L-4 over to Howard on my next day off.

It was a beautiful sunny morning and, as I lifted off the black-top runway, I looked forward to the one-hour flight. Puttering along at 60 miles per hour was not the most exciting way for a fighter pilot to fly, but not having to stay in formation and going "low and slow" gave me a chance to indulge in a little gawking.

The direct course took me out over the Pacific a short distance. I climbed to 5,000 feet, reasoning that, if the engine quit, I would be within gliding distance of the beach. Since it was still early, the air was smooth; the cockpit was warm from the morning sun. The L-4 trimmed out nicely and would almost fly itself, hands off. I relaxed, half asleep, as I droned along. I noticed the outline of a fish swimming just beneath the surface of the water. I watched it idly for several seconds before I realized, with a start, that what I took to be a mere fish from 5,000 feet was fully 15 feet long and was no mere fish. It was a shark and it was a granddaddy. My contentment evaporated as I hastily turned toward shore. I began to notice strange noises coming from the engine. I knew they were in my head and not beneath the cowling. Still, they persisted until I was once again over the shoreline. And there I stayed until I got past Albrook Field and landed at Howard.

When Frank and I met, we shook hands warmly. He was a staff sergeant, having enlisted before Pearl Harbor. Since I was a commissioned officer, a thin but real barrier stood between us. I was reluctant to go with him to his usual haunts, and he couldn't go to mine. So we went to the PX and strolled around, talking for an hour and a half. It was long enough. After the first hour, we had been over all the news about mutual friends and had caught each other up on our own doings. The conversation began to lag as we walked back to the ramp where the L-4 was parked.

As we stood at the edge of the concrete hangar apron, saying our good-byes, I noticed something in the dirt at my feet and stooped to pick it up. It appeared to be a coin, but it was not round—its edge had four curved sides only approximating a circular shape. Without giving it another thought, I put it in my pocket. Back in my room at La Jolla, curiosity got the better of me. I took out a piece of blitz cloth and began working away at the coin, removing the outer stain. It was a coin all right, but like nothing I had ever seen. It was silver and very old. Its thickness was uneven, and the four sides bore the marks of a curved chisel, which had been used to cut it out of a silver plate. An audience of three or four guys had formed by now. One man offered the information that he had seen a coin like it in a museum; it was a Spanish piece of eight.

"Didn't you find any more?" he asked.

They all groaned disgustedly when I admitted that I hadn't looked for any more.

"Never mind," I alibied, "I'm going back there in a month or so, and I'll give the place a good going over. I know exactly where I found this thing. Maybe I'll even borrow a shovel."

But I never went back to Howard, and I left Panama soon after. I at least should have written to Frank and told him to go out and search around the spot where I'd picked up the piece. But I did nothing. For years afterward, I convinced myself that mine was the only coin there, that it had fallen out of the pocket of some conquistador who had come that way three centuries earlier. Absolute nonsense, of course, but the story shielded me from having to wonder about a fortune that may have slipped through my fingers from stupidity and thoughtlessness.

One unhappy memory from La Jolla involved my flight commander, a mean little SOB. He had that Napoleonic manner so common in short men, as if he had to make up in hauteur what he lacked in stature. Little Napoleon had a penchant for terrorizing new pilots. On one occasion, with a new pilot on his wing, Little Napoleon put the flight in line astern and then went into a Lufbery circle, pulling it in as tight as he could. From a vertical bank, high-g turn, the P-39 had a nasty habit of stalling with little warning. As the flight lost altitude, Napoleon kept reefing it in, placing the rest of the flight in a very dangerous position. Suddenly, around 1,000 feet, his wingman stalled. There was no time or room for any recovery action; the machine just snap-rolled right into the ground. The site was not far from the field, and most of the pilots went out to help clean it up. It wasn't very pleasant duty. When the plane hit, the engine tore loose and came forward through the cockpit. A crash site has a smell that is unmistakable: a mixture of hot oil, moist earth freshly torn up, and burning flesh. I will remember the smell of that crash as long as I live. The incident probably went into the books as an accident. I called it something else.

Little Napoleon took it all in stride, showing not a bit of guilt or remorse. I had heard of another accident he had caused a few months before our arrival at La Jolla. The 43d was engaged in a joint exercise with Army ground troops, and he was leading a simulated strafing attack on a column moving down a dirt road. As soon as the troops spotted the aircraft, everyone scattered along both sides of the road, taking cover. All except one. Why he stood in the middle of the road watching the approaching P-39s is anybody's guess. Maybe for the same reason boys stand on the tracks when a train is coming. But standing there was a mistake. A bad mistake. As he made his low pass, Napoleon hit the soldier in the head and killed him. Napoleon didn't hit him with the prop, but with the underside of his aircraft—not that it made any difference to the GI how he was killed. Why was it necessary to get that low on a training exercise? Couldn't he have pulled back on the stick a sixty-fourth of an inch when he saw the soldier standing in the road? I didn't understand; it was not necessary for a second lieutenant to understand the behavior of captains. But his conduct was as enigmatic to me as that of the captain at the jungle strip where I made my emergency landing. Maybe it was simpler than I thought—maybe all captains in Panama were crazy.

All the news wasn't bad, however. Orders came through from Fighter Command Headquarters that the Moore Field bunch, including those at the other squadrons, was going back to the States for reassignment to a combat theater. So the ultimatum "Off the Isthmus by Christmas or through the Locks in a box" was fulfilled; we left Panama the first week in December 1943.

A ten-day delay en route was authorized, so everyone headed for home. This was another great chance to impress friends and relatives, and I was certain that I would be up to the task. I fancied myself a returning warrior, even though I hadn't heard a single shot fired in anger. No matter, I'd been out of the country flying fighter planes, had a nice tan in the middle of winter, and was ready with an inexhaustible supply of adventure stories to tell. I was never without my brown leather A-2 flying jacket, which sported a colorful hand-painted squadron insignia on the left breast. I was not disappointed in its ability to provoke questions, which I answered archly with something about, "My outfit, the 43d Fighter Squadron." It was contrary to dress regulations to wear flying clothes off post, but on leave everyone wore what he pleased or what he fancied the well-dressed warrior of 1943 ought to wear.

My little boy, Gary, was almost a year old, and June was carrying a second child, mute testimony that her trip to McAllen in May was not without consequence. There wasn't much to do in Wisconsin that winter, what with gasoline and food rationed and all our friends gone, but we were content to enjoy each other's company and occasionally visit relatives. Hardly before I had unpacked, it was time to board the train again, saying the same good-byes to family and parents. This time, however, there was an added element of uncertainty: I knew that, somewhere soon, I was finally going to get my taste of combat. Leaving home a few days before Christmas was not easy, but we all accepted the circumstances without undue complaint. *C'est la guerre.*

PART II

Fighter Pilot

The eagles rose on silver wings
With fellow fliers free,
To trace white lace
In airless space
Where never men were meant to be.

7

When the group reassembled at Dale Mabry Field, Tallahassee, Florida, it seemed that each new arrival was greeted as a long-lost comrade who had been out of touch for years. The usual outrageous tales were passed back and forth about hometown ventures and adventures. One of the funniest stories was told by Tom Hardeman.

On the way down from the Midwest by train, Tom was in a chair car, staring at the bleak landscape rushing past, when the conductor came through asking for a doctor. Before Tom joined the aviation cadets, he had spent two years in premed training, which qualified him for such useful tasks as dissecting frogs and tracing the arteries of a cat. At any rate, the conductor readily accepted Tom's volunteered services. A passenger had suffered a heart attack, and the conductor was more than willing to be quit of responsibility for him—even if the only volunteer's medical qualifications were highly suspect. Tom put on his most officious manner and directed the conductor to lead him to the stricken man. The poor fellow was stretched out in the lounge of the men's room in the Pullman car. In his best bedside manner, Tom stroked his chin and decided that the conductor should go through the train and find some nurses. He returned shortly with two: a comely young thing and a rather plain middle-aged lady. Tom inquired where the man's accommodations were and was shown a top berth. He then made some assignments. The older nurse was to take the first shift, sitting up with the patient right where he lay, while Tom and the pretty one would get some sleep in the patient's upper berth, in preparation for the second shift. Certainly a most prudent and practical division of labor.

Somehow the conductor got wind of the arrangement. He came back to the berth, jerked the curtains aside, and informed the startled medical team that that sort of thing would not be tolerated on any train of his. Tom leaped out of the berth, pulling on his pants, and retorted indignantly, "Sir, how dare you insinuate that anything improper was going on!" He was still upset the next morning when he took the young lady to breakfast in the dining car; all the heads that had popped out of the curtains during the previous night's commotion now bobbed above their menus disapprovingly. He never did say what happened to the patient, and I guess we never asked. Forever afterward he was known as Doctor Tom.

When Goehausen reported at Dale Mabry, he brought along his sweetheart, Miriam, from back home in Webster Grove, Missouri. She was a very fine young lady, soft-spoken and shy, but she had her share of spunk, too. The first time she heard me call Walter Little Henry, she said nothing. But I understood in short order that she did not approve of the sobriquet, so I was careful thereafter to call him Walter whenever she was present. They had made up their minds to be married before Walter went overseas. They had also decided not to make a general announcement about their intentions except to those of us who were participating: Al Franek and his wife, who was to be the bridesmaid, and me, as best man. It was a simple ceremony held in the base chapel, but they loved each other. In spite of the wartime air of impermanence that existed everywhere, their commitment was total; forty-seven years later they are still married. Even the lack of a honeymoon did not seem to dampen their spirits. Walter had to spend his nights on the base with the rest of us, but they spent the days together, wandering about the town and enjoying each other's company.

The only thing we accomplished at Dale Mabry Field was to satisfy a directive that every officer going overseas had to be qualified with the .45-caliber automatic pistol. Some did well; for me, it was Matagorda all over again. I think I put a few rounds in the target next to mine. I know I put one in the paste pot sitting innocently beneath my target, and once I caused a seagull, who showed the poor judgment to be flying in the vicinity of my target, to do some unscheduled aerobatics. However, the requirement was only that the familiarization course be completed, so this time I received no unearned medals.

Shortly after New Year's Day we moved up to Camp Patrick Henry, near Norfolk, Virginia, a sprawling complex that was one of the principal embarkation points for the European Theater. Here we were issued full field equipment, including steel helmet and liner, backpack, blankets, canteen, and leggings. I wondered why we needed all that stuff. It certainly was not my conception of what the well-dressed fighter pilot was wearing that season. I don't think any of us realized that beds and sheets and PXs and Officers' Clubs were not essential to fighting a war. This fact was to be brought home soon enough.

Finally it was the day for embarkation. We were moved down to the dock in trucks. When I saw the ship at dockside, I couldn't believe we were going to cross the ocean in something that size. She was a Liberty ship, which wasn't all that small, but I'd seen too many newsreels of troops boarding the *Normandie* or the *Queen Elizabeth*. I went about telling anyone who would listen that this was the boat that would take us out into the harbor to the "regular" ship. Of course, this was nonsense, as we all soon discovered. The ship did put out into deep water that evening to rendezvous with the rest of the convoy, but by morning the gentle rolling motion told us we were under way. I'll never forget the exhilaration of stepping out on the deck that first morning. The sea was calm except for a gentle swell, the sun was sparkling on the water, and the fresh breeze carried the salty tang of the ocean to my nostrils. There was no land in sight, only ships in all directions as far as the eye could see, moving together at nine knots.

The Liberty ship was not designed for use as a troop transport, so the accommodations left something to be desired. In the forward hold, infantrymen were stacked five bunks deep, a terribly crowded condition. We lieutenants fared a little better. There were two rooms about 15 feet square and twenty-four of us. That meant that twelve had to be fitted into each room. The bunks were in each corner, three deep. This arrangement allowed almost no floor space. Only two or three could stand in the room at one time, requiring a great deal of patience and not a little careful planning. Even though we were all close friends, each individual's habits and personal hygiene came in for some close scrutiny.

There wasn't much to do on board except eat, but even that didn't provide much respite from boredom since we were served only two meals per day. Some of us volunteered to act as supernumeraries on the gun crew. In spite of interminable practices, walk-throughs, and drills, we saw no sign of enemy submarines or aircraft—much to our disappointment.

During the crossing I struck up a close friendship with Jim Brooks, one of the group whom I had known only casually in flight school and our tour in Panama. He was from Roanoke, Virginia, and slightly older than I. He had blond wavy hair, bright blue eyes, and a boyish charm that did not go unnoticed by the ladies. It didn't seem to make any difference whether they were teenagers or in their thirties; somehow they gravitated in his direction, and he wound up the center of the attention of the nicer-looking women present. It was a good thing for all concerned, especially him, that he didn't recognize the extent of his talent and use it to the maximum. He would never have had the time or energy to pursue his flying.

We liked to spend the evenings away from the rest of the crowd, sitting on the after hatch or some other out-of-the-way place, talking about the past, such as it was; the future, whatever that might be; and singing. Jim had a good ear for music, and he taught me the harmony for many old minstrel tunes. Doctor Tom often joined in, and singing those old songs gave us many hours of enjoyment during the long crossing.

The convoy split just before reaching Gibraltar; part of it peeled off northward toward England. Since we continued on into the Mediterranean, it became clear for the first time that we were destined for the Mediterranean Theater. Twenty-one days after leaving Hampton Roads, we docked in Oran, Algeria.

Our temporary jumping-off place was Camp Canastel, a cluster of buildings and tents on the heights above Oran. Even though I had come to expect primitive living conditions, it was a shock when we were unceremoniously marched down to the supply tent, given an empty mattress cover, and told to stuff it at a straw pile at the edge of camp. That, with the two blankets we had been issued, were all the help we were going to get to keep off the North African winter chill. We did have tents with beds, which were knocked-together two-by-fours with slats across. In retrospect, these accommodations were not bad at all; a great many people in the forward areas would have considered them luxurious.

The first night none of us was able to sleep for the cold, shock, and discomfort—in spite of being fortified with some perfectly awful Algerian wine. One by one, we crawled out in the early morning darkness and made our way to the mess area. The cooks had lighted fires under garbage cans full of water, which, when hot was used by each diner to wash out and sterilize his mess kit. We huddled around these fires, miserably trying to get warm. When it was finally light, I decided to tidy myself up a bit. There was no plumbing in the open shack that served as a washroom; the only available water was from a Lister bag, a great rubberized canvas pouch suspended from a tripod. The lower end was fitted with numerous spigots, which made it resemble an oversized cow udder hanging there. No washbasins were to be seen either, only mysterious depressions on the top of a long concrete bench. I inspected one carefully. There was no drain hole in the bottom and anyway, they were far too small to serve as washbowls. To find out how the arrangement worked, I decided to mill around until a long-time resident showed up. I didn't have long to wait. An infantry officer came in, yawning and scratching, a towel over his shoulder and his helmet on. He nodded to me absently, pulled off his helmet, filled it at the Lister bag, set it in one of the depressions, and began to wash. My face must have been very red as I followed suit.

Another reminder that our gentlemen's existence was over was the shortage of certain creature comforts we had come to accept and expect. Things like cigarettes and whiskey. And things like toilet articles and writing materials, which heretofore we got merely by stopping by the PX. No longer.

The tiny PX here had a very limited inventory; indeed, many articles were absent altogether. Not just the state of the shelves determined the availability of goods to us, however. We were issued ration cards, which had to be presented to the clerks when we made a purchase. In addition to taking "funny money"—Military Payment Certificates (MPCs)—they asked for the ration card and crossed off the quantity purchased.

I still have a card issued to me at the 1st Replacement Depot at Oran. It is a curious bit of nostalgia, not only because it provides an insight into the kinds of things that were rationed, but because it lists certain items that are completely unavailable today. The card proudly proclaims that it is good anywhere in NATOUSA—North African Theater of Operations, U.S. Army. In the category of "Every Week" are listed such items as smoking ration, candy bar, soft drink, and chewing gum. Under "Every Two Weeks" are soap and razor blades. The "Every Four Weeks" category includes a dozen items like toothpaste, matches, writing tablet, envelopes, and pipe cleaners. The list for "Every Eight Weeks" covers the back of the card and consists of 60 items such as band, watch; belt, money; book, note; brush, shaving; brush, tooth; brush, hands—and some necessities, too: cards, playing; and dice. Among the oddities are mirror, trench (which was of polished metal); nib, pen; pen, fountain (to be filled by pressing a side lever to squeeze a rubber interior bladder while immersing the tip in a bottle of ink, also rationed); and pencil, styptic.

Later, things improved considerably, but cigarettes, beer (when available at all), and Coca-Cola were always meted out grudgingly and guarded jealously.

The trip from Oran to Constantine took a couple of days in a dilapidated train of World War I vintage, which bumped and chugged its way across North Africa. After suffering the sounds and smells of so many densely packed bodies, Jim Brooks and I sought relief during one of the numerous stops. We broke open a boxcar door and settled ourselves among great rolls of paper inside, finishing the journey in relative comfort. Our destination was the Fighter Training Center at Telergma, Algeria. The trucks that picked us up at Constantine did not arrive at our new station until around midnight, but the mess was kept open and huge piles of peanut-butter–and–jelly sandwiches were waiting for us. After subsisting for several days on canned "dog food"—C rations eaten cold—the sandwiches and coffee ranked as one of the finest meals I had ever eaten. With our arrival at Telergma we reached the last rung up the ladder toward combat.

A replacement pilot's first weeks in an operational unit were difficult for the individual, and they worked a hardship on the unit as well. The step up from routine, "bore a hole in the sky–type" flying to combat was truly a quantum jump. The step was magnified when the new pilot had to be checked out in an aircraft different from the one he had been flying. Front-line units just didn't have the aircraft, instructors, or the patience and time to handle transition training. To reduce the impact on pilot and unit, Twelfth Air Force Headquarters had set up a rear-area central facility, the Fighter Training Center (FTC), at Telergma.

The permanent installation at FTC looked like a movie set from *Beau Geste*. In fact, the site *had* been a French Foreign Legion outpost. A high wall completely surrounded it. Several buildings were arranged with their backs against the wall, leaving a fair-sized open area in the center of the post. The headquarters and permanent party were housed within the encircling walls; a row of tents outside provided billets for the pilot-trainees. Most of the tents were equipped with homemade heaters, installed by prior occupants. The previous tenants of our tent must have been Eskimos or very lazy fellows, because it was stoveless. My tent mates and I paid a visit to the next-door tent to examine its heater. It consisted, outside the tent, of a large raised can from which 100-octane gas was piped through a valve. From the valve, aircraft tubing carried the gas inside the tent and through access holes punched in a cut-down steel drum. The end of the tube was pinched shut and bent under to form a gooseneck. A row of holes had been punched into the last six inches of the tube. As the gas seeping out of the holes burned, the flames preheated the incoming gas until only escaping vapor was burning. We pronounced the construction simplicity itself and set about building our own heater.

We managed to scrape together the necessary parts at the boneyard of a neighboring bomber base where French pilots were being checked out in the Martin B-26. That particular combination of pilot and machine assured a generous supply of wrecked aircraft from which to scavenge. Finally, since a couple of test runs had been more or less successful, we decided to leave the heater on all night, being careful to place a pan under the gooseneck to catch any drips. When morning came, the tent was just as cold as ever. The damn heater had gone out during the night, leaving an inch of gasoline in the catch pan. From deep in his sack, a pilot we called George suggested that I get up and dump it outside. But I had a better idea. I could just reach the stove without getting up, so into its mouth I pitched a lighted match. The pan flared with a whoosh and began burning brightly. As the thing heated up, the flames, alarmingly, began to leap a foot or two out of the steel can.

At this juncture I suspected that I might have made a mistake. I ran outside in my undershorts to get a fire extinguisher. By the time I got back, my tent mates were sitting atop the blankets and warming their feet by the flames, which were now licking five feet up the tent pole. I worked the stirrup pump furiously but failed to produce a single drop. The damn extinguisher was empty. Luckily, the fire started running out of gas and finally subsided, leaving a badly charred tent pole. A near miss, considering what might have happened if the tent pole had burned through and collapsed the tent. I thanked my tent mates, dryly, for all their help. No one responded except George, who wanted to know if I would provide the same service on the following morning. I told them all to go to hell.

★

For a change, we trainees had to be given aircraft assignments before training started so that each of us would be trained in the type of aircraft with which his future unit was equipped. There were two American Spitfire groups in the Mediterranean Theater, the 31st and the 52d Fighter Groups. The Spits were used for air-to-air combat rather than ground attack; I opted for the Spit training. Fortunately, this preference was not shared by all. In an informal, hand-raising session where preferences were expressed, my close friends and I succeeded in getting assigned to Spitfires.

The fighting units were equipped with Spit Mark VIIIs and IXs. The Mark Vs at the school must have been combat castoffs. Decrepit or not, they were honest-to-goodness Spitfires, and our enthusiasm for flying them was unbounded. Telergma had only a few Spitfire instructors. They were on temporary duty from the 31st and 52d Groups. Of the two from the 31st, I remember one, Van Ausdell, very well, since it was he who checked me out for my first flight. He was soft-spoken, patient, and treated me as a fellow fighter pilot instead of with the "I know it all and you don't know anything" attitude commonly found in flight instructors. Perhaps it was because he was not a flight instructor, but a combat pilot.

In many respects the British fighter was a marked departure from its American cousins. Instead of manifold pressure in inches of mercury, the engine-power setting was controlled by reference to a boost gauge graduated in pounds. In the Spit, 14 pounds of boost approximated 30 inches of mercury. The brakes were not applied by toeing the rudder pedals but by operating a hand lever on the stick similar to a motorcycle brake lever. The grip on the end of the stick was not the familiar pistol type but a circular handle fitted with a rectangular button. The button, pressed by the right thumb, fired the guns. Pressing up fired the four .303s, pressing down fired the two 20mm cannons, mashing full in fired everything. The compass was not mounted on the instrument panel; it swung in a horizontal position forward of the stick, very much like a marine compass. But probably the biggest change was that the gear-retraction handle was on the right side of the cockpit. On takeoff the pilot had to shift his left hand from the throttle to the stick to free his right hand to raise the gear. For those who were not flying, it was great sport to watch each fledgling take off. Invariably, at 15 to 20 feet of altitude, the Spit would make a sudden dip toward the ground as the pilot switched hands and reached for the gear handle. Our guardian angels must have been accomplished pilots, because no one clipped the ground during this strange maneuver.

The landing gear was very narrow, so the pilot had to stay on the rudders long after the plane had quit flying. If the Spit got away to one side or the other, it was virtually impossible to stop a ground loop.

We all got through our first flights without difficulty. Thereafter the instructors left us pretty much on our own to practice formation flying and get ourselves well into the aircraft comfort zone—to achieve that level of competence and familiarity where we flew instinctively, without conscious thought. In the air the Spitfire was a pure joy to fly. It was an honest airplane, highly maneuverable and instantly responsive to the slightest control pressure.

We took turns leading four-ship flights out over the trackless waste of desert. When it was my turn to lead, I came within an inch of getting the four of us into trouble. I've forgotten what we were doing—probably rat-racing, a kind of follow-the-leader in line astern where we chased each other all over the sky. When it came time to start for home, I had only a vague notion in what direction the field lay. The low, jagged ridges and alkali flats all looked the same and seemed to stretch to the horizon in all directions. Fortunately, there was a direction finding (D/F) station near Telergma, which I contacted. The operator replied promptly, giving me a steer back to base.

I was almost due south of the field—the course given me was 345 degrees, north northwest. I rotated the cover glass on the compass and set its two parallel lines to the desired heading. But when I turned the aircraft to align the pointer on the card between the lines, I put the little index arrow at the wrong end.

Unbeknownst to me, I was flying the reciprocal, away from the field instead of toward it. When I gave the D/F operator another count, six or seven minutes later, he gave me the same steer but said my transmission sounded weaker. I thought his did, too, and one close look at the compass told me why. In my embarrassment and frustration, I wracked into a 180-degree turn, momentarily scattering the other three planes. Another count five minutes later confirmed that we were inbound, and soon after that I began to recognize landmarks. Someone in the flight called out the field just as the fuel supply was getting to be worrisome. None of my three mates said anything after the flight. They didn't have to. We all knew what I had done wrong, and it was a profitable lesson for all.

Finally it was completed, this Spitfire indoctrination, and we were moving on again, for the last time. With fifteen or twenty hours in Spits, we pronounced ourselves ready for the Luftwaffe's finest. However misplaced such juvenile overconfidence was, I have since come to the conclusion that without this attitude, a pilot would be better suited to bomber or transport aircraft than fighters.

But were we really ready, I wondered? I remembered reading about World War I and being astonished that, in 1917 to 1918 the longevity of pilots at the front was something like three weeks—less than that for new pilots, who often lasted less than a few days. Even the Red Baron, Von Richthofen, took a cavalier attitude toward new pilots, if the stories could be believed. He simply told them to get up there and do the job or be killed.

"Well," I assured myself, "I didn't come all this way to become Messerschmitt meat or Focke-Wulf fodder. Maybe some of the others, but not me."

8

A C-47 was scheduled to take us from Telergma up to Naples. I, along with seventeen other pilots bound for the 31st Fighter Group, were only passengers, so we went where the C-47 went. Where it went was to Siracusa, Sicily, and there it stayed for the night. Claude, Doctor Tom, and I found our billets, washed up, and were wondering just what one did for amusement on an evening in Siracusa. One of the guys who had been out scouting returned with the news that a party was in progress, and he would show us where it was. We started out on foot to find this bit of Sicilian high life.

As we walked along the narrow, half-dark street, it became apparent that we were not in, nor were we going toward, any center of night life. We were going into a residential area. I was convinced that our guide was lost and I was for turning back immediately; Doctor Tom was not so sure, and Claude was for pressing on regardless. Finally we turned in at what looked to be a middle-class house, and our knock was answered by an older man who welcomed us with open arms and cries of delight, as if we were long-lost friends or relatives come home at last. Everyone—the family and some of our gang—was crammed into what appeared to be a large dining room, around whose central table everyone ranged on a variety of seats. The air was thick with American cigarette smoke, the atmosphere gay and festive, no doubt aided and abetted by a seemingly inexhaustible supply of vino brought out by our host—for a price, of course. I was no wine connoisseur, but I thought that it tasted suspiciously like grape juice that had been fortified with some kind of alcohol. No matter. It went down and produced the desired effect.

Our host had a cousin—or was it an uncle?—living in Brooklyn, and he assured us, more than once, that, "finish *guèrra*, me go America, too." And the talk continued in this vein as we worked our way through wads of lira and piles of bottles. Doctor Tom seemed to be making some progress with a young lady who, though not particularly shapely or pretty, was nevertheless our age, which was recommendation enough considering his heightened libido and impaired sobriety. I was not so far gone that I didn't see what was going on, and I got worried when he and the young lady quietly departed for another part of the house. I half expected the old man to come unglued and perhaps extort some hush money or, worse, start hollering for police or MPs. But no one seemed to take notice, although their departure was certainly observed by everyone. I suppose the old man was, by his own ethical standards, a man of honor, and to half of Europe in 1944 honor lay in doing what you had to do to survive.

Tom returned shortly thereafter, and we all bade our new friends good night soon afterward. He was full of remorse, disgusted with himself for what he had done ("Shit, what did I do that for?"). More important, he confided as we lurched down the silent, narrow street, "I forgot to pick up a prophylactic kit from the medics before leaving Telergma."

Claude volunteered the information that he had heard that, as an emergency measure, washing one's self with a handful or two of whiskey would do the trick. But we had no whiskey, either. Only the half-full bottle of vino Claude had carried away with him.

"Well," Tom spoke up resignedly, reaching for the bottle, "I guess that'll have to do. It's better than nothing."

So Claude and I stood there and watched the last of our wine run through Tom's fingers and down his pants legs. The resultant sticky mess further confirmed my suspicions that it was grape juice, but perhaps there was enough rubbing alcohol or antifreeze in it to do some good. Something did, it turned out. Tom got off scot-free.

★

In the spring of 1944, the airfield at Castel Volturno was the home of the 31st Fighter Group. So, on March 31, 1944, after being flown to Naples, we were trucked up to the 31st billeting area. Of the eighteen pilots assigned to the 31st, Claude, Little Henry, Doctor Tom, George, a pilot named Jack Edge, and I were the six who went to the 308th

Squadron. Jim Brooks and his buddies went to the 307th, and another third went to the 309th.

The front lines were hardly 20 miles away, and the sounds of heavy artillery were unmistakable in the soft, warm air of the Italian spring-time. As I lay on my bunk, I tried to imagine what it was like up there at the source of that incessant booming. The noise up close to the guns must have been earsplitting, and the artillerymen who served them must have been in a continuous state of shock.

The group had gone off operational flying in preparation for a move and a change of aircraft type. I was disappointed to learn that the 31st was giving up its Spitfires, re-equipping with P-51 Mustangs, and moving to the east coast of Italy near San Severo. Both the 31st and the 52d Groups were being trans-ferred to the newly formed 306th Fighter Wing of the Fifteenth Air Force, joining the P-47s of the 325th Fighter Group and the several P-38 groups that were already opera-tional and engaged in bomber-escort missions.

Most of the pilots were away on a ferry mission to Casablanca to bring back the first consignment of P-51s, but those few who were available would do nicely for our purpose; anyone who had flown even one combat mission was someone to be attended and listened to. We had little to do during this stand-down except hang around the flight line and prompt the older heads to talk about their experiences. As part of the Twelfth Air Force, whose mission was ground support, the 31st had provided air cover over the front line and the Anzio beach-head. The missions consisted of patrols of relatively short duration, limited by the fuel capacity of the Spitfire. From listening to the talk, I gathered that when enemy aircraft were encountered, a lot of sparring took place that didn't always end in a fight. Like all good little fledgling combat pilots, I kept my mouth shut, but I couldn't help wondering at this. I had always been told that the essence of the fighter pilot credo was to find 'em and have at 'em straightaway. Was this so much BS pumped into us by rear-area training people who never had to put their necks on the line? I didn't know. But I did know one thing: I was going to find out for myself very soon.

One day I walked the half mile to the mouth of the Volturno River. It was not a nice day; low stratus hung in the air overhead, obscuring the sky and casting a darkening gloom over the scene. A light rain had fallen earlier and, although it had stopped, the grass and brush were still wet to the touch. I sat down anyway, unmindful of the dampness. Suddenly I was back in my hometown again, back in Wisconsin.

It must have been in the fall of '40 or the spring of '41. The day was cool and rainy as I walked the two and a half miles from home to downtown. A captured Messerschmitt had been set up in an open park on the lake front, just behind Hotel Racine, as part of a touring display. The purpose was to stimulate interest in Bundles for Britain, or Lend-Lease, or some other such cause of which I had scant knowledge and less interest. But that plane interested me.

A wooden platform with steps had been set up beside the cockpit, and there was no admission charge; it was free. The attendant, an RAF sergeant, was deeply engrossed in conversation with a young lady, the only other person around. He waved one arm perfunctorily, as if to say, "Help yourself; I'm busy right now."

I walked around the outside first, impressed by everything—the large identification crosses on the sides of the fuselage, even the small legends printed in German at various places. Then I climbed the stairs and leaned in as far as I could, staring at the instrument panel, the controls, and all the knobs and levers. When I looked for the sergeant to ask him something, he was crossing the street with the young lady, heading for a nearby coffee shop. Well and good. The "Do Not Enter" sign surely did not apply to me.

I threw a leg over the cockpit edge, climbed in, and sat down. I grasped the stick, put my left hand on the throttle, slid my feet forward onto the rudder pedals, and sat transfixed.

Who had sat like this before me? Did he squeeze this trigger and shoot these guns? Had he shot down a Hurricane or a Beaufighter? I had no love for the Luftwaffe, but I was flying with that German pilot in the skies over Europe—touching the things he touched, looking through the same sight he once looked through. I felt close to The War, in on momentous events far removed from Racine.

The mood was broken by the sergeant, who had returned unseen by me while I was at 3,000 meters over the English Channel in that Messerschmitt.

"Out," he commanded with a jerk of his thumb, and I hastily obeyed.

As I walked home, I came back again and again to that cockpit and that feeling of participation.

Now, surveying the beach and the riverbanks, I tried to reconstruct in my mind's eye the scenes of a few scant months before, when a terrific infantry battle had taken place on this spot. But the quiet desolation of the place, the rusting, abandoned equipment, belied the noise and death that had been here. The feeling that I sought, of recapturing the event and being a part of it, eluded me. I went back to the base and the only guidance I could turn to: the memories of the combat-seasoned pilots.

The older pilots had flown the Spit in combat for many months or years, had great confidence in it, and had adopted tactics that were best suited to the strong points of the aircraft. Since maneuverability was the forte of the Spit, the tactics of the group seemed to center on out-turning the German fighters—dogfighting, actually.

The old-timers were guarded in their view of the P-51. They had heard all the praise and all the pep talks from the upper echelons, but they also remembered their days in the P-39 and were completely unimpressed with the attempts that had been made thus far to field a really first-class American fighter. From the few hours accumulated during the ferry flights, they recognized that the P-51 was a different breed of horse, but it did not have the sweet feel of their beloved Spitfire. Of those pilots who were eligible, most elected to pack it in and go home. The ones who stayed had to learn to fly differently and fight a completely different air battle—not an easy task. For a bunch of wild-flying young men from Panama who had nothing to unlearn, however, it didn't matter a bit what we were mounted on, just so we got to point the business end of it at the bad guys.

The record of the 31st at the time it ceased Spitfire operations was impressive. From August 1942, when the 31st traded in its P-39s for Spitfires, until this day, April 2, 1944, the 308th Fighter Squadron had shot down 67 enemy aircraft, including a couple of French Dewoitines in North Africa. The 307th had 65; the 309th, 56½. Adding in the 6 scored by headquarters pilots brought the group total to 194½—not especially big numbers at the time, but respectable, and every one of them had been earned the hard way.

A few days after our arrival it was time to pack again, this time with the whole group, for our move to San Severo. There was an old Spitfire Mark V still assigned to the 308th and, since there were just enough squadron pilots available to fly the new Mustangs from Castel Volturno to our new base, one of us new guys was going to get to ferry the old Spit. The operations officer asked which one of us would like to take the flight. All six of us jumped up, so he resorted to having us draw lots. I won. The others gave me a couple of verbal parting shots about getting lost and went off to find their trucks. I was handed a chart. A pencil mark showed the location of the field. Then I was on my own.

No sweat. I could handle the Spit, and I sure as hell could fly 100 miles without getting lost. I began to fantasize about running into an Me-109 that had happened to stray too far south into the area of my direct route. In my mind's eye, I got onto his tail and sent him crashing to the ground in short order. All the way over I kept a sharp lookout, especially to the north, but there was nothing up there to be seen, and I was finally brought down to earth when at last I caught sight of the pierced steel planking (PSP) runway at San Severo. I lined up with the runway for my initial approach. As I crossed the boundary at 500 feet, I pitched up into a tight 360-degree turn, chopped the throttle, and dropped gear and flaps as I continued around. I rolled out just over the end of the runway. As I lost airspeed and the nose came up, the wheels touched, skipped, and began to roll. I had landed at San Severo, the first of many, many such landings. Before my last, I was to see, feel, and do things that I would not have believed that day, April 3, 1944.

The town of San Severo was not much, but it did boast an opera house, making it a place of some substance in that poorer part of agrarian Italy. San Severo had probably changed very little in the last centuries; even the standard Italian tomato paste was made in the same way as ever. The processing of tomatoes went on indoors, but the resulting thick red soup was spread on wooden boards and placed in the sun before each dwelling, at the angle where the sidewalk met the wall. The ubiquitous red squares were always out there, unprotected from the equally ubiquitous flies, which caused more than one of us to swear off any locally prepared meals.

Our housing area, eight or nine miles from the town, was formerly an Italian Army post, so there was a cluster of permanent buildings—various administrative facilities and housing for the officers. The spaces between them were filled with the enlisted men's tents. The housing structures were masonry with tiled roofs, the long narrow interiors broken up by walls into a series of rooms. They were dark and gloomy inside, devoid of creature comforts other than Army cots. The stark interiors and hard, cold floors, which produced a faint echo when walked upon, combined to give the places a look and feel of monasticism. The living quarters hardly seemed those of high-spirited young men.

The airdrome, four miles away in the general direction of San Severo, was sited next to an olive grove and had a single PSP runway. The parking area for the 31st was an open dusty clearing on the northeast end of the field. The opposite end was occupied by a photoreconnaissance ("recce") outfit. A wooden structure served as a control tower, but since we didn't have the crystals for the frequency on which it operated, traffic was on pretty much of a scramble system. The 31st took off in one direction and the recce outfit took off in the opposite direction.

During the first week of operation at San Severo, when we were still making familiarization flights in the Mustang, this dangerous situation almost cost Little Henry his life. He was waiting on our end of the runway to take off while, unbeknownst to him, a Mosquito was waiting on the other end to do the same. Both pilots were waiting for a B-25, which was making an approach to land toward Little Henry. After the B-25 touched down, its pilot pulled off the PSP and onto the dirt apron and began taxiing back to the recce end. His plane kicked up a great cloud of dust, which drifted across the runway. As soon as the B-25 was clear of the runway, both Little Henry and the Mosquito started their takeoff rolls. To those of us standing in front of the operations tent, the drama seemed to be unfolding in slow motion. We stood transfixed with mouths agape as the two aircraft gathered speed toward each other—all of us except one older pilot, who started running futilely, waving his arms and yelling, "No, no!" at the top of his lungs. What happened next was quicker than the time it takes to tell. The Mosquito pilot spotted Little Henry bearing down on him and horsed his machine in the air at stalling speed, just managing to stagger over the onrushing Mustang by a hair's breadth. When the Mosquito passed the B-25, the 25 pilot pulled out onto the runway to taxi the rest of the way on the PSP. So, just as Little Henry raised the tail of his aircraft and saw the Mosquito flash over him, he was confronted with a B-25 pulling into his path. Now it was Little Henry's turn to haul his reluctant aircraft into the air before it was ready. It was all over in a second or two, but we spectators were badly shaken. The old type, who had gotten 15 to 20 feet toward the runway, was on his knees retching. Little Henry took the incident in stride, seeming none the worse for his experience. One good thing that resulted from this near miss was the establishment of a common tower frequency for all locally based aircraft.

We soon found out that the P-51 Mustang was indeed a different breed of airplane. It was fast, for one thing. The Mustang indicated 250 to 260 miles per hour at low altitude, compared to about 210 for the P-39 and the P-40 at cruise power. The P-51 was redlined at 505 and, though it was no Spitfire, its turning ability wasn't bad at all—especially if you sneaked down 10 degrees of flaps. It was pretty good in the climbing department, too, and accelerated very fast in a dive. But the thing that really set the Mustang apart from any other fighter, friend or foe, was its range. With a 75-gallon tank slung under each wing, it could perform the unheard-of: It could fly *six-hour* missions!

Physically it was pleasing to the eye and looked fast, even sitting on the ground. Power was provided by a V-1650 Rolls-Royce Merlin engine built under license in the States by Packard, the luxury automobile company. The V-1650 was a fine engine and could be taken up to 61 inches of manifold pressure at 3,000 RPM for takeoff or, if needed in combat, 67 inches for up to five minutes in Emergency Power. Normally aspirated engines tended to run out of power as altitude increased, usually between 15,000 and 20,000 feet. The P-51 had a two-stage blower in the induction system that was controlled automatically with a barometric switch. Around 17,000 feet, when the throttle had been advanced almost all the way forward just to maintain normal cruise, the blower would kick into high, the manifold pressure would jump up, and the climb could be continued to 30,000 feet. The P-51 could be taken a lot higher than that, but above 30,000 feet the power was way down and the controls had to be handled gingerly.

The landing gear was wide set and sturdy so that it took a lot of doing to screw up a landing, and a ground loop was all but impossible. Control of the tail wheel provided a new wrinkle that none of us had seen before. The wheel was steerable for minor turns while taxiing but, to make a sharp turn, it could be unlocked by pushing the stick full forward. An unlocked and free-swiveling tail wheel enabled the aircraft to pivot around on one wheel. With the stick returned to a neutral position, as the aircraft began rolling straight ahead, the tail wheel trailed and then locked again, allowing slight left-right travel.

The only blemish that kept the B model from being superb was the armament. Only four .50-caliber machine guns were installed, two in each wing. The laminar wing section, whose thinness gave the plane its exceptional speed, was not without its cost; the guns could not fit upright and were canted over at an angle. Thus, the ammunition feed trays had to make a slight curve upward and then down again to enable the link-belted rounds to enter the gun a right angle. This arrangement could cause jamming under certain conditions. Later on, in combat, it created a potentially dangerous situation for me when all four guns stopped firing.

The aircraft identification markings of each of the squadrons had been assigned in England in July 1942 and had remained unchanged. Our P-51s were painted accordingly:

Squadron	Designator
307th	MX
308th	HL
309th	WZ

The squadron designator was placed on each side of the fuselage, forward of the national insignia, and the individual aircraft letter was aft of it. The group marking first tried was a single red diagonal stripe across the vertical tail surface, angling down and back from the forward tip. However, this did not prove to be sufficiently visible. Within days, three more equally spaced stripes were added, giving the tail a sort of barber-pole look.

The 308th's call sign, Helpful, was briefly changed to Broker and then to Border, which it remained. The 307th's was Playboy and the 309th's was Woodbine. The CO of the 307th reported that on a mission to Toulon, immediately after calling a turn by using the squadron call sign, Playboy, he heard a female voice on our radio channel. The voice remarked plainly, above the normal chatter, "My, what cute names you Americans have." I couldn't vouch for the story because I didn't hear the transmission, but we knew the Germans were monitoring our radio channels.

My indoctrination with the P-51 was typical of that of the pilots in the group, since, with the exception of some ferry time, no one, not even the old heads, had any experience with the Mustang. There were no flight manuals, either—at least none that I ever saw. Thus we learned by doing and exchanging information with each other.

My flight records show two local flights on April 5 and 6, 1944; practice formation flying from April 7 through April 11; and high-altitude test-firing on April 12. A full-scale formation flight in group strength was laid on for April 14 and handled exactly like the real thing. Another followed the next day. That training flight proved to be the last for us, since it prompted the higher-ups to pronounce the group ready for combat operations. I had logged a grand total of fifteen hours in the P-51, of which four and a half had come on the two group practices.

Despite the short training neither I nor any of the rest of us felt unready; I think we would have gone into combat sooner than that if it had been left up to us.

9

Finally the day arrived. On April 16, 1944, the newly Mustanged group and I were to share a first together, a sortie over enemy-held territory. The pre-flight activities that day were typical and were to be repeated, with slight variations, over and over again, each time the group went out to do battle.

On April 16 the mission order was received from higher headquarters four to six hours before takeoff. It contained the essential information needed at the 31st to complete the operational planning: the target; rendezvous point and time; group task, such as target-area cover or close escort; and the bomber groups to be escorted. The mission order also contained such information as the initial point (IP), the point from which the bombers would start their straight run to the bomb-release point; the direction of turn off the target; and the withdrawal route. With this data the group operations and intelligence officers did the detailed planning and prepared the displays in the briefing room.

The pilots scheduled to fly were awakened about an hour before the briefing. But everyone, even the ground officers, was caught up in the excitement of our inaugural mission, so they all turned out and bustled around, getting cleaned up and dressed. Breakfast was a hurried affair—all the basic rations were either canned, dried, or powdered, and there was not much a cook could do with so little to work with. The standard fare was creamed chipped beef on toast (which went by a variety of nicknames, all of them vulgar) and powdered eggs, powdered milk, cereal, and so on. Though I would have preferred to drink milk, the coffee was strong and plentiful and I claimed my share of it.

In flying school most of us had picked up the cigarette habit. I don't think I was enslaved by Demon Tobacco, at least I didn't lapse into a nicotine fit if I had to do without, as some fellows did. Smoking was just something we all did mindlessly and could afford—the cost was one dollar for a carton of Lucky Strikes, Old Golds, Chesterfields, or Camels, the popular brands of the day. After breakfast, everyone lit a cigarette if he had one or bummed one if he didn't, and straggled by twos and threes over to the nearby briefing room.

The largest building in the complex was divided roughly in half by a solid interior wall. The northern part, with a tiny bar in one corner, served as the group Officers' Club and on Sundays doubled as a chapel for Mass and other denominational services. The other, slightly larger part was the briefing room. Ordinarily, it could accommodate the fifty-odd scheduled pilots, but today the chairs and benches, which extended from just in front of the low stage at the front of the room all the way to the back, were filled to overflowing. Standees ranged down the sides and across the back of the room. On the front wall, behind the stage, was a huge map of the southern half of Europe and a blackboard on which was chalked the variable mission information of the day.

The briefing, called for two hours before takeoff, was opened by the senior officer who was to lead the group—or, more correctly, to lead the lead squadron. He covered all the operational details: engine-start times, order of squadron takeoff, form up, headings, rendezvous and IP times, and the bomber groups and tail markings of our assigned part of the bomber stream. He often referred to the map behind him, on which the complete mission track was laid out with colored string. On this, our first go, we were assigned to escort B-24s to Turnul Severin, a city at the Iron Gate, a narrow, steep-banked stretch of the Danube separating Yugoslavia and Rumania. It was a milk run, actually, but that string represented a 400-mile flight each way over strange territory held by the enemy.

The senior officer talked about radio discipline and the need for absolute radio silence until rendezvous or unless engaged by enemy aircraft. Any transmission the Germans intercepted would help them deduce our intended target and the strength of the attacking force. A half hour, even fifteen minutes, additional warning time would be helpful to them in preparing to meet our massed formations. Then the officer gave us a time hack, and everyone set his watch on signal.

Next the intelligence briefer gave his guesstimate of the expected opposition. Flak was supposed to be light, and no enemy fighters were reported in the vicinity. Then it was the weatherman's turn. He forecast some cumulus cloud buildups over the mountains of western Yugoslavia, immediately beyond the Adriatic, but nothing that would interfere with the mission. The target was to be clear.

Then it was time to get on with it. Everyone filed out and headed for the transport vehicles for the fifteen-minute ride to the field and the respective squadron "dispersal areas." Each of the three squadrons had its own open field to park in, but tagging them as dispersal areas was taking some liberties with the term. There were no hardstands, no revetments, no perimeter track—not even designated taxiways. Just an open, dusty field with twenty-five P-51s scattered about. Adjacent to our parking area was a large pyramidal tent that served as the squadron operations, or ops, center. It was here that we spent the final minutes before going out to man our planes.

I was to fly on the wing of the squadron leader, Major James "Stick" Thorsen. Since he was leading Red Flight, my call sign would be Border Red Two. I noted the identity of the aircraft I was assigned to fly; its location; and the location of Thorsen's P-51, which I would be following out of the parking area. The air that pervaded the ops tent was one of expectancy, but everyone, at least the veterans, seemed relaxed and at ease. The mission had been planned to be a walkover, with no opposition, but milk run or no, I was excited, although I tried not to show it. I was going to fly a combat mission. Finally. After all the indignities of Pre-flight, the trials and tribulations of flight training, and the sometimes hair-raising experiences with the P-39. Now, at long last, I was on the threshold of the one thing that had been my goal since I first raised my right hand in Milwaukee and was sworn into the Army Air Corps. No matter that there were no enemy fighters expected or that I was going as a lowly wingman. I was going and I would be mounted on one of the latest and best front-line fighters with hot guns, and that made my heart beat a little faster.

Out at the aircraft the crew chief—the mechanic who had charge of that plane—and the armorer were waiting. Perhaps they were as excited as I was; if they were, I couldn't tell. Only their quiet confidence showed. They had been out there for an hour, running up the engine and checking the mags, the oxygen system, the radio, the sight, guns, gun heaters—everything that could be checked. They knew the equipment was ready. They could do nothing more for me now but help me into my parachute and shoulder straps, plug in the radio and mike cords, and wait for engine start. It seemed as though we sat there for a long time, making small talk, but it couldn't have been more than a couple of minutes. Then it was time.

Battery switch on. A short pump of the primer. Fuel-pump switch on. Crack the throttle an inch.

"Clear!" I shouted, leaning my head out to warn anyone to get clear of the propeller.

Mag switch to the Both position. Start switch held on. The prop began turning slowly. Then, as the engine fired, I moved the mixture control forward and the engine roared to life, sputtering and belching clouds of blue smoke from the exhaust stacks, gradually smoothing to a steady, smokeless idle. Some of the acrid exhaust swirled into the cockpit, stinging my eyes, but it was all familiar and I felt good. Oil pressure and fuel pressure looked okay. With raised fists together, thumbs extending right and left, I gave the crew chief the "chocks out" signal and then waited while he clambered up onto the wing for the ride out to the runway.

Then he was jumping down, and I pulled out onto the PSP behind Thorsen. The takeoff and join-up were a blur, accomplished more by rote than by a conscious effort on my part. I stuck to Thorsen like glue, hardly seeing anything that was not in my field of vision while looking at the side of his aircraft. I know we met our bombers at the rendezvous, and I did get to see the bombs drop away. Then I saw a row of four black flak bursts at our level several hundred yards to our left. Seconds later a row of four again, this time a little closer in but lower and farther aft. Then nothing. I had never seen flak before. It looked pretty close to me, but Thorsen took no notice; he didn't even bother to change course or altitude. The flight was otherwise uneventful, and four hours and twenty minutes after my wheels had left the steel runway at San Severo, they touched down again. I dropped my chute and flying gear at the personal-equipment tent, then I sought out Thorsen and stood by while he made his post-flight report. Afterward I asked him about the flak.

"Most likely 88s," he said, "a battery of four guns probably laid by radar. If you can't hear the bursts, they're not close enough to worry about. If you're directly over them, they have a ghost of a chance of getting lined up on you. But if you're passing even a mile or two to the side of their position, it's pretty tough for them to hit anything." I took his word for it, but I still felt that those black puffs looked awfully menacing.

All in all, I had to admit, the mission was pretty tame stuff, except for a misfortune that happened in the 309th. While crossing over the top of the B-24s, 1,500 feet above them, the P-51s were fired upon by some of the gunners. Two of the fighters were hit, and one of the pilots had to bail out over Yugoslavia. An important lesson to remember, I thought: It isn't only the German fighters and flak that can knock you down. To our practiced eye, the Mustang didn't look anything like a Messerschmitt. They both had in-line engines, however, and to the nervous gunners, who were accustomed to seeing only the blunt-nosed P-47s and the twin-tailed P-38s, that similarity was enough to draw their fire.

I was quite satisfied with my own performance. I had seen Fortress Europa from 25,000 feet, had kept my wing position smartly for four hours and twenty minutes, and was pleased at having mission number 1 under my belt. Now I had the privilege of regaling my Panama buddies who had not gone on the mission with endless recitations of the minutest detail until I had exhausted the subject, if not the audience.

★

The second mission was to escort B-24s attacking the marshaling yards at Sofia, the capital of Bulgaria. I wasn't going, so I had to cool my heels, standing around and waiting. The mission turned out to be a huge success. Colonel Charles "Sandy" McCorkle, the group commander, drew first blood for the re-equipped 31st, scoring two victories. He flew with the 309th, so I didn't get to hear his combat report firsthand. But the news went through the group like wildfire. This was it! This was the real thing! My outfit had closed with the enemy and had something to show for it, and I was a part of it, however vicariously. I was really pumped up.

The very next day, April 18, 1944, I was again on Thorsen's wing when the 31st was scheduled to support P-38s strafing the airdrome at Udine, Italy. Our course would take us northward up the middle of the Adriatic Sea, crossing the coastline between Venice and Trieste. Udine lay in the plain bounded by the sea and the Dolomite Alps, and there were reported to be large numbers of fighters and bombers there. The distance to Udine was about 375 miles, and I guess Fifteenth Air Force Headquarters did not like an enemy airdrome that close to Italian bases plump with juicy targets. To my knowledge, we had no fighter-interceptor capability at all in the area and only the most rudimentary antiaircraft weapons were in place. The idea was to punish the Luftwaffe into pulling back into Austria and Hungary. On the Udine mission we didn't engage enemy aircraft, but on the radio-telephone (R/T) I could hear other pilots in the group calling out bogies and bandits. I was very unhappy that we went about our business as if we were alone in the sky.

We had been plagued by bad weather all the way up to the target. Coming home, Thorsen went down through a hole and we came back under an overcast, flying at 300 to 400 feet. The weather was dark and threatening with occasional showers spattering the windscreen. I was relieved when it began to lighten up as we neared San Severo.

After we landed, I brazenly asked the major why we hadn't made any attempt to find the enemy aircraft called out. I took pains to hide my disappointment. He just smiled and said something about a long war. He knew what he was doing, which was to perform the squadron's assigned task; he was not about to go flogging all over the sky, looking for a couple of Me-109s.

The 308th lost two pilots on this mission. They were homeward bound down the Italian coastline, trying to stay under the bad weather, when they crashed near Ancona Point. No one knew for sure if they were victims of the low ceiling and visibility or if they were hit by the antiaircraft fire for which Ancona was famous. They were listed as MIA.

The 308th Squadron tallied its first victories in P-51s on the Udine flight—one each scored by two of the flight leaders, Fred Trafton and Tommy Byrnes. But more important to me was the news that Doctor Tom, who was flying a wing position, got off a couple of bursts at an Me-109 and claimed a damage. I was so disappointed on missing the action, I didn't even congratulate Tom. I don't know if it was just thoughtlessness or jealousy.

When I got to know Major Thorsen better, I developed a keen liking and respect for him as a man and as a squadron commander. He was undistinguished physically, tending toward the stout side, with none of the bombast everyone had come to associate with a good combat leader. But he was not interested in appearances, only results. Even though he lived apart from the rest of the officers, he seemed to have a sixth sense about what was going on in the squadron; he knew who wanted to fly and who didn't, who should lead and who should follow. He never tried to explain unpopular decisions, even though he must have known about the grumbling and second-guessing that went on. He was friendly enough but a very private person—an enigma to the new guys. His aircraft was named *Nightshade*, which I thought was a stupid name because it sounded vaguely like a window covering. I asked him what it meant, but he turned my question aside without a direct answer. Years after the war, I learned that it is a highly poisonous plant common in England and usually referred to as deadly nightshade.

In April 1944, Captain Roland Lamensdorf, one of the ground officers, was officially the 308th Squadron intelligence officer. Because he was older and wiser than anyone else in the squadron (he was thirty-one years old), Lam was actually a kind of guardian–father confessor to the rest of us, especially the new pilots. He was already a lawyer before he entered the military service and, having been in the 31st since September 1942, he knew the ropes pretty well. He was a good guy, and we liked and respected him very much.

Whenever anyone complained about something at San Severo, Lam could always be counted on to restore some perspective, beginning each recounted episode with, "If you think this is rough, you should have been at Thelepte" (pronounced "Tell-EP"). Thelepte Airdrome in Tunisia was the home of the 31st in February 1943, and apparently the living conditions were awful—the worst that had to be endured before or since. Besides the annoyance of daily German fighter attacks and frequent sandstorms, water had to be trucked from Tebessa, 45 miles away. Each man was allotted only one gallon per day for drinking, cooking, washing, and shaving. Food consisted of canned C rations, usually cold. To make matters worse, the *Afrika Korps* broke through the American lines at Kasserine Pass, forcing the 31st to evacuate all personnel and equipment just hours ahead of the advancing German Army. After listening to such a litany of hardships, it was difficult to be unhappy with conditions at San Severo.

Right after the group became operational, a major from the 4th Fighter Group in England came down on temporary duty. His name was James Goodson, and he had a wealth of experience in fighter escort of heavy bombers. He had heard his share of shots fired in anger, having been a member of the Eagle Squadron in England before the United States entered the war. He already had a sizable string of ten victories at the time he arrived. Acting the consultant is not an easy job, but Goodson had the personality and good sense to pull it off. His experience must have been invaluable to the squadron COs and the group staff. He never said much to us underlings, preferring to watch and listen, although he was always available to anyone who wanted to talk or ask questions. He went out a couple of times with the 307th, and on one mission he got two Me-109s. The armorer was dumbfounded when he opened the gun-bay doors and discovered how few rounds Goodson had used. They were good kills, too, confirmed by others who witnessed them. He left after two weeks and often thereafter I kicked myself for not making an effort to cultivate his friendship. He was one of the good guys.

★

The ground rules for victories were well understood by all the pilots, but I can't remember if they came out of 306th Fighter Wing Headquarters officially or were just something that had evolved in the group. I know Lam administered them in our squadron and, in the course of the post-flight briefings, established the individual claims that were approved by the squadron CO, forwarded to Group, and thence to Wing.

To claim a confirmed victory, one of the following must have occurred:

    a. The enemy fighter must have crashed into the ground
    b. The enemy pilot must have bailed out
    c. The enemy aircraft must have been enveloped in fire
    d. The enemy plane must have lost structural parts, such as a wing or tail surface

These conditions had to be either corroborated by another pilot or clearly visible on the gunsight aiming point (GSAP) camera film.

A claim of a probable was allowed if, as a result of numerous hits:

    a. The enemy aircraft was in a steep dive at low altitude or clearly out of control or
    b. It was losing glycol or oil but was otherwise flying in a controlled manner

A claim for an enemy aircraft damage was allowed whenever hits were observed but the aircraft escaped while it still appeared to be operating.

Of course there was some judgment exercised by Lam and the CO, especially on marginal claims. And a lot depended on who was making the claim; more leeway was generally given to veterans who had already scored several victories. In some cases a confirmed victory was credited if there was such a concentration of strikes in the cockpit area that it was considered impossible for the pilot to survive, even though the engagement may have been broken off at high altitude.

The armorer removed the film magazine from the GSAP camera in the wing root immediately after the fighter landed. He marked the magazine with the pilot's name and aircraft number, date, and claims. Group headquarters had no film-processing capability, so it was all sent over to Wing, at Torremaggiore. There it was developed, titled, and spliced together so that each group's film formed a separate segment. The following morning it was reviewed by the wing commander, Brigadier General Dean Strother, and his staff. Then each segment was sent back to its respective group. Group Operations ran the movies as soon as they arrived, but the pilots didn't get to see the film until the evening after the mission, before the main feature, when it got dark enough. The side of a building served as a movie screen.

Our guns were loaded with armor-piercing incendiary (API) ammunition. When an API round struck the target, the heat energy generated ignited an incendiary pellet in the end of the projectile, which caused a bright flash. The pellet ignited any volatile material nearby. As the film was shown in the evening for everyone, it didn't take a specialist to figure out who was doing all the scoring, since every hit caused a flash. The images of some of the enemy aircraft maneuvered on the side of the building in slow motion, with nothing to indicate they were even being attacked. Some others, like those of the planes Trafton and Byrnes had gone after, showed such a play of flashes on them that no doubt remained about their ultimate fates. *That* kind of scoring, I decided, was what I wanted to do.

10

Whenever I was down at the flight line, I liked to go out and talk to the mechanics or just climb up and sit in one of the planes. One day, as I sat in the closed cockpit enjoying the warm sun and the quiet, I looked around me and suddenly realized that, more than any other aircraft I had known and flown, I felt comfortable in the P-51 Mustang. It was like a favorite warm jacket or an old pair of shoes; everything was friendly and familiar, the feel, the look, even the smell. With my eyes closed I could see every gauge and dial, find every switch and lever merely by reaching out and putting my hand to it.

The engine instruments were pretty much the same as those for all liquid-cooled engines, even the old P-40s at Moore Field: manifold pressure and tachometer, fuel and oil pressure, oil and coolant temperature, and hydraulic pressure. Ditto the flight instruments. Although the turn and bank and the artificial horizon were frequently used going through an overcast, the compass and directional gyro, the altimeter, and clock were the key gauges now.

They were key because there were no navigational aids on the ground—no beacons, no low-frequency ranges, no Omni ranges, nothing—unless you wanted to count railroad tracks. That left dead reckoning and pilotage as the only means of finding the way across half of Europe. You flew your heading for x number of minutes or hours and watched for prominent checkpoints. Considering the distances flown and the poor information that was available on winds aloft, there was plenty of room for error, especially if an undercast, or broken cloud layer, obscured the ground. And it wasn't only the group and squadron leaders who had to worry about getting lost. En route to the rendezvous point, only the group leader was actually navigating. But, on the way home, flight leaders, element leaders, even individuals might well have to find San Severo on their own.

The large amounts of fuel the Mustang carried eased many of the worries about navigation. An awful lot of navigation errors could be rectified by the simple expedient of changing course, hunting around a bit, or even backtracking, if necessary.

The great range of the P-51 was provided by the internal fuel it carried: 92 gallons in each wing and 85 gallons in the fuselage tank. This was supplemented by two 75-gallon external tanks slung from bomb shackles under the wings. The fuel-tank selector, which had five positions corresponding to the five tanks, controlled fuel flow. The selector was in the center, below the instrument panel, just forward of the stick.

The Mustang was a far cry from the PT-19, in which we had learned to fly in Primary Flight School, and yet one of the fundamental lessons of our days in the PT-19 was to pay big dividends with the Mustang. That lesson was fuel management. The PT-19 had only one tank in each wing, and the instructors insisted that the quantity of fuel in each tank be kept very nearly the same on both sides. The cadet had to learn to switch the tank selector at approximate ten-minute intervals. This was not as easy as it sounds. Each cadet, to a man, was absolutely absorbed in trying to do his air work perfectly. How could the poor student remember to change tanks every ten minutes? Each cadet had to develop a sort of timer in his head that ticked away, regardless of what he was doing, until the interval had passed and he reached for the fuel selector. Like everything else about flying, we learned.

Now fuel management was a little more critical. The fuselage tank, an 85-gallon design afterthought, was behind the cockpit. With so much weight aft, the P-51 behaved very badly in tight turns with a full tank. Immediately after takeoff, even before switching to the jettisonable tanks, the pilot had to move the tank selector to "Fuselage" and monitor the fuel quantity until it was down in the 30- to 35-gallon range. If the pilot was forced to drop the external tanks and fight with a full fuselage tank, he was in serious trouble. Even in the hands of an average pilot, the Me-109 could easily outmaneuver a Mustang that had a full fuselage tank. On the other hand, if the pilot was distracted and ran the fuselage tank low or dry, he ran the risk of running out of fuel if he had to drop tanks at maximum range with significant amounts of fuel still in them.

One other fuel-management problem could rear its ugly head, especially when new, excitable pilots realized a fight was imminent. If the fuel selector was on one of the External positions when the tanks were dropped, the engine didn't run very well when it started sucking air. No permanent harm was done, but the momentary silence in the cockpit invariably rattled an already wrought-up new guy. If the truth be known, it rattled some old guys, too.

If a pilot encountered no enemy aircraft, he retained the external tanks and carried them home. If so, airspeed suffered on the return flight, but this penalty was far outweighed by the drastic reduction in the consumption of tanks and the reduced work load of the mechanics who had to install them. When a pilot wanted the tanks off, however, he wanted them off *right now*. They could be jettisoned electrically by arming the bomb circuit and toggling them off with the thumb button on the stick, or they could be manually salvoed by pulling a lever on the left side of the cockpit, below the instrument panel. Sometimes one or both tanks would fail to release by either method. During the early missions, having one hung tank was certainly the most common ailment of the Mustang, and the condition occurred at exactly the wrong time to have to start pushing levers or pulling positive g's to try to shake the tank off. In a fight, this was an invitation to get shot down and could not be tolerated.

The culprit in the hung-tank mystery turned out to be excessive zeal on the part of the mechanics, who had little or no previous experience with American external tanks. The feed lines were secured by clamps at the wing fitting and at the tank. To ensure that the tanks would feed properly and not leak, the installers tightened these clamps as hard as they could. Occasionally, an overtight clamp was enough to keep the tank from falling free. When the installers learned the technique of tightening just enough to prevent feed problems but not so much as to cause separation problems, the hung tanks were history.

Our personal flying equipment was the standard RAF gear we received at Telergma, where we started to learn to fly the Spitfire. The British parachute was different from its American counterpart in that it had a single-point quick release in the middle of the chest. The shoulder- and leg-strap terminal fittings were pushed into the release and were locked in place by spring-loaded latching pins. If a pilot bailed out and a strong wind was blowing on the surface, the extended canopy could act like a sail and drag him along, causing serious injury. The RAF chute could be released by rotating a three-inch metal disk on the quick-release mechanism to unlock it and then striking it with a sharp blow of the fist. This freed the shoulder and leg straps. The harness, with the shrouds and canopy attached, separated from the pilot as a unit. On a water landing, with the ever-present danger of becoming entangled in the shroud lines, the ability to get clear of the chute in one motion was particularly attractive. I had always considered the standard water-landing procedure with the U.S. chute to be a Mickey Mouse operation. The pilot was supposed to undo his leg straps and chest-snap hook at 100 feet above the water, keeping his arms down to prevent himself from slipping out of the harness. Then, at 10 feet, he was to throw his arms straight up and plummet into the water. The chute, freed of its burden, would drift away downwind, clear of the pilot struggling in the water—or so it was said. But, to me, judging the above-water height without knowing the state of the sea seemed like a pretty haphazard operation. I often wondered how many pilots dropped into the water from 100 or even 200 feet. Of course, the quick-release type harness had its downside, too. At the Fighter Training Center we were all warned more than once: "If you bail out, look down at the D ring, grab it, and give it a yank. Do not, repeat, do not get excited and try to open the chute by rotating and striking the quick release."

That made sense to me.

The RAF flying boots were well made and well designed, and I kept mine until I was finally ordered to turn them back in to Supply. The lower part was leather, like a regular shoe, and was worn directly over the sock. The calf portion of the boot was attached to the lower part by a neat row of stitches. If a pilot were shot down, he could cut the stitches and discard the upper portion of the boot. What was left was an ordinary-looking Oxford shoe, far less likely to attract the attention of the local populace or German soldiers than the American issue, which was a large, fleece-lined, zippered boot.

I knew nothing about electronics and radio other than to key the microphone when I wanted to talk and let up when I wanted to listen. Radio communication in training and in Panama was always less than satisfactory. Glass amplifier tubes were notoriously prone to damage from vibration. Like light bulbs, they just naturally burned out. Since there were very many of them in a transmitter and receiver and any of the tubes could cause some kind of mischief, the loss of radio communication was not uncommon. On the ground a technician could replace a burnt-out tube easily. He simply removed the radio cover, pulled out the old tube, and pushed a new one in after aligning the multipin base with the corresponding holes in the socket. But the ease with which tubes could be changed on the ground was no consolation to the pilot in formation who had to resort to hand signals or to waggling his wings at the tower to communicate.

The four-channel VHF set in the newer fighters was an order of magnitude better than its predecessors. On the P-51, the control box was mounted on the right side of the cockpit and connected by cables to the microphone in the oxygen mask and the earphones in the helmet. The transmit button was on the throttle. I suppose that back in some dimly lit laboratory somewhere, not so dimly lit professors were working on all sorts of good stuff. They certainly did a hell of a fine job on the four-channel set. Its clarity and fidelity were excellent, the static nonexistent, and communication seemed a whole lot more reliable. Perhaps they'd figured out how to ruggedize the fragile parts, or maybe the maintenance of the sets was better. But better they were. The A channel was used as the Fifteenth Air Force common for communicating with other groups; B was our 31st Group working channel; C was set to the tower frequency; and D was the emergency channel for contacting Air/Sea Rescue or the direction-finding station, Big Fence. Having only four channels was restrictive. But when you could hear and understand each time you used the radio, all other inconveniences were tolerable.

11

My first real baptism of fire came on April 21, 1944, with the first visit of the 31st to the Ploesti oil fields of Rumania. The milk runs were over.

During the briefing, all eyes were on that red string stretched across the huge map on the front wall. It ran from the spur of the Italian boot easterly across the Adriatic, across Yugoslavia to the bomber rendezvous point, and ended finally above Bucharest—almost 600 miles. No one in the group had ever flown that kind of mission before, particularly in a formation of forty-eight aircraft. The German war machine had to have gasoline and lube oil, and most of it came from the Balkans, from Ploesti. The oil fields as well as the extensive refineries that supported them had to be destroyed, even though they were American-owned. We dutifully jotted down the compass headings and times. In addition, I wrote down the engine start, or PT. *PT* was a term carried over from Spitfire days, when the start and ignition booster buttons were side by side and had to be pushed simultaneously. PT meant Push Tits.

The intelligence briefer took the stage and talked about flak installations and concentrations of enemy fighters in the immediate vicinity of the target. His wording was a masterpiece of hedging worthy of the best Philadelphia lawyer. A statement such as "Sixty-three large-caliber antiaircraft guns are believed to be in the area south of the target" always set me to wondering. Believed by whom? And did he really believe that there were sixty-three, or was that a nice number somewhere between fifty and a hundred? I had the feeling that someone was trying to measure a fly speck to three decimal places with a yardstick. Granted, intelligence work was an inexact business, and I am sure that, if any better information was available, we would have gotten it. Still, I waited—in vain, as it turned out—for someone, just once, to stand up on that stage and say, "I don't have a damned clue as to what you're going to run into up there."

The forecast was for bad weather all the way to the target, but that was nothing new either. In the absence of reliable data, I think the weatherman played safe and called for bad weather everywhere. That way he was in a position to take the "I told you so" route if the weather was stinko. Or he could take credit for surprisingly fine conditions, as if he had had something to do with the improvement. At the end of the briefing, we piled into the several jeeps available for the ride to the airdrome and squadron operations.

In the operations tent, the aircraft assignments were posted. As always, each pilot noted the location and marking of the aircraft he was to follow out of the parking area. Thorsen went over the flight positions again and discussed where he wanted the other three flights. The 308th was the lead squadron today, so he would also lead the group. Each squadron was to put up sixteen aircraft and two spares, which were to turn back at the Yugoslavian coast if no one aborted. In the standard formation, the sixteen Mustangs were grouped into four flights of four aircraft each. The lead flight was called Red Flight, and its supporting flight was Yellow; the second section consisted of Blue, and it was supported by Green Flight. As before, I was Thorsen's wingman, so my call sign was Border Red Two.

Lam, the squadron intelligence officer, issued each of us two small packets that could just fit into flight-suit pockets. One was an escape/evasion kit, which contained some concentrated food bars, Benzedrine, a morphine syringe, and other like bits and pieces. The other was a package of used and rumpled money of the countries we were to fly over. There was a little more fiddling around, and then it was time to go. I walked out to my machine in a highly excited state, heart thumping, but I also felt elated and full of expectation. No more milk runs. No more silhouettes, like the aircraft recognition exercises. Now I was going to see the real thing.

The pre-flight check was a cursory, tire-kicking affair. Then I had to urinate, except it was the second time in two minutes and, in spite of the urge, I was able to manage only a few drops. The crew chief helped me into my bulky RAF Mae West life vest and parachute harness. Then, when I was in the cockpit, he held the shoulder straps so I could thread the ends onto the lap belt and cam it down. I felt as if I had to go again, but I knew nothing would come of it, even if I did get down and try. So I made my cockpit check, picked out *Nightshade*, and concentrated on its propeller until it started to move. I cranked up; gave the chocks-out signal; and, when the crew chief was safely seated on the wing, moved out and fell in behind Thorsen as he essed his way toward the end of the runway. The long nose of the Mustang made forward visibility very poor, and with sixteen aircraft kicking up dust, it was absolutely essential to keep essing and watching the mechanic on the wing for hand signals. At last we were at the runway. The crew chief jumped down and gave me a highball—a hand salute— and I was pulling out into takeoff position. As soon as Thorsen was halfway down the runway, I wiped my sweaty palms on my flight-suit thighs; made a rolling mag check; and pushed the throttle to the gate, 61 inches. I was off.

I closed rapidly on Thorsen and tucked in tightly, sneaking an occasional glance beyond him at the rest of the squadron as each succeeding airplane caught up and dropped into position. Finally, the major rolled out on course. When I loosened my position so I could look around a little, I got a real thrill: Our squadron was in perfect formation and, on either side above us, the other two squadrons were equally well formed. The Adriatic sparkled below and was dotted with the white sails of the Italian fishing boats. As we gained altitude, the Italian coast gradually fell away. Ahead to the east, a buildup of cumulus clouds marked the Yugoslavian coastline. Soon we were at our cruising altitude. As the weather deteriorated, the squadrons began to maneuver around the towering buildups while trying to stay in contact. My attention was completely devoted to keeping station on Thorsen's wing, so I had only a sketchy idea of what was going on. Unbeknownst to any of us, Fifteenth Air Force Headquarters had recalled the mission because of the weather, but the B-24s and the 31st had failed to get the word and pressed on to the target.

Rendezvous with the bombers came off without a hitch. Each squadron took up position over the bomber stream, flights scissoring back and forth, trying to stay out of the clouds but without overrunning the slow-flying B-24s. Shortly after rendezvous, someone broke radio silence to call out enemy fighters. I tried in vain to spot them by sneaking quick glances away from Thorsen's machine, but I couldn't see anything except clouds and more Mustangs. The next thing I knew, the traffic on the R/T increased in volume and intensity to bedlam; everyone was cursing and shouting at once. "Here they come! Break, *break right!* Passing under you. Watch out, four o'clock level,

Blue Leader. A whole bunch of the sons o' bitches. . . . Red Leader, break right! You got him. You got him! Where the hell are you, Green Four?"

The shrill cacophony in my headset made my hair stand on end, but I was totally absorbed in staying with Thorsen as he went through some very high-g maneuvers. My vision was blurry from the stresses. Clouds and bits of the horizon went by in very strange places. I saw what I took to be tracers going over my wing between Thorsen and me, and I wanted to shout a warning. But I couldn't think of the right words to call a break. I just choked.

After a few minutes, which seemed like hours, it was all over, and we were trying to re-form. I was soaked with sweat and in such a keen state of sensitivity that the first sound of a routine radio call made me jump perceptibly. I finally got my nerves under control, but I felt nauseated as we set course for home. I was still twitchy when we started our descent and, after I pitched out and made my pattern, I just drove it down on the wheels and let it roll.

All the crew chiefs were waiting in a knot at the end of the runway. As each one's aircraft came in, he mounted the wing for the taxi ride back to the parking area. When I was chocked, I shut down, unbuckled, and headed for the operations tent for debriefing. Luckily, no one was interested in quizzing me. I really hadn't seen much of anything except the side of Thorsen's *Nightshade,* and I would have been embarrassed to admit it. I found out that the group had engaged two gaggles of thirty aircraft each and had destroyed sixteen of them. We had lost four of our own. One of the lost pilots was Jackson, a classmate from Moore Field who had been assigned to the 309th when we had come up from Telergma, three weeks earlier. He was the first combat casualty of our Panama bunch but certainly not the last.

The 308th had done well, bagging four of the attackers and getting four probables into the bargain. Claude got one of the probables, which bettered Doctor Tom's claim of a damage three days earlier. I was feeling down, having seen nothing and shot at nothing. One of our Panama guys was going to get a confirmed victory one of these days, and I just knew that it wasn't going to be me.

Lying in my sack later that evening, I thought about the events of the day and tried to sort things out. I could see one thing clearly: Flying such close formation that I wouldn't get lost or separated kept me from doing my job, which was watching and keeping my leader's tail clear. I was going to have to loosen up and take my chances on staying with him. I also recognized that, in the heat of battle, there was no time to think about things. The time to do the thinking was on the ground.

If I didn't do something instinctively, it wasn't going to get done. Anticipation was the thing. Be ready. I had to act without hesitation when the time came. Get the gun and sight switch on with the first bogey call. Get the tank jettison switch armed early so that the drop tanks would be away a split second after the command. Be ready for a hung tank. Be ready to go mixture auto-rich, full throttle, and RPM. And above all, be ready to call a break instantly when bounced by enemy aircraft, using the right call sign so I didn't scatter every other flight in the sky.

On the next mission—two days later—I was scheduled to fly on Johnson's wing as Green Four. I didn't know whether I had been graduated or demoted. No explanations or comments were forthcoming, so I chose to believe that Thorsen had okayed me for general wing flying and was taking on a new guy to fly his wing. Johnson had the reputation for being a tiger in the air, so I knew I would not want for action. We were going to Wiener Neustadt, a modern city near Vienna where Me-109s were assembled. That probably meant that we were poking a stick in the hornet's nest. Vienna—or Wien, as it was known to the Austrians—was 450 air miles from San Severo, almost due north. The direct route would take us across the Adriatic and over the Yugoslavian coast just west of Split. After crossing the coastal mountains, we would pass almost over Zagreb, in the plain of Croatia. The very large and unmistakable Lake Balaton would lie in the distance to the east, in Hungary. Much nearer, almost beneath our track, would be the city of Graz, Austria, only a scant 75 miles from Wiener Neustadt.

The takeoff and join-up were routine. As the group climbed northward over the sea, I had ample opportunity to look around. Forty-eight airplanes plus six spares made a formidable force and took up a good part of the sky. I was glad that I was a part of it instead of having to look at it from an Me-109 or FW-190 cockpit.

Up near the Yugoslavia-Austria border, bogies were called out at one o'clock, slightly below. This time, I got a good look and saw about twelve Me-109s passing from one o'clock toward three, fairly close. As the squadron started to turn into them, Johnson let go his tanks, cut sharply inside our lead flight, and started down after them. I just had time to sneak a look at our lead flight on the outside as I rolled to follow Johnson. I was horrified to see the rest of the squadron turn back to the original heading, leaving us hung out to dry. I shot a glance back at Johnson. He was already getting away from me, turning in a tight vertical bank and closing rapidly on a 109. I pulled it in as hard as I could. But, if I was to stay with him, I knew I was going to have to keep reefing it in. The 109s on the outside of us, which Johnson was expecting the lead section of the squadron to engage, could easily drop in behind us. But I figured that, while pulling four or five g's, I was relatively safe. Hauling back on that stick for all I was worth and in a semicrouch, I was tightening my stomach muscles—tightening *all* my muscles—trying to hold my head up against the vicious, unrelenting force of magnified gravity. I no longer knew if I was in the same piece of sky as Johnson; the positive g's were draining the blood from my head and I was sightless. After another second or two, I eased the back pressure on the stick until I got some vision back, hoping Johnson would still be in front of me. No joy. That part of the sky was empty. At eight o'clock, a mile or two away, I saw a parachute. A good bit closer, two aircraft were coming at me. They had no deep central air scoop but two flat, shallow radiators under the wings and close to the fuselage, exactly like the recognition silhouette. They were unmistakably Me-109s! I went to War Emergency—67 inches manifold pressure—and made for a bank of clouds over on my left. I beat them into the clouds, a stratus deck that was fairly smooth inside. I was safe for the moment; visibility wasn't 20 feet.

If I had chased someone into cloud cover, I would pop up on top, fly straight ahead, and watch for him to come out. Expecting them to do the same, I pulled the throttle back and started a turn, rolling out when I had reversed course. After a couple of minutes I pulled up into the sunlight and made a violent 90 left and then a 90 right to clear myself. I was alone. I had no idea where they had gone, but I really didn't care. *Now* what? I decided I would go the short distance to the target and join on someone rather than risk flying all the way home alone. Setting course for the target area, I climbed back up to the group's altitude, turning often to look aft and constantly scanning the sky for those fast-moving black dots. The target area could easily be spotted by the dark cloud of flak bursts, and the heavy bombers could be seen from miles away.

I moved in gingerly toward the first flight of Mustangs I came upon. The large letters *WZ* on the side told me they were from a sister squadron, the 309th. The leader gave me a short glance, raised his gloved hand to acknowledge my presence, and went on about his business. I felt like the lost kitten that had found its mother. But I couldn't help wondering what had happened to Johnson. Was that his chute or a German pilot's?

After I had landed and parked, I walked slowly toward the ops tent for debriefing, dreading the interrogation and my admission that I had lost my element leader. I told my story to Lam as completely as I could while he took notes. Johnson wasn't back and no one had reported seeing him. Two of the older heads who had completed their tour in Spitfires and were waiting to go home seemed interested in the fact that I had outrun the 109s in level flight. I asked one of them—he was the squadron's leading scorer, with six victories—if that had been the wrong thing to do. He laughed and said, "I guess not." I didn't sense any of the reproach from the rest of the pilots that I had expected. True, I hadn't deliberately left Johnson to take a shot or some such thing; still, I did lose him, and he wasn't back yet. Some of the older pilots questioned his action in dropping tanks and getting sucked into a fight before bomber rendezvous.

I went outside, sat on a wooden bench, and watched the late afternoon sky for one more Mustang. After a half hour, Lam came out and asked me if I wanted a ride back to the housing area. Everyone else had already gone, so there were just the two of us in the jeep. We rode back in silence. I felt pretty bad.

Two other squadron pilots besides Johnson failed to return: Trafton and Hughes. Although no one knew it then, Trafton was wounded, but he had successfully bailed out and was to return to Italy three months later. Hughes was dead. He had remarked to Lam before going out to his airplane, "Isn't it a beautiful day to get shot down?" Did he have a premonition, or was it just an offhand remark? Who knows. But he was right about one thing: It had been a beautiful day.

12

During the rest of April I was airborne three more times. We went back to Ploesti and then to Piombino on the northwest coast of Italy, but neither of these missions produced any fighter opposition. Also we went to Toulon, in southern France, where we did get some action. Almost as soon as we picked up our assigned bombers, we saw a lacework of contrails ahead and the R/T came alive. In response to a bogey call-out in our squadron, I sneaked a look from my wing position and saw two Italian Macchi MC.202 fighters at nine o'clock. They seemed perfectly content to sit on the sidelines and watch the show, even doing some slow rolls, secure in the knowledge that we would not leave the heavies to chase them. They were right. Despite the hollering and screaming on the R/T, my flight didn't get into any of the fighting; we stayed with our big friends until well away from the coast. The other squadron flights engaged some Me-109s and destroyed two of them.

For the Panama guys, the most exiting event to close out April happened on a mission I did not fly. The target was Milan, and Goehausen, having some kind of problem, was coming home alone down the east coast of Italy. Around Ancona Point he spotted a twin-engined Ju-88 skimming along just above the waves. He made a firing pass. Although Walt didn't see much damage done, the 88 promptly crashed into the Adriatic, becoming the first victim and victory to be scored by one of the un-Spitfire pilots. When Walt got back to the airdrome, he made a low pass down the runway and did a slow roll—

the traditional victory ritual—before landing. Because of the many accidents that occurred throughout the Air Forces, this was absolutely, positively forbidden, and he knew it. But at the moment his elation could not be bridled by rules and regulations. To make matters worse for him, everyone was down at the field awaiting the group's return. Everyone was treated to the spectacle. Walt was grounded immediately. His friends were really worried about him, remembering Eric's fate in flying school. After a couple of days, however, Goehausen was returned to flying status, much to everyone's relief. Of the nineteen pilots in the squadron, two were in the hospital and two were away on ferry duty to Casablanca, which didn't really leave enough warm bodies to put up four flights. Exactly why there was a shortage of pilots in a front-line unit when there were thousands of them running loose in the States I never fully understood.

★

The group was making almost daily five-hour flights above 25,000 feet. My principal training in the physiological effects of high-altitude flight had come in the high-altitude chamber at Albrook Field in Panama. The oxygen system in the chamber and in use on the fighters did not amount to much. The mask was a smallish affair, just covering the mouth and nostrils. A rubber bladder hung down from the mask about six inches. The oxygen, conveyed from the aircraft to the mask by a thin rubber hose about the width of a pencil, was mixed with the exhalant in the bladder and then inhaled on the next breath. Thus the bladder expanded and contracted as the pilot breathed, and the amount of oxygen reaching the pilot was controlled simply by turning a knurled knob to open or close the oxygen inlet valve. It was a kind of Rube Goldberg contraption, actually, that allowed the pilot to live and breathe at altitude, but only just.

The pressure-demand system in the P-51 was a vast improvement over the old. The mask was much larger, covering most of the lower face, and it was fed by a one-inch corrugated hose whose end snapped into a companion fitting on the aircraft. And for good measure, a microphone about the size of a quarter was permanently installed in the mask.

The regulator, mounted on the right side of the cockpit, had a lever with two positions: Normal Demand and 100% Oxygen. In the Normal Demand position, the regulator "sensed" the altitude and metered the correct amount of oxygen into the regulator. In the regulator the oxygen mixed with cockpit air and then was conducted to the mask. As altitude increased, more oxygen and less air entered the regulator.

At very high altitude, the system supplied 100 percent oxygen. With the regulator switch in the 100% Oxygen position, the system overrode automatic mixing and a faint flow of pure oxygen flowed to the pilot, regardless of the altitude. Of course, this mode of operation tended to rapidly deplete the oxygen supply and had to be used judiciously— only in an emergency or when the pilot suspected the onset of hypoxia, or lack of oxygen.

The pressure-demand system made two displays available to the pilot. A gauge, low on the right side of the instrument panel, showed the pressure in the oxygen tank. As oxygen was used or leaked, the pressure decayed. The pilot used the gauge to determine the amount remaining in the tank and the time he could continue at altitude. The other indicator gauge consisted of an oval opening behind which were a pair of "eyelids." The lids came together when oxygen flowed from the regulator to the mask and popped apart when there was no flow. When the hose was connected and the regulator was delivering oxygen, the eyelids blinked in time with the pilots breathing, assuring him that the system was functioning properly.

Although oxygen wasn't needed until 12,000 to 13,000 feet, the Air Force required that it be used above 10,000 feet. Above 20,000 feet, hypoxia was always lurking. If the truth be known, I suspect that many pilots were lost because they lost consciousness from hypoxia or because the onset of hypoxia slowed their thinking and reflexes during air fighting.

Along with my Panama buddies, I had been exposed to the effects of hypoxia in the altitude chamber at Albrook Field. After reaching the equivalent of 25,000 feet of altitude, each of us in turn removed our masks and began writing a fixed text on a pad of paper. As I watched the two or three men who preceded me quickly slip from perfectly normal to physical and mental sluggishness to unconsciousness, I was shocked. More shocking still was my own stint at doing without oxygen. Afterward, when my mask was put back on my face and I had recovered my senses, one look at what I had written told the whole story.

On the pad my writing began as neat, legible script. Quality began to deteriorate after one line, the letters getting bigger and more poorly shaped. Finally, my writing became an illegible scrawl, wandering off the edge of the sheet. And most shocking of all, I had no recollection of any danger signs, no forewarning of "losing it"; I remembered only a sense of well-being and satisfaction. The intended lesson found its mark: Hypoxia was bad news for a fighter pilot, alone in his aircraft, and was to be avoided at all costs.

But this lesson had to take its place alongside all the others that posed a threat to life and limb. We knew and respected each danger individually, but there were just too many of them to be of constant concern. For the most part we acknowledged them only subliminally and got on with the business of flying.

I should have recognized the signs of hypoxia in myself earlier than I did, but I suppose they were lost in the excitement of beginning combat flying. The blinking eyelids, or lack thereof, should have told me all I needed to know, but I missed the signal. On one of the first missions to southern France, when we had been at altitude for an hour and a half, I was having trouble holding my position. I frequently fell well behind the flight and lacked the sense or will to put on enough power to get up where I belonged. When we met another flight during the scissoring maneuver above the bombers, I got confused and wound up flying with the other flight, without quite figuring out what had happened or how. Even after we descended, I had only a hazy, dreamlike recollection of the whole mission.

I took my chewing out from the flight leader in silence. I deserved what I got. But I knew I could fly better than my performance indicated and that something was very wrong indeed. I looked at my equipment.

The mask I was using was the British model issued to me when I was a Spitfire trainee. Why I continued to use it, I cannot say; American masks were available. Perhaps I was clinging to the residual glamor of the Spitfire and the RAF. The British mask had been adapted by me for use in the Mustang. But unbeknownst to me the mask did not fit my face properly and had begun to split where it met the bridge of my nose. And my nose was no small thing (I choose to call it merely prominent)—it could almost have earned me the nickname Beak or Schnoz. My nose held the mask high on my face and left a slight gap at the hollow between the nose and cheek. When I inhaled, instead of drawing oxygen from the regulator through the hose, I was partially breathing the rarefied, unpressurized cockpit air.

After discovering the problem, the solution was simple: Discard the deteriorating RAF mask and use the U.S. one, which was new, fit my face better, and was designed for American systems. As an added measure of safety, I pulled the adjusting straps so tight that the edges of the mask clamped down against my face. It wasn't very comfortable; after each mission, when I unhooked the mask, a deep ridge remained on my nose and cheeks where it had pressed in. But the symptoms of hypoxia disappeared, and no one ever complained about my flying again.

★

The Fifteenth Air Force went back to Ploesti on May 5. I can't remember whose wing I was flying that day, but I was finally feeling comfortable enough to move out a little and take a good look at everything around me. The B-17s and B-24s were an impressive sight, the largest concentration of bombers I had ever seen. This mission was the first 1,500-ton raid from Italy—640 heavy bombers attacking several targets in Rumania. As usual, the target was defended by massed antiaircraft guns that seemed to be sited perfectly to inflict the maximum damage on the bombers. From the looks of the dark cloud of spent flak bursts, the Jerry batteries were putting up barrage flak, as fast as they could fire, into a cube of air space that straddled the intended line of flight between the IP and the target. The bombers had to fly right into the flak to get to their release point. We stayed well off to the side—there was no point in our going into it. Certainly, no German fighter was going to be in there.

It was horrifying to watch the bombers disappear into that block of smoke. Occasionally, one would fall out the bottom, out of control—sometimes spinning, sometimes afire. We all watched for chutes, and someone would count them aloud on the R/T: "There's three of them. There comes another. There's two more." Long pause. "I guess that's it."

The carnage must have been awful. Even those who came through and rallied off the target sustained damage. Though the defenders had laid down a dense white smoke screen covering a wide area around the target, the thick, oily black columns boiling up through the smoke indicated that at least some of the bombs had found their mark.

Our other two squadrons became heavily engaged by German fighters, but the 308th got into it only at the very end. My section didn't get to fight at all. We stayed with our bombers until we were well clear of any possible fighter attacks, and then we set course for home.

When we got back into San Severo, we learned that Emery had scored the only 308th kill, although the group had gotten a total of nine. I cringed at the thought of having to listen to my friends in the 307th and 309th lay it on us. But that's how it went. As my uncle used to say, "Chicken dinner one day, feathers the next."

The very next day, we went to Brasov, in the South Carpathian Mountains, about 50 miles north of Ploesti. This was my fourth mission to Rumania, so I began to recognize landmarks and feel comfortable with the route. There weren't that many cities, and if weather permitted they were easily visible from 25,000 feet. After starting for home, the city of Craiova, Rumania, would gradually appear almost dead ahead. Then, a little farther on, the pencil line of the Danube angled northward. Though the Danube was most definitely brown, not blue, it was nevertheless unmistakable. To the north lay Turnul Severin at the Iron Gate of the Danube, and farther along, just visible to the south, was the city of Nis, Yugoslavia. Then the mountains began, and then the Adriatic coast. The coastal cities of Dubrovnik and larger Split made good marks. Vis, an island about 40 miles southwest of Split, was never occupied by the Germans and had a short landing strip that could be used in an emergency. I don't think many of us used the charts after that. We knew the headings by heart.

Then for five straight days we went to northern Italy, pounding the rail system. We encountered no fighter opposition. On one of these missions I came close to wetting my pants—and not from fright, either. I don't know what went wrong. The flight certainly was not one of the longer ones I had been on, but long before we reached the target the pressure in my bladder told me that I was in trouble. A relief tube was installed beneath the seat, but my previous attempts to use it in the P-51 and other fighters had been less than satisfactory. The device consisted of a plastic cone fitted with a small rubber tube, which, in theory at least, conducted the urine to a vent on the underside of the fuselage. Using the tube involved undoing the lap belt and the leg straps of the parachute, unzipping and peeling back layers of flight clothing, finding the plumbing fixture (no small feat in a sitting position), and tucking into the cone—all with the left hand while flying with the right. To maintain formation, however, the throttle had to be tended almost constantly with the left hand. Trying to use the tube was like the comedy routine of the one-armed wallpaper hanger.

I didn't even try; instead, I chose to tough it out. Gradually the pressure increased to the level of pain and beyond. Finally we started for home. I briefly considered letting go all over myself, but somehow I couldn't bring myself to do it. By the time San Severo appeared, I was clenching my teeth in agony. I got onto the ground and into the parking area as quickly as I could, but the crew chief had to lift me out of the cockpit because I couldn't straighten up. Right there beside the plane I went—and went, and went. Then I took a couple of steps and went some more. It was several hours before the pain in my abdomen went away. On the next several missions I was worried about the scenario recurring, but I never had the problem again. Perhaps my bladder stretched or I managed my liquid intake better, but even on six-hour flights I endured nothing like that. And I never used that damned relief tube, either.

13

Colonel Sandy McCorkle, the Group CO, had gotten a request from a P-38 group for a flight of P-51s to put on a demonstration at their base. They were celebrating an anniversary and were making a holiday of it. McCorkle gave the duty to Captain Tommy Molland, who promptly scouted up Doctor Tom and me to fly his wing positions. We had a skull session and then took off thirty minutes early so we could practice a little before taking the stage. The repertoire was the usual aerobatics but, since we were performing under the critical gaze of other fighter pilots, low and in extra-tight formation. The pièce de résistance was a little different. We backed off behind the trees, lined up with the runway and then we opened up a little to let Tommy flip his machine over. Just as Doctor Tom and I closed back in, we crossed the field boundary and went roaring down the runway at an altitude of 20 feet, with the leader of the three-ship vee upside down. I don't know about the spectators on the ground, but I was impressed.

In the months ahead Tommy and I were to draw closer, flying often together and, in quieter moments, sharing our thoughts and sometimes even our feelings, which, in itself was a rarity. I felt privileged that he sought me out. By a strange coincidence, he had graduated from Moore Field also, but almost a year earlier. There must have been twenty-five to thirty such flying schools in the country and the graduating classes were quite small. I developed an intense loyalty to Tommy as a military superior and a great fondness for him as a friend. I like to think he reciprocated.

★

Even as the first missions were being flown, the work of improving the facilities at the airdrome went on apace. Because San Severo was a semipermanent base, everyone turned to with a will, knowing that work put into improvements would not be wasted. The dirt began to fly soon after our arrival, and it wasn't long before shallow slit trenches dotted the field, within a few leaps of each man's working area. Perhaps being so well prepared for bombing and strafing staved off the need to ever use the the trenches. We endured no enemy attacks at San Severo during the stay of the 31st.

Other, more routine attacks—the gastric kind—occurred on a daily basis. We had to assuage them in open-air latrines dug a suitable distance from operations and maintenance. The plywood crates in which fuel tanks were shipped proved to be an excellent source of building material. In no time at all our latrines were enclosed so that the users could sit in peace, like Rodin's statue, The Thinker. I think visitors, especially the Red Cross girls, appreciated this new concession to modesty.

One second-rate setup that lasted far too long was housing squadron operations in a pyramidal tent that was too small. Not only did pilots meet there before and after missions; the tent housed the aircraft status board, a typewriter, flight records, intelligence files, mission reports, claims—the whole administrative apparatus. The operations officer and two clerks worked there. When a windstorm came up the last week in April and blew the tent over, the result was a real mess. The tent could be suffered no longer, so during the second week in May, ops was moved into a Quonset hut erected on the same site. It was a prefabricated building about 20 feet wide by 30 feet long, semicircular in cross section and formed out of curved, corrugated steel panels. The hut was a great improvement appreciated by the pilots but especially by Lam and the clerks.

★

The mechanics and armorers—all of the enlisted maintenance men—were a special breed. Their jobs held no glory, no decorations, few promotions, and certainly no easy living conditions. Most in the maintenance crew had been overseas since 1942, and they had little chance of going home until the war was over. In some respects they were treated as second-class citizens, always having to defer to the officers in matters of privilege. Though military discipline was generally more relaxed in front-line organizations than elsewhere, certain lines between officers and enlisted men were never crossed. We ate and slept separately. Only in the line of duty was there personal contact. I had learned that one of the mechanics in the 308th, Petersen, was from Racine, and I vaguely remembered him from one of the sailing clubs. He received occasional copies of the hometown newspaper, which he offered to lend me. I stopped over at his tent sometimes (never the other way around), and we developed a friendly— albeit correct—relationship. I liked Pete and I enjoyed talking to him about common acquaintances and interests back in Wisconsin, but I realized that my presence was an imposition on his tent mates, who must have been uncomfortable while I was there. I never stayed long.

All the maintenance men in the squadron were a professional lot. They believed in what they were doing, however small the contribution to the total war effort, and were intensely proud of the job well done. It was a point of honor with them that the aircraft and pilot came first; no task was too hard, too long, or too insignificant if it affected the ability of the aircraft to function or the pilot to survive. Individuals felt personally disgraced if their work was found to be wanting, and they suffered the double indignity of peer disapproval. There were no screw-offs; they were simply not tolerated.

I don't think that many of us pilots realized how good the maintenance crew was, and how dedicated. I know I didn't. We all thought the perfect condition of the planes and guns was something that just happened naturally, by itself. No way. The determination and sweat of the technicians created the perfection. I wish that, just once, I had gone to my crew chief, my armorer, or the line chief; looked him squarely in the eye; and said, "I know. And I appreciate what you are doing."

★

A curious thing happened toward the end of May—perhaps *bizarre* would be more descriptive. Pilots were allowed two ounces of whiskey for each mission completed, but we didn't have to down it immediately after landing; it could be saved and taken in any quantity the stomach and common sense would permit. The flight surgeon, Doc Roth, kept the books and dispensed the medicine, which was known as operational rye, or Old Overshoe, a corruption of the name of the only brand available, Old Overholt. One Saturday night three of us pooled our ration and, with the two bottles we got from the Doc, sat around the officers' mess, polishing it off. In the bleary stages of the evening, my flight commander, Emery, came by. He seemed to be worse off than any of us, which convinced me to stagger off to find my bunk while I was still able. In that twilight world of waking-dreaming, I heard an aircraft flying very low and close overhead, repeatedly. Then there were running footsteps and shouting. Later, when I finally was wide awake, I found out what had happened.

At first light, about 0430, Emery had gone down to the airdrome, fired up his machine, and really beat up the housing area, buzzing the buildings at treetop level time and again. Stranger still, he had flown away, and no one had seen him since. He just vanished. We heard rumors that a lone P-51 had strafed a town in Yugoslavia or Hungary that Sunday morning, but the rumors were never confirmed. In fact, the whole incident was sort of hushed up. I suppose the affair posed a problem: Should Emery be classified as a combat loss, an accident, or what? What was the best way to spare the feelings of his next of kin back in the States? Apparently Emery had some personal problem. But, if anyone knew what it was, he wasn't talking. The aircraft Form 1, the pilot's maintenance log, was all that was left of man and machine. On the cover Emery had scrawled "Good old Pacey, the best crew chief a man ever had" and then tossed it on the ground in the parking area.

Emery had picked up a runty, short-haired bitch (four-legged) at Pomigliano, and he and Peanuts, as she was called, were inseparable. A few weeks before Emery flew off, Peanuts, in the midst of delivering a litter, had seen Emery approaching and had tried to waddle over to him though she had half a pup protruding from her—she was that glad to see him. For a few days she moped around looking for him and then allowed Jacobs, a friend of Emery's, to look after her. But I don't think she ever forgot Emery or gave up trying to find him.

The day after Emery flew off, the order announcing the award of decorations was received from wing headquarters. Emery was up for the Distinguished Flying Cross (DFC), which was also given to Ricks, Johnson, and Trafton, but none of them was left to claim his medal. Perhaps that should have told us something about the price that had to be paid for decorations, but it didn't. We all thought we were immortal; we suffered from the everyone-but-me syndrome.

★

Mail from home ranked just ahead of the evening movie as a recreational institution. The mail did come through on a regular basis now, and the old guys always reminded us that this was a luxury to be thoroughly appreciated. When the 31st was on the move continuously during the North African campaign, it was a wonder that any mail at all found the group. The list of bases the group had occupied since leaving Africa—nine in nine months—illustrated the nomadic nature of the 31st:

Place	Arrived	Departed	Stay (Days)
Gozo, Malta	June 28, '43	July 14, '43	16
Ponte Olivo, Sicily	July 14, '43	July 19, '43	5
Aggrigento, Sicily	July 19, '43	Aug. 2, '43	14
Termini Airdrome, Sicily	Aug. 2, '43	Sept. 8, '43	37
Milazzo, Sicily	Sept. 8, '43	Sept. 20, '43	12
Montecorvino, Italy	Sept. 20, '43	Oct. 14, '43	24
Pomigliano, Italy	Oct. 14, '43	Jan. 18, '44	96
Castel Volturno, Italy	Jan. 18, '44	April 2, '44	74
San Severo, Italy	April 2, '44		

Even after the 31st settled in at San Severo, it was hard to believe that a letter could find its way to it from Arizona or Iowa. All the writer had to do was address the envelope like this:

308th F.S. 31st F.G.
APO 520 NY, NY

With the advent of V-Mail, the time letters were in transit was reduced to a couple of weeks. To be sent by V-Mail, the letter had to be on a standard form, a single-sided page. Somewhere in the postal system, it was microfilmed. Then the film was sent by air to the overseas theater, and there it was photographically printed on a sheet about four inches by six inches. The writing was pretty small and, if the penmanship was poor, reading the whole letter took a while, short as the message was.

The outgoing mail, of course, had to be censored. Lam, whose duty it was to administer the censorship program, collected all the outgoing mail and then, once a day, assembled several of the junior officers to read each letter. Taboo were the exact location of the unit, details of the aircraft's performance capabilities, and mission details. I figured German intelligence already had this information, but it was important, we were told, that it not be confirmed by an authoritative source. Lest any of us amateur censors sign and seal the envelope without carefully scrutinizing the letter, we were assured that all censored outgoing mail was rechecked on a spot basis. If any forbidden information was found, the squadron censor and the writer would be court-martialed. Although this sounded a little farfetched, the threat was sufficient incentive for thoroughness. When Lam sat us down around a table and handed out the stacks of letters, we got on with it.

Perhaps, back home, receiving letters with incised portions gave the recipient a feeling that the friend or relative was in the thick of things that were very hush-hush and important to the war effort. Posters everywhere in the States proclaimed that "A slip of the lip can sink a ship" and depicted spike-helmeted Germans or toothy Japanese behind a wall or telephone pole, an oversized ear cocked to listen in on war secrets. But the need to cut things out of letters was extremely rare.

When I read each of the letters I was reviewing, I tried to skim through it, looking for forbidden phrases without actually reading the letter. But that was a losing battle—like trying to avert your eyes from something that you didn't want to look at while observing all the details. It couldn't be done. At least I couldn't do it.

Each letter was a story in itself, only one half the story to be sure, but it didn't take much imagination to supply the missing half. There was tragedy and humor, but mostly just news or whispered endearments reaching out to someone 5,000 miles away. Some were tentative and self-conscious, the writer painfully aware that the letter had to be left unsealed so a stranger could pore over the words. Others seemed quite oblivious to the threat and went on, openly, about what they wanted to say. I thought one of them, obviously written to a wife, was a model of uncomplicated, straightforward communication—an ultimatum, actually. It read in part: "The day I get back to the States, the day the ship docks, there's going to be a whole lot of screwing going on, and if you want to be in on it, you better be there."

Many of the letters dealt with problems of love, and replies to Dear John letters were not infrequent. I don't know where *Dear John* originated, but it was applied to the letter received from the wife or girlfriend back home who confessed to finding someone else. Some of the recipients replied with outrage, some with pitiful pleading. There was nothing to be done except put words on paper, which was little enough because he was here and she was there.

Sometimes little curly "watch springs" were taped or pasted onto the page—freshly plucked pubic hair, no doubt. I was always careful to preserve this whimsical bit of nonverbal interchange. One day, in the midst of our labor, George handed me a letter he was reviewing. It was from my armorer, Langlois, to his wife. Toward the end he mentioned some of the pilot losses and asked her to pray "for Lieutenant Goebel, my pilot." Even though we did not socialize and met only at the aircraft, I felt closer to him after that. It had never occurred to me that anyone other than the folks back home and my immediate pilot friends were concerned about me.

We did the best job of censoring that we could, never discussing anything we had read. But I was never comfortable in the role of official keyhole peeper and was much relieved when letter-reading duty finally passed to the next bunch of replacement pilots.

★

Out on the Isle of Capri, off Sorrento in the Bay of Naples, was a rest camp, a spot where combatants could go for a few days and forget the war. It was to Capri that Sheehan—one of the older, ex-Spitfire pilots—went in late May. He was back two days later, and he was not in a good mood; he'd ridden a truck across the mountains to Naples and then all the way back again without ever getting to the camp. The boats that ran back and forth from the shore to the island were nowhere to be seen. He could get no explanation of why the boats were no longer running; he got only shrugs, resigned looks, and gestures.

Sheehan tried to make the best of it, bumming around the streets of Naples, looking for entertainment. But that turned out to be a bust, too. The place was crawling with MPs who seemed to be everywhere, stopping anyone in uniform and demanding to see dog tags and undershirts. There's no telling whose idea that was, but the enforcers took a perverse pleasure in carrying out the harassment, especially when they encountered Air Corps lieutenants wearing wings. Flyers were not well liked; perhaps ground soldiers subconsciously resented the pilots' glamorous public image. Whatever the reason, it seemed that air crews were considered non-Army and fair game for whatever botheration could be cooked up. Small wonder that Sheehan came back a little more unrested than when he left.

14

The missions continued unabated, and I went out almost every day. After pounding the northern Italian rail system, it was to the port cities of southern France we went, three times running. On flights to France, it was common practice to stop at one of the numerous fields on Corsica to refuel and stretch the legs. On one of these flights, we landed at Ghisonaccia, about midway down the east side of the island. While milling around waiting for the refueling crew to finish, I again found a coin in the dirt. This time it was not silver, but copper. The coin was a five-centime piece, about the size of a quarter, dated 1854, with the image of Napoleon III on one side of it. From the look of it, it had lain there a long, long time. I stuck it in my pocket, and I managed to hang onto it through my combat tour and bring it back to the States. I still have it.

As pilots, we all continued to grow in experience and confidence. I finally learned to spot other aircraft in the air at maximum distance, but I'm not sure when I learned. The realization that I had acquired this talent dawned on me only gradually. I had known since Panama that I was missing something. There the flight commander had called me aside one day and told me that he had noticed that on practice intercept missions, I was never the first to call out a bogey. Little Henry spotted them often, almost as often as the flight leader. This was saying something, considering that a wingman spent most of his time looking at the aircraft he was following.

Then something happened to me at San Severo that I couldn't explain. I became one of the few in the 308th who could pick up bogeys when they were almost indistinguishable from fly specks on the canopy. It had nothing whatever to do with visual acuity—we all had 20/15. I remember trying to describe this newfound ability to Claude and giving up in frustration. It was like trying to describe the color red—I knew what it was, but I just couldn't put the means of recognition into words. One difference I did recognize was that I moved my eyes much more slowly, in a deliberate, methodical way, instead of the quick scan I used to use. It was as if they were out there, and I knew they were, and it was only a matter of seizing them with my eyes. Whatever, I had finally learned what Goehausen had known all along.

With pilot losses and people completing their flying tours of duty, there were plenty of vacancies. Major Thorsen, in his usual quiet way, was bringing us sophomores along as quickly as possible. It was not long before I was leading an element and finally, on my twentieth mission, I was scheduled to lead a four-ship flight. The target was St. Etienne, France, and, although the mission provided no special thrills, the chance to lead a flight was reward enough. I was quite satisfied with myself.

The next day, I led Green Flight again, this time to Montpellier, France, on the south coast between Marseille and the Spanish border. Again the Luftwaffe failed to appear. The excitement of leading a flight had worn off by now, and I felt comfortable with the new responsibility. All I wanted now was an encounter with some enemy fighters to test my hand and my eye—and my nerves, too.

On May 29, I was scheduled to lead again, but this time I approached the task with some trepidation. For one thing, I was going to lead Blue Flight, which meant that I would have eight aircraft to worry about; my own flight and Green Flight. For another thing, the target was Wollersdorf Airdrome (A/D), 22 miles west northwest of Vienna. Since we would be overflying Wiener Neustadt, where Me-109s were assembled, it was a pretty good bet that we were in for a fight.

While flying a wing position, the opportunity to fire was practically nonexistent; even in an element-lead slot, the chances were few. But as Blue Leader, I would be on my own once we were engaged, free to pick my target and tactics. Close support of heavies may have made the bomber crews feel warm all over; they must have liked being able to see a fighter umbrella above them. But to the escorting pilots the rigid requirement to stay so close was just too confining. Providing area cover was the more desirable job, since it allowed the freedom to roam the target area, looking for mischief.

We didn't have to do much roaming and looking on this mission; a cluster of tiny, fast-moving dots away to the north, in the direction of Vienna, plainly foretold of the Luftwaffe's determination not to let this intrusion go unchallenged. I turned immediately to a heading that put us on an intercepting course. We shed our tanks. I began breathing a little faster. Gun switch on. Mixture to auto-rich. RPM and manifold pressure up, climbing, trying to get a height advantage. Suddenly, at 28,000 feet, the two formations collided, springing at each other like animals in the wild, and the fight was on.

There was no feinting on their part, no attempt to slip past to get at the bombers several thousand feet below and three or four miles away. The German pilots were extremely aggressive—they had come to fight, and so had we. The dogfight was the damnedest melee I had ever been involved in, with fighters of both sides intermingled, attacking and taking evasive action. Adding to the confusion was the saturation of the radio channel, with screamed warnings to break, pleas for help, and shouted instructions. I had everything firewalled, my left hand pressing the throttle and prop control as far forward as they would go, my right hand pulling hard on the stick, in a high-g turn. I struggled to keep my head up against the g forces as I made a quick check to clear behind. Okay. As I partially rolled out of my turn, I spotted two 109s crossing in front of me, 800 to 900 yards away. Immediately I wrenched my plane into a turn, cutting inside to shorten the range as quickly as possible. One, who I took to be a wingman, was lagging behind the other and seemed to be having trouble staying with his leader. I fastened my teeth on him, closing steadily through some wild, evasive maneuvers. Then the leader made a sudden, violent turn reversal, which his wingman failed to follow. A bad mistake. I was down to what I judged to be 350 yards. I opened fire, hosing away at nearly 30 degrees of deflection. The lead necessary for such a shot made him just barely visible between the sight ring and the nose of my plane. I concentrated on keeping the sight pipper steady out in front of him, on his line of flight, and was rewarded by a few strikes on the forward fuselage. His canopy came off, followed instantly by a dark hurtling figure. I broke to clear my tail and, when I looked forward again, I could not pick up either the other 109 or the falling pilot. He must have delayed opening his chute to a much lower altitude; no white blossoming canopy was anywhere to be seen. After the first few missions, I had prided myself in keeping pretty cool in the air. Now I babbled excitedly, and disgracefully, on the R/T, calling for my flight to witness my first victory.

Although my flight was scattered a bit, they were still with me. We quickly re-formed. The sky was empty of fighters except for a few P-

51s over in the direction of the target. By the time we climbed back up and returned to the bombers, they had rallied off the target and were homeward bound. We stayed with them as long as we could, finally leaving them near the Yugoslavian border. I had regained my composure by then, but I still felt a grim satisfaction at finally getting on the scoreboard. I was a virgin no longer.

The radio chatter made it obvious that a general engagement had occurred. After I got back to operations to write up my claim, I found out that Claude had scored, too. Edge had a probable and a damage. All told, the squadron tallied seven victories and three probables.

The B Model P-51 that we were flying had an optical sight with a 70-mil reticle—too small, really, for any angle-off shooting. With only four .50-caliber machine guns, it was a low-percentage shot that I had taken. But the result of that encounter couldn't have been better, even if I had known what I was doing. The result was another example of the old adage "I'd rather be lucky than good."

Besides having only four guns, the P-51B had another shortcoming that was to cause me embarrassment even though we were all forewarned of the problem. The Mustang's wing was too thin to accommodate the .50-caliber machine guns in the normal upright position, so they were canted over about 30 degrees. Because the ammunition feed trays for the .50-calibers had to curve up and then down again, the chances for a gun jam were excellent if the guns were fired while pulling about four g's. On the Mustang, there was no way to cycle the guns from the cockpit; if one or more of the guns jammed in flight, you were out of luck until you landed.

I guess I am one of those people who learn by doing. Well, I did and I learned. On one of the next missions, I got into a wild melee and was taking all manner of ridiculous shots. Suddenly all four guns stopped firing. My heart stopped beating a split second later. Talk about a tiger turning into a rabbit! I was stunned, and for an instant I could think of nothing better to do than follow my quarry through his aerial gymnastics, with only the GSAP camera going. I figured that I better let go before he got wise to my problem and gave me an even bigger one. He made a sharp turn to the right and I went left, diving away at full throttle. Nothing quiets the nerves like putting a little distance between you and the nearest enemy fighter, especially when you are impotent.

We saw the gun-camera film from that mission at the evening movie, before the regular feature. When my film came on the header said:

Pilot:	Goebel
Attacking:	1 Me-109
Claim:	None

And there, big as life, was the image of the 109 cavorting around on the wall of the building for several seconds, without any strikes on him at all. My armorer, Langlois, told me afterward that he had taken a good razzing about the gun jam from his fellow armament buddies, but of course it hadn't been his fault at all.

★

We were tabbed to go back to Budapest on June 14, 1944. We were to escort a B-17 wing that was attacking oil refineries and an airdrome up there. Since my one and only victory, I had led Green Flight for three straight missions—to Ploesti, Rumania; Oradea, then in Hungary; and Trieste, Italy—all without encountering any enemy fighters. This June 14 mission was my fourth Green lead, and again the skies were empty—of German fighters, that is. The ever-present flak still had to be reckoned with, and it was accurate and intense over Budapest. We watched helplessly as the heavy bombers plodded, relentlessly, into that blackened piece of sky. Aircraft were sometimes lost in one blinding flash, sometimes in a slow, spinning final dive.

As we came out of the target area, we gave our attention to a straggling B-17 that had dropped out of formation and was steadily losing altitude. If there were any Me-109s prowling about in the vicinity, they were sure to pick on such cripples, who could do little to defend themselves and had no covering fire from the rest of the formation.

As we crossed the Hungarian border into Yugoslavia, the straggling B-17 was already several miles behind the formation and down to about 10,000 feet. The B-17 wasn't going to make it. The two flights of Blue Section were split at this point. Blue stayed with the main formation; Green, which I was leading, dropped down to the straggler to give him close escort and perhaps, a little moral support. We closed in, near enough to read the straggler's tail number, which was 770, and to see bits of equipment falling away from the waist windows as the crew tried to lighten the aircraft. But it didn't do any good. Two engines were feathered, and there was no telling what the other two were doing. Not enough, because the descent continued.

When the B-17 was down to about 5,000 feet, the pilot must have seen a level patch he thought was big enough to get into. He started a long shallow turn, rapidly losing altitude. Finally, he leveled off very low, with flaps down and gear up. From several thousand feet above, he appeared to touch down slowly and smoothly, leaving several trails of brown earth behind as he ploughed along the green field. Finally he slewed to a stop. We made a final low pass. The crewmen were all out by now, waving. As we started a climb for home, I threw one last look back and saw our countrymen scurrying about, getting organized for their evasion effort.

"Poor buggers," I thought, "I hope you haven't used up all of your luck. You're going to need a lot more."

His call sign, ironically, was Moses 13.

★

Of the Panama guys, Little Henry had scored the first victory. Now he had achieved another first: multiple victories on one mission. It was on our June 15 mission to La Jasse, in southern France, and although I was up that day, I didn't see any enemy aircraft. Not so for Henry. He told me his story in Corsica, where we both stopped to refuel on the way home.

His section had engaged ten to twelve Me-109s. He had gotten one of them straightaway but lost the rest of his flight in the wild melee that followed. Hardly before he could decide on his next move, he was aggressively and expertly attacked by several 109s. They were no amateurs. They had him dead bang, although he fought back the best he could, giving as well as he got. He exchanged fire with two of them on head-on passes and finally dove away at very high speed at full throttle. The possibility of a pullout from the dive was iffy until the last moment. When Henry was sure that he had it made, skimming over the wavelets of a lake, he looked back just as both of the 109s hit the water in quick succession, sending up twin geysers. He circled upward and, with his GSAP camera, took pictures of the two sets of concentric rings spreading from the impact points.

We walked over to look at his plane. From only a cursory inspection, I could see that he'd taken a couple of 20mm rounds in his right wing. One had gone through the leading edge backward and downward, obviously the result of a near head-on shot. The other, which I could put my fist through, was from the rear through the right flap, about two feet out from the fuselage. From the looks of the hole, Henry must have had some flaps down when he took it, but he didn't remember. I mentioned casually that the hole wasn't all that far from the cockpit. He laughed in agreement, allowing how it had been a pretty sporty proposition for a while. He didn't seem the worse for his experience, at least he didn't show any ill effect. So, when the fuel trucks finished topping us off, we saddled up and headed back to San Severo.

Knights of the Road: With Glen Nelson (r.) in Galveston, Texas, as we prepare to start our trek back to Wisconsin.

My high-school graduation picture, taken about six months before Pearl Harbor and a year before I joined the Aviation Cadet program.

This photograph of my wife, June, left home with me when I went off to flight training and it stayed with me all the way through Panama and Italy.

Aviation Cadet Goebel during Primary Flight training at Corsicana, Texas.

My cousin, Gil Gorski.

Brown Forbes (r.) and I as we await our turn to fly at Corsicana.

My mother and I on the day I earned my silver pilot's wings and gold lieutenant's bars.

With June and our new son, Gary, during my post-graduation leave in Racine in May 1943.

My "bent bird" following my first flight in a P-39 at La Jolla, Panama.
(Official USAF Photograph)

Lieutenant Al Hayes in a P-40 at Aguadulce, Panama. Al was killed in a P-39 two months later during a practice dive-bombing mission at La Jolla. *(Official USAF Photograph)*

P-51Bs of the 31st Fighter Group's 307th Fighter Squadron taxi out for what must have been the group's very first combat mission in Mustangs. *(Official USAF Photograph)*

The cockpit area of my P-51B, showing details of the "greenhouse" enclosure.

Lieutenants Johnson (l.) and Ricks in the bivouac area at San Severo, Italy. Ricks was killed on the group's second mission, which was to Udine, Italy. I was flying as Johnson's wingman when he simply vanished while attacking enemy fighters during the fifth mission, to Wiener Neustadt, **Austria.** *(Compliments of Walter Goehausen)*

Lieutenant Fred Trafton (l.) and Captain Roland Lamensdorf. (*Compliments of Walter Goehausen*)

A B-17 of the 5th Bomb Wing's 99th Bomb Group. *(Official USAF Photograph)*

B-24s over Ploesti, Rumania, on May 31, 1944. The two dense columns of black smoke are from fires in the tank storage area and the pumping station of the Concordia oil refinery. *(Official USAF Photograph)*

This B-24 was hit by flak in action over Central Europe in April 1944. It has rolled almost inverted and the left wing has just buckled. *(Official USAF Photograph)*

The Enemy: This Me-109G of the elite Hungarian Puma Group is about to scramble from Veszprem Airdrome, near Lake Balaton, in July 1944. *(Compliments of Karoly Faludi)*

Colonel Charles "Sandy" McCorkle, the 31st Group commanding officer at the time of my arrival in Italy. *(Official USAF Photograph)*

Major James "Stick" Thorsen, the 308th Fighter Squadron commander in the Spring of 1944.
(Compliments of Walter Goehausen)

Captain Tommy "Twig" Byrnes, Thorsen's operations officer. Tommy was shot down and killed by an Me-109 near Vienna in June 1944. *(Compliments of Walter Goehausen)*

Captain Leland "Tommy" Molland, my close friend and mentor, and eventually the commander of the 308th Fighter Squadron. *(Compliments of Walter Goehausen)*

308th Fighter Squadron pilots on the steps of our quarters at San Severo: (l. to r.) Joe Sheehan, Tommy Molland, Bill Shelton (on bottom step), Jack Edge, Claude Greene, and Bob Goebel.

This B-25 was "acquired" by the 31st Group for use as a support aircraft and personnel hauler. From its combat markings, it appears that it had been put out to pasture as a reward for years of loyal service. *(Compliments of Walter Goehausen)*

In flying suit just before donning my Mae West and parachute at the aircraft.

Wally Goehausen took this photograph of me while he was straddling the nose of the *Flying Dutchman* just aft of the propeller. *(Complements of Walter Goehausen)*

**A flight of 308th Fighter Squadron D-model Mustangs in echelon over Italy.
HL-C is Tommy Molland's *O Kaye*.** *(Official USAF Photograph)*

**These were the photos I carried on missions to facilitate the
fabrication of false identification papers by the underground.
The only civilian coat, shirt, and tie available were used by all
pilots in the group when the photographs were taken!**

Lieutenant Jim Brooks.

Five of my closest friends: Charley "George" Bushick, Jack Edge, "Doctor Tom" Hardeman, Jim Brooks, and Joe Sheehan. *(Compliments of Walter Goehausen)*

In the cockpit of the *Flying Dutchman*, ready for takeoff. Note the external tank and the .50-caliber machine guns. A very small opening on the leading edge of the wing near fuselage is the gun-camera port.

Lieutenant Wally Goehausen, with his ten aerial victories marked on his P51-D, *Miss Mimi*.
(Compliments of Walter Goehausen.)

Mustang Ace.

PART III

Ace

They found the foe and joined the fray.
It finally came to pass,
To test their hand
As dropped the sand,
Through each appointed hour glass.

15

My first respite from the daily routine of combat flying was a couple of days in North Africa to bring back a brand-new D model P-51. The big depot was at Casablanca, where the cocooning and other preservatives were removed from the aircraft after transport across the Atlantic by ship. After cleaning, the new Mustangs were inspected, run up, fueled, and generally made ready for the ferry flight to Italy. I had never been to Casablanca before. Since Jim Brooks, from the 307th, was also going, we buddied up and looked forward to the change of scenery. Counting the guys from the 52d Group, whom we had picked up on the way, there were perhaps a dozen of us who wound up at Casablanca, milling around the airfield. The drill was for each of us to make a local flight in our assigned aircraft and, after satisfying ourselves that the machine was going to run, to get on back to our home base the best way we could.

We had a night to spend in the city, so Jim and I started out to find an Officers' Club or dining facility to while away the evening. We were directed to one such place. As we walked along the street, trying to get our bearings and shooing away the swarms of boys yelling "Baksheesh," we fell in with two young ladies, fairly well dressed for that time and place. We should have known better, but Jim was at least as big a Virginia yokel as I was of the Wisconsin variety. When he tried to make conversation and asked them if they were French, the one with the fur stole (in summer in North Africa?) replied in heavily accented English, "Nah, F- - - the French."

That was okay with us, but clue number 2 went right over our heads. So we steered them to the club, which we finally found, and went in to treat them to dinner. It didn't take long after we seated ourselves to realize that something was very wrong—and they called its name pariah. After twenty minutes of being ignored, we were pretty well convinced that the neglect was deliberate. The place was busy but not that busy. Finally Jim spotted an MP standing just inside the entrance, so we excused ourselves and went to find out what kind of leprosy we had. In my naïveté, I thought that we were non grata because our khaki uniform shirts were open at the neck—we had no neckties with us. The MP smiled, almost laughed, at the question.

"No," he informed us, "that's not the reason. It's the girls you're with. They're bad stuff. Pros they are, but the worst kind. They get arrested for prostitution and then have to work in a prison brothel to pay off their fines."

I didn't understand how that could be and wanted to pursue it with him further, but Jim had heard enough. He gave a tug on my shirtsleeve and we sidled toward the door, without looking back. We didn't get to eat—but hell, who wanted to eat, anyway? We found a couple bottles of wine and a loaf of bread somewhere and headed back to the field, calling it a night.

Next morning we were away early, to the Maison Blanche Airdrome at Algiers, then to Cagliari, Sardinia. Finally we landed at San Severo. It felt good to put the wheels down onto the familiar strip of PSP and then to taxi in to my own squadron parking area. I really felt at home here, and I was glad to be back. Casablanca was a nice break from the daily grind; yet I was no sooner out of sight of Italy when I began to think about the 31st and San Severo. Where are they going tomorrow? I wondered. Who is going? Is there likely to be a fight?

The competition to pile up missions and, hopefully, victories was keen. All the while I was gone, I had worried about what I was missing. Upon my return, I was happy to learn that I hadn't missed a thing. By a great stroke of luck (to my thinking), the group had been stood down for five straight days while I was gone. I also drew smug satisfaction from the fact that the very next day, when I was not yet scheduled to go back on operations, the group went to Trieste but because of bad weather was diverted to some piddly-assed alternate. No enemy fighters were sighted.

★

Accountability for equipment in a theater of operations was nothing like the rigid bean-counting mentality so common in the rear areas and the continental U.S. I knew all about that mentality. I had lost a Colt .45 automatic in Panama and had filed the necessary papers to drop accountability on it. The official response ("Disapproved") followed me all over the States and caught up with me at Telergma, where the cost of a new one was duly taken out of my pay.

The Colt .45 incident wasn't at all consistent with how materiel seemed to move around mysteriously in the Mediterranean Theater. Equipment appeared and disappeared without the benefit of requisitions, shippers, or other documentation. For example, rumor had it that a couple of Spitfires were parked with a B-25 group in Corsica or North Africa. A B-25 sat awkwardly among the swarm of P-51s at San Severo. No one seemed to know where it came from or how it came to be there. Officially, the 31st didn't even have a B-25; unofficially, the twin-engine, twin-tail medium bomber was parked out at the field.

The B-25 was a fine utility aircraft. We used it all the time to haul people to Bari, Naples, or wherever. Wing Headquarters must have known about it, but who wanted to rock the boat when a successful fighter group showed a little ingenuity in getting the equipment it needed to operate effectively?

Right after the move from Castel Volturno, the squadron CO, Stick Thorsen, showed up at San Severo with a small Italian biplane, a Saiman 200. He had great fun flying it low and slow and gawking at the sights, such as they were, in the Foggia–San Severo area. To me puttering around the countryside in an open cockpit and feeling the slipstream in my face sounded exhilarating. I was getting up the nerve to ask Thorsen if I could take the Saiman up. But, before I could, it disappeared as mysteriously as it had appeared.

Long after we had given up the Spitfires, one of them remained and was reserved for the exclusive use of the group CO, Colonel McCorkle. It was a Mark IX, and all the pilots—veterans and new guys alike—cast covetous eyes on it to no avail. No one—but no one— except Colonel McCorkle was allowed to fly it. I don't know how he managed to flimflam higher headquarters as long as he did, but eventually he must have run out of excuses for keeping it; it too disappeared.

I was sent down to Cerignola to bring back a P-40 that one of the bomb groups was being stripped of. It had been a while since I had flown a 40, but that didn't concern me. I thought that I could fly anything with wings, so long as the propeller went round and round. After I got the P-40 fired up, I wasn't so sure.

I sat in it for a few minutes, refreshing my memory. The engine sounded pretty lumpy while I taxied out. When I checked the mags, I got twice the allowable RPM drop on both right and left. I should have taken it back to the ramp, but—what the hell. A goodly number of air crew and mechanics were watching, and I thought that it was up to me to uphold the honor of the 31st. I had decided to get the tail up on takeoff and then hold the plane down on the runway, letting the speed build in a level attitude. If the gear was raised just as the plane began to skip, the illusion was that the gear had been sucked up into the aircraft, suddenly thrusting it into the air. Hot stuff! But I hadn't done a very thorough pre-flight inspection, considering the abundant evidence of misuse. I didn't check the friction lock on the throttle quadrant, and that turned out to be a big mistake.

The tower gave me a green on the Aldis lamp, so I pulled out onto the runway and tore ass. Just as I reached for the gear handle with my left hand, the engine sound started to fade quickly. I was shocked, and it took me a split second to figure out what had happened. The throttle friction lock was so loose that the throttle would not stay in the forward position; it moved back toward idle as soon as I let go of it. Gone were any thoughts of grandstanding. I was pretty well down the runway and not airborne yet. I shoved the throttle back up smartly and held it there. After I'd gotten up a couple of hundred feet, gained some airspeed, and tightened the friction lock, I finally retracted the gear and headed for home. Some exhibition I had put on. The Cerignola guys were probably laughing their heads off. The plane ran just well enough for the fifteen-minute flight to San Severo. In a few days that P-40—like the Saiman and the Spitfire—was gone.

It wasn't only complete aircraft that were subject to misappropriation. Later in the month our B-25 went to Cairo and was three days late coming back. Captain Upzak, the squadron engineering officer, was along and, when he went out on the ramp to check over the aircraft the morning of the return flight, he discovered that one wheel was missing. How can you, at a strange base, get a new wheel and tire for an airplane you're not supposed to have? It's a wonder they got back at all.

16

My second victory came on June 23 on a return visit to Ploesti, my seventh trip to Rumania. I was leading Blue Flight and, as soon as we got past Craiova, I knew we were in for a fight. The sky ahead was filigreed with the contrails of maneuvering aircraft much higher than we were. Suddenly the R/T came alive:

"Playboy Leader, Playboy Red Three here. Bogies eleven very high."

"Roger Red Three, I got 'em."

A short time later I called Twig Byrnes, who was leading the squadron.

"Border Leader, this is Border Blue. More bogies at twelve high."

"Border Blue, Red Leader. Rog."

Those 109s and 190s were really up there; even from our altitude they looked like specks at the end of the contrails. They worked around to the side and then behind, and then the contrails thinned and stopped.

"Here they come. They're comin' down!"

The high-pitched fragments of shouted warnings saturated the radio channel, further quickening my pulse. Tanks off; throttle, everything forward. They appeared to have broken up into smaller groups so that they could attack the bomber stream at many points simultaneously. A loose formation of four 109s, the nearest ones to us, came down in a steep dive, heading for the bombers. Even though I turned to intercept, dropping the nose at max throttle, they went by us very quickly and continued on down through the bomber formation, making a steep, high-deflection firing pass as they went through.

The gunners in the bombers exchanged fire with the attackers, but I saw no serious damage done on either side. As a general rule, escorting fighters weren't keen on going anywhere near the bombers, especially in close to Me-109s. Turret gunners were notoriously unbiased when it came to firing on any single-engine aircraft, painted insignia and silhouette notwithstanding. Even when they did recognize the difference, the gunners often made the common mistake of not giving the German fighter enough lead. Instead they sprayed bullets perilously close to a pursuer, for whom the lead was just right.

But all those considerations were nothing now. I had latched on to the last 109 before it had turned into the bombers. I was 800 yards back, but gaining—and I was determined to get him. As he leveled off and then started to climb, I closed rapidly to 300 yards from dead astern. Since I was about 15 degrees above him, I put the pipper out in front about a half radius over his cockpit. Now! I opened fire with a long burst—three or four seconds—and saw some scattered flashes on the 109's right wing. Coolant began streaming from its underside. Though the German was still flying, I knew he had no more than five minutes until his engine seized. I kept after him, squeezing off several short bursts, but failed to hit him.

He kept on diving. At a few thousand feet, he slowed abruptly. I suddenly found myself overrunning. Even though I jerked the throttle back to idle, I came sliding up alongside him. He was in a turn to the left; I was on his right, not 50 feet away. I looked over and could see him plainly—black-helmeted, goggled—looking back at me. As I began to drift aft, I noticed a stylized Prussian eagle, short wings and talons outstretched, painted on the right side, just behind the cockpit. When I was able to slide over to a six o'clock position, I fired again. As my rounds began to kick up the dust in front of him, I realized he was making a forced landing. No wonder he was slow. I was shocked; I had gotten so absorbed in looking at him through the sight reticle that I had not noticed how low we were. If he had dived into the ground, I would have gone in right behind him.

I quit firing as he touched down in a great cloud of dust. Although it didn't look good for him, the 109 did come to a stop, finally, without breaking up. I cast one last look back as I passed over him, but he had not gotten out yet. Well, I wasn't waiting around.

After satisfying myself that I was alone, I went up to takeoff power, keeping my airspeed up and gaining altitude as rapidly as I could. I was about 15 miles north of Bucharest, which I could see on my left. Traffic on the R/T had dropped to the point where I was able to contact my number 3 and arrange for a rendezvous with him and his wingman. My wingman was with him, too. The four of us rejoined and headed for home. I wasn't sure whether the 109 was destroyed or not, but—as far as I was concerned—I had shot him down. At the debriefing I was not a damn bit bashful about claiming an enemy aircraft destroyed.

The debriefing after a mission must have been a trying time for Lam. Recording statements taken from returning pilots was easy; the hard part was fitting the statements together so that the whole made sense. The perceptions of pilots who had witnessed the same event were astonishingly different. Many of the differences were understandable: The arena was three-dimensional; every observer was in a highly excited state; and, after the fact, placing events in the correct time sequence was very difficult. Then, too, certain observations, like the results of one's attack, were certainly colored by the hopes and wishes of the individual pilot involved.

The need for detail was always greater than what was available. I remember standing around listening to a post-flight interrogation after a mission I had not flown. Tommy Molland had already given the interviewer his rundown but was being pressed for more detail. Exactly how many of them were there? What was your altitude and airspeed when you started firing? What time was it?

Finally Tommy called a halt—with a great deal of forbearance, I thought. He never raised his voice.

"Look," he said, "I'm perfectly willing to tell you what I saw on the way up—how many barges were on the Danube, how blue the sky was, when and at what altitude we made rendezvous. But when I say twenty to thirty enemy aircraft, it's because I didn't stop to count them. The time I guessed at because it was between rendezvous and the IP. My altitude was between 26,000 and 16,000 feet. Airspeed was 250 to 450, depending on what second you're talking about. The location of the crash I also guessed, because I had the feeling, the *feeling*, that we had worked eastward during the fight. If you don't like those numbers, put in your own. They'd be as good as mine, anyway."

That was the end of that debriefing. I couldn't have agreed with Tommy more. Once the fight started, everything was relative—either you were behind him or he was behind you. The only relevant aspects were your relative position and the distance apart. If you saw the ground, you were probably going straight down; if you saw the sky, you were probably going straight up. You didn't look back inside the cockpit until five minutes after it was all over. Those who did were probably sitting in a POW camp.

After Lam put the facts together at best he could, his report went to Group Headquarters for integration into the official 31st Fighter Group report to Wing; to Fifteenth Air Force; and, ultimately, to posterity.

The following group report—for the June 23, 1944, mission to Ploesti—was typical:

HEADQUARTERS
31st FIGHTER GROUP
APO 520

24th June 1944

Mission No. 566 – 31st Fighter Group
307th, 308th, 309th Squadrons
Ploesti, Rumania - 23rd June 1944.

1. MISSION AND TARGET: To provide target cover and withdrawal escort for the 5th and 47th Wings attacking Rumana Americana and Dacia Romana Oil Refineries, Ploesti, 1000 hours.

2. AIRCRAFT AND CHRONOLOGY: 50 P-51's took off from San Severo A/D at 0745 hours. Four aircraft returned early for mechanical reasons. 46 aircraft were over the target from 0950 to 1035. One P-51 lost, pilot safe (Air Sea Rescue).

3. ROUTE: Base, direct to target and return.

4. RENDEZVOUS, FORMATION AND ASSAULT: P-51's arrived at Ploesti at 0950 hours at 25,000 feet. The bomber formation was good and the assault was made from the NE to SW at 22,000 feet with the rally to the left. The bombers were escorted to NIS where they left at 1140 hours between 18,000 and 20,000 feet.

5. RESULTS OF BOMBING: Not observed.

6. STRAFING: None.

7. ENEMY AIR RESISTANCE AND ACTIVITY: At 0955 hours, 307th Squadron sighted 8 aircraft in three groups: 3 Me-

109s, 4 FW-190s, a lone Me-109. The aircraft were at
12,000 feet over Ploesti. When attacked the enemy aircraft
attempted to dive away but were followed by P-51s which
destroyed 4 and damaged the other 4. At 1010 hours 3 FW-
190s were seen by the 308th Squadron, 10 miles north of
Bucharest going west at 22,000 feet. They were attacked
and two were destroyed. At 1015 hours 2 twin-engined
aircraft were observed north of Bucharest going west at
27,000 feet. P-51s started going after them, whereupon 2
Me-109s were observed approaching from 12 o'clock from
the direction of the twin-engined aircraft. These Me-109s
were observed at 12,000 feet going east just north of
Bucharest but were not engaged. At 1020 hours 309th
Squadron sighted 2 FW-190s making an attack at the last
group of bombers. As the enemy aircraft pulled up they
were attacked and one was probably destroyed, the other
damaged.

8. FLAK: M[edium] to I[ntense], I[naccurate], H[eavy] at
target.

9. SIGNIFICANT OBSERVATIONS:
ENEMY:

(a) Naval and Shipping: A large barge was observed in
the Danube River at 1100 hours.

(b) Enemy Ground Activities: Effective smoke screen
over Ploesti.

(c) As in Para 8.

(d) Other: An unidentified single-engined aircraft was
seen spinning down trailing smoke and glycol at 1100
hours. Two chutes seen at 1100 hours. Two chutes seen at
1117 hours.

(e) Enemy Airdromes and Aircraft on Ground: 6 single-
engined and 8 twin-engined aircraft observed on Bucharest/
Pipera Airdrome and 19 single-engined aircraft on
Bucharest/Otopzvi Airdrome at 0950 hours from 25,000
feet.

10. WEATHER: En route, over Yugoslavian mountains, 10/10 cloud to 17,000 feet and another 10/10 layer at 21,000 feet, improving to 15,000 feet in target area.

11. AIR SEA RESCUE: Lt. McElroy bellied in at 1210 hours at 41 deg. 15 min. N - 17 deg. 0 min. E due to mechanical reasons. "Mayday" was given by Lt. Creswell, who circled Lt. McElroy and saw him get into his dinghy. Lt. Creswell was low on gas and landed at Bari. Word was received that Lt. McElroy was being brought to Foggia for return to the unit, but he did not return on the 25th.

12. RADIO SECURITY: Satisfactory. Jamming experienced on "B" channel in the target area.

13. FRIENDLY AIRCRAFT LOST OR IN DIFFICULTY: None.

14. AIRCRAFT SEEN DESTROYED BY OTHER GROUPS: None.

CONCLUSIONS:

15. VICTORIES AND LOSSES—

VICTORIES:

DESTROYED

2 FW-190s	Lt. Riddle 307
1 Me-109	Lt. Brooks 307
1 Me-109	Lt. Surrett 307
1 Me-109	Lt. Goebel 308
1 Me-109	Lt. Goehausen 308
1 FW-190	Lt. Voll 308
1 FW-190	Capt. Byrnes 308

PROB. DESTROYED

| 1 FW-190 | Maj. Warford 309 |

DAMAGED

1 FW-190	Lt. Baetjer 309
2 FW-190s	Lt. Riddle 307
1 Me-109	Lt. Brooks 307
1 Me-109	Lt. Schanning 307

TOTALS:

4 Me-109s destroyed   1 FW-190 probably destroyed
4 FW-190s destroyed   3 FW-190s damaged
2 Me-109s damaged

LOSSES:

	Fighters	Flak	Other
Lost	0	0	0
Missing	0	0	0
Damaged (Repairable)	0	0	0
Damaged (Washout)	0	0	0

Lt. McElroy bailed out at 41 deg. 15 min. N - 17 deg. 0 min. E believed due to mechanical trouble.

16. SORTIES: 46

17. FORMATION LEADERS AND FLIGHT LEADERS:

307th Squadron: Lt. Col. Daniel (Group Leader) with Maj. Brown, Lts. Bohn and Schanning.

308th Squadron: Capt. Byrnes with Lt. Col. Tarrant, Lts. Goebel and Goehausen.

309th Squadron: Maj. Warford with Lts. Cloutier, Wilhelm, and Carey.

18. COMMENTS: Lt. Goehausen scored his fifth victory on today's mission to reach "Ace" status.

19. CORRECTIONS: None.

> Albert D. Levy
> Major Air Corps
> Group Intelligence Office

I could never have figured out what had happened from reading the "activity" paragraph, and I was on the mission.

On June 24, 1944, we went back to Bucharest, on a fighter sweep. Strangely, no enemy fighters were up. The following day we were out again, this time going the other way, to Avignon, France. It was no dice again. For our trouble all each of us got was a sore ass and another five and one-half hours in the Form 5, the flight log.

17

Captain Thomas Byrnes had become the squadron operations officer at the beginning of June. He had completed a combat tour in the A-36, a dive-bomber version of the Mustang, while in the Twelfth Air Force and had joined the 31st shortly before the group moved to Castel Volturno. He was a combat veteran who learned quickly and flew boldly.

Byrnes knew Stick Thorsen from somewhere. I assumed that Stick had something to do with bringing Byrnes into the 308th Squadron. Byrnes brought the nickname Twig with him. It had been given to him as the diminutive form of Stick—Little Stick, so to speak.

A diminutive name was appropriate for Byrnes. He was short, like my cadet pal, Brown Forbes. And, like Brown, Byrnes must have squeaked by the minimum height requirement with nothing to spare. His boyish face radiated good humor. His slightly protruding front teeth giving him a vague resemblance to Mickey Rooney, a youthful movie star of that period. Twig and I had hit it off from the first. We thought alike, liked to fly together, and enjoyed each other's company on the ground as well.

Byrnes had scored his first victory on the group's second P-51 mission, and he had gotten a second enemy fighter a month later, up near Vienna. On June 23, he was leading the squadron to Ploesti when he bagged his third, an FW-190. I never knew Tommy Byrnes to shirk a fight or his responsibility as a leader in the air. Perhaps that was his undoing.

On June 26, 1944, on a mission to Vienna, he had taken it upon himself to play guardian angel to a lieutenant colonel, newly arrived from the States. Twig was going to lead Blue Flight and had scheduled the colonel to fly on his own wing so that he could look after him. At the post-flight debriefing, I learned what happened.

Some 15 miles northeast of Lake Neusiedler, Twig's flight got into it with a formation of Me-109s. Twig shot down one of them and was hotly pursuing a second one. The colonel saw another 109 lining up on Twig and called for him to break, which he appeared to do. The colonel last saw him in a steep dive at low altitude.

The Operations Report said: "Captain Byrnes was last seen near 48 degrees 05 minutes North, 16 degrees 55 minutes East going in from 2000 feet." Not much of an epitaph.

I felt the loss of Twig keenly, and in my own mind I held the colonel responsible for his death. This was patently unfair. It was an accepted fact that, with a new guy on your wing—regardless of his rank—you had better look after yourself; he would probably be too excited and confused to be of any use. But I was not interested in being fair. I had to blame someone, and the colonel was it. Turning my anger on the German pilot who killed Twig never entered my head. That was different; that was one of those things. But the colonel—he should have done better by Twig, I thought, and I did not forgive him. But there was no time for mourning or recrimination. The war went on.

The next day, June 27, saw my fifth go in as many days. The assignment was a target-cover mission to Budapest. I had been to Budapest once before, in early June. We encountered no fighter opposition then, so I had been able to get a good look at the route and the area around the city. Budapest was about 450 miles from San Severo in a northeasterly direction. Lake Balaton was the principal landmark, lying to the west of the direct course, about 75 miles southwest of Budapest. The city straddled the Danube River and was really two different cities, Buda and Pest.

This time the B-17s of the 5th Bomb Wing were to attack the marshaling yards; the 31st was to provide target-area cover. The new group CO, Lieutenant Colonel Yancey Tarrant, was flying with our squadron. I was flying as his number 3. He was another alumnus of an A-36 group and had come over to the 31st as deputy group CO a month before. Everything went as scheduled, and soon we were patrolling the target area at 28,000 feet. I called out an Me-110 twin-engine fighter that was passing beneath us. Since the colonel had only started a steep turn, I cut inside him; dropped down on the German fighter; and, from almost dead astern, cut loose. I lighted him up pretty well along the slim aft fuselage. There was no return fire, so I must have silenced the 7.9mm machine gun manned by the rear gunner. I hadn't noticed many hits on the right wing. But, as I broke off, I could see his right engine burning as he banked away steeply to the right and started down into a spiral. Unbeknownst to me, Goehausen had made a simultaneous attack on the same plane. I didn't see much point in chasing the 110—it was done for—so I rejoined on Tarrant, and the remainder of the mission was uneventful.

On the way home I began to regret my rash behavior in cutting my leader out of a shot. On my way from our aircraft to the operations shack, I caught up with Colonel Tarrant and started to apologize. He stopped me with a wave of his hand. It wasn't an angry gesture—more likely it meant "That's okay. You did what you had to." Tarrant was a good group CO. Although his administrative responsibilities limited his time, he continued to fly missions, performing creditably on every one. I think he took as much pride in his pilots' successes as he did in his own.

At the interrogation I found out about Goehausen's firing on the 110 I had hit. I knew that I had cut my flight leader out of a shot, but I was really surprised that I had not seen Goehausen during his firing pass. He was equally surprised; he hadn't seen me, either. It seemed incredible to me that two pilots flying curves of pursuit on the same target could be completely unaware of each other. Each of us must have concentrated so completely on the Me-110 and the sight picture that we had come very, very close to colliding in midair. Because Goehausen and I had both made significant hits, Lam decided to credit each of us with half a victory.

The next day I noticed that I was given full credit on the board. Apparently, Goehausen had gone to Lam and graciously conceded his half. That brought my total to three. Henry already had five.

★

My mother used to say that there was no rest for the wicked. I didn't think I qualified as being wicked, but there was no rest for me or any of us in the squadron. In quick succession we went back to Bucharest; to Blechhammer, Germany; and then to Budapest—with only one day off in between to go swimming. There was no action on any but the last mission, on July 2.

It was my 41st mission, and I had begun to get careless. Maybe not careless, but—well, jaded. Incautious, perhaps. I knew that it was a damned dangerous business, this flogging the air all over Europe in a single-engine plane. But going out almost every day as I did, I think I began to get complacent, to lose that sense of hazard that makes one careful. However, this mission, by the time it was over, got my attention. And, having been brought back to reality, I don't think I ever again lost my focus or grew contemptuous of danger.

With the full 85 gallons of fuel in the fuselage tank, the aft center of gravity (CG) in a maximum-rate turn caused a stick reversal; the plane tended to wrap the turn tighter without any back pressure on the stick. In short, the plane behaved like a pregnant sow. The standard procedure was to burn the fuselage tank down to about 30 gallons immediately after takeoff, even before going on the external tanks. That way, if the external tanks had to be jettisoned unexpectedly, you were already in a condition from which you could fight.

On July 2 we were taking the B-24s of the 55th Bomb Wing up to Budapest to hit the marshaling yards and industrial areas. The route was familiar to me; I had been there twice before and fuel had not been a problem. Why, then, did I leave 50-plus gallons in the fuselage tank on the climb out? I don't know. I suppose I thought I was getting some kind of edge in the hunt for victories, being able to hang around the bombers in the target area longer. I glossed over the aerodynamic effect. That was for new guys to worry about.

Our assignment was to provide close escort for the penetration, target area, and withdrawal of the bombers. The rendezvous point was over northern Yugoslavia, at 0916, with a planned bomb release at 1014. That was a long time to be providing close escort. Because of the 100-mph difference in speed between the heavily laden bombers and the fighters, it was not possible to just fly along above them. Nor was it a good idea to pull the throttle back to stay with them; at that speed the Mustangs would be at a tremendous disadvantage if forced to defend against enemy fighters. The standard tactic was to split into flights, crossing over the top of the bombers as we scissored from one side to the other, so that no part of the bomber formation was ever uncovered at any time.

We approached rendezvous on time, but the bombers were obviously late. The group leader elected to make a very shallow 360-degree turn, to kill time and keep the three squadrons more or less intact. Rendezvous was finally made at 24,000 feet at 0925. As we split up to begin our escort duties above our assigned bombers, I noted that the sky was a clear, brilliant blue. In the distance to the north, however, were several thin layers of cirrus at about our altitude.

The run to the IP, east of Budapest, seemed to take forever. After 30 to 35 minutes of monotonous patrolling, it became progressively easier to lose your edge, to get complacent. Finally the bombers made their left turn off the IP and began the assault from east to west. As the first bombs began to fall, the lead squadron broke radio silence by calling out fifteen to twenty Me-109s away to the northwest and high, at 32,000 feet. Everyone stayed with their part of the bomber stream, which had gotten strung out. Although the bombers were not attacked, everyone sat up a little straighter in the cockpit and redoubled their vigilance.

The increasing cloudiness above and below our altitude made doing our job progressively harder. Scattered clouds lying below the bombers allowed them to bomb visually, but the clouds above occasionally caused us to lose sight of the B-24s. In addition, the clouds were a potential screen for lurking German fighters.

Quite suddenly, without anyone calling them out, we collided with a formation of eight to ten Me-109s. It didn't seem like a bounce; it was more like the two formations just blundered into each other. I don't think anyone even called a break. It was instant pandemonium. The radio was useless, absolutely saturated by a half dozen pilots trying to transmit at once. I broke sharply, without even looking back; got my tanks off and my guns on; and went to full power. In the vertical turn the Mustang felt a little rubbery. I immediately remembered the fuselage tank, but it was too late to worry about that now; I was going to have to play the hand I had dealt myself. A lot of airplanes—both kinds—were going in all directions. In the brief instant I looked around, I couldn't pick out the rest of my flight.

What I did see was a 109 close on the tail of a 51 below me at about ten o'clock, 600 to 700 yards away. A string of tiny smoke puffs strung out behind the 109 told me the German pilot was already firing. As I took after them, I could see that the 51 was doing a lot of jinking. It hadn't been hit. Not yet. I was about 450 yards from the 109. With the spread harmonization the group used, I was still too far away to shoot—the inboard guns crossed at 250 yards and the outboard at 300. But waiting for a proper shot might prove fatal for the Mustang pilot. I tried to make a guess where the rounds would go at that range and snapped off as good a shot as I could get. The one-second burst produced one or two hits on the German's left wing, enough to make the pilot break off. Just as he did, I got off another burst, again getting a few strikes back in the tail area. Now he was turning *hard!* I tried to follow, but no way. My P-51 started shaking immediately. When I tried to force it into a tighter turn, it quit flying and fell out. The recovery was easy enough, I just let it go and it started flying again. The 109 was still there, above me now and still turning, almost opposite me. I thought I could see a thin streak behind him. Coolant! Was it my imagination? Was I merely seeing something I desperately wanted to see?

Reef it in! We became locked in a plain old-fashioned turning duel, a Lufbery circle. I was working hard, sweating. My heart was pounding as I tried to outturn him, playing the stick just to the point of a high-speed stall. Was it enough? He seemed to be closing on me a little, but then I saw that thin streak again. He really was losing coolant! But could I hang on long enough to get some help or until he overheated?

He was definitely gaining on me. One-third of the circle was between his aircraft and mine, two-thirds between mine and his. In my semipanic I pulled the stick back hard again. Again I literally fell out of the sky and had to direct my attention to regaining control of the plane. Nose down, ease the stick. We were flying again. Now where the hell was he?

He was gone and so was everyone else. Several sharp turns confirmed it. I switched the fuel selector to "Fuselage," eased myself into a cloud bank, and burned off the fuel in my fuselage tank as fast as I could. I was still pretty excited and not doing a very good job flying on instruments. The needle and ball went their own separate ways; the only time either one was in the middle was when it was passing from one side to the other. I was all over the sky. I just concentrated on keeping the wings level and dropped the nose slightly until I came out into the clear. I was still alone.

It didn't take long to get the fuselage tank down to 20 gallons, at which point I reduced power to normal cruise and went looking for the rest of my flight. I spotted the 24s straightaway. Since the R/T traffic was down to normal, I arranged for a meeting with the other three members of my flight and used the bombers as a marker. In a surprisingly short time, we re-formed.

I unhooked my mask momentarily and wiped the sweat from my face with my sleeve. My heart rate and breathing had slowed almost to normal. Finally, my aircraft was ready to fight, but I wasn't. Fortunately, no one was left to fight with—all the enemy airplanes were long gone.

Later, when I was telling Lam the substance of the encounter, as well as I could piece it together, I said I wasn't sure what kind of claim to make.

"If you hit him and you saw glycol, why not claim a probable?"

That was fine with me; Lam's offer was more than generous. A bit much, perhaps, almost getting my ass hammered and still making a claim. But who could resist an offer like that?

I couldn't forget my close call; I went over it again and again in my mind like a cow chewing its cud. Had the extra fuel made that much difference? Or was the 109 pilot that good? I had caught a Tartar, that much was certain. My brush with my own fallibility made me think of an old cowboy line: "There never was a horse that couldn't be rode, never was a cowboy who couldn't be throwed."

So much for leaving the fuselage tank almost full, I thought. It'll be a cold day in hell before I try that again.

But it was all of two months.

★

The next day, July 3, I was airborne again. This time it was back to Bucharest. We were to provide escort for the 304th Bomb Wing's B-24s, which were going to have a go at the Malaxia Locomotive Works and the Titan Oil Refinery there.

Takeoff from San Severo was at 0933, somewhat later than usual. This was to save fuel because we were going to have to take our bombers in and back out again without any relieving fighters. While providing close escort—scissoring back and forth over the bombers—the fighters actually had to fly much farther than the distance made good by the bombers. Thus, the fuel consumption for distance traveled was greater than it would have been if the fighters had been flying to the target on a straight course. At some small risk to the bombers, we often improved our fuel margin by moving the rendezvous point closer to the target and having the fighters take off later than the bombers.

The July 3 rendezvous was made 40 miles east of Craiova on time at 1141. After rendezvous, the R/T traffic began to pick up with a steady stream of bogie call-outs, so I called for my flight to drop tanks. About 15 miles northwest of the target, a gaggle of fifteen Me-109s approached the bombers in small groups from the direction of Bucharest, at 26,000 feet. I spotted two Me-109s above at about one o'clock. I think the leader saw my flight about the same time. He had balls, I'll say that for him. The two 109s started down to attack either the bombers below or the four of us; it was a rash act indeed. Perhaps he had recently come from the Eastern Front and had no fear of Russian fighters, but we were not the Yaks or MiGs he was used to fooling with.

We broke into them. In thirty seconds he had discovered his mistake. As soon as we broke, he pulled straight up into a loop. Then, as he got over the top and started down, he rolled out, doing a sort of half Cuban eight. He lost his friend in this maneuver; the wingman continued diving, and I'm not sure anyone picked him up. I tried to follow my man, but I didn't have enough speed. In military-emergency power, I just managed to stagger over the top of the loop. But once I got the nose down, I accelerated rapidly. He had opened quite a lot of sky between us, but I had kept him in sight. Now I began to close the distance. We were in a long shallow dive. His wingspan gradually grew within the bright orange circle of my sight. A quick glance down at the gun switch verified that my guns were hot. I stayed slightly low in his blind spot. He may have mistaken my wingman, who was quite far back, for me, because the German continued in his descending, high-speed run. Although my wingman *was* way back, he was well out to the side, and my numbers 3 and 4 were wide on the other side. We had the poor bugger boxed in.

Now the 109 almost filled the sight; I had to be in range now! Surely I was no more than 200 yards away. I had the pipper low in the center of his fuselage when I squeezed off the first short burst. No strikes. Thank God our group did not put tracers in the normal load, or they would have given me away. I didn't like tracers anyway; they tended to draw the eye away from the sight. The pilot invariably wound up holding the trigger down, trying to steer the tracers onto the target—a nearly impossible task. Quickly raising the pipper almost to the tip of his tail, I fired again and was rewarded this time with strikes quick-flashing around the fuselage and wing roots. Then his prop wash threw me off him momentarily.

Before I could get the sight back on him for another burst, the pilot left his airplane. The 109's nose dipped suddenly, catapulting him out. His chute blossomed. I could plainly see him suspended beneath it, a dark, toylike figure, swaying gently as he floated down. I told my number 3 to take my wingman and his and to pull off a ways so I would be free to maneuver around the chute. Putting the gun switch in the Camera Only position, I made a pass at him, being careful to break off so my slipstream would not collapse his canopy. As I passed to the side of him, I raised my gloved hand in a half wave–half salute and then re-formed my flight.

It occurred to me as we started for home that he may have thought I was going to shoot him out of his harness when I lined up on him. Poor bastard; he must have really puckered up. We had heard that some in the Eighth Air Force were shooting Germans in parachutes, but I didn't believe it. I knew for sure that nobody in our group did it, and I never heard of an instance of it in our wing. I don't think we would have tolerated anyone who pulled a trick like that. Leaving chutes alone was not a written policy, just an application of the Golden Rule—no one knew when his turn to bail out was coming.

This latest victory brought my total to four.

18

When the pilot strength of the group finally rose to an acceptable level, a few pilots from each squadron were occasionally relieved from ops to make use of the R and R facilities both in Italy and the Middle East. My turn finally came—a trip to Egypt and Palestine. Tommy Molland was going too, as was Doctor Tom and Edge.

Captain Leland "Tommy" Molland was one of the few remaining pilots from Spitfire days and was, by any scale of reckoning, a fighter pilot's fighter pilot. He had joined the 31st in June 1943 at Korba North in Tunisia and had fought through Malta, Sicily, and the landing at Salerno. Three victory crosses decorated his Spit by the time the group left Castel Volturno. He was one of the few old-timers who took the change in aircraft in stride, continuing his outstanding combat record in the Mustang. He became an ace over Ploesti on April 21, 1944, when he scored twice.

Tommy looked the fighter type: handsome, of average height but lean, and he moved easily, with the certain grace that marked him as an athlete. He was not given to idle chatter, generally remaining quiet unless he had something to say and never using two words when one would do. But he could fly that machine; he was a great pilot and a courageous and resourceful leader in the air. I was pleased that Tommy would be part of the R and R group.

After an uneventful flight across the eastern Mediterranean in a war-weary B-17, our magic carpet, we were installed in quite a nice hotel in Cairo. We were within walking distance of Shepheard's Hotel, whose lovely garden beckoned and to which we hied ourselves most afternoons. We passed the time sitting in the shade and sipping our drinks. It was very pleasant.

We did make a halfhearted attempt at sightseeing, of course. We were taken in tow by a hotel employee who spoke passable English. At least, I *think* he was a hotel employee. He sported an official-looking brass badge, which proclaimed him to be a dragoman (whatever that was). I don't remember what he charged, but it was not much and he earned it. He did all the negotiating with taxi drivers and tradespeople, gesturing wildly and speaking rapidly in Arabic. The discussions were often heated, but I don't think it was a show for our benefit; the prices he got for us were considerably lower than those paid by more adventuresome travelers.

We went out to see the pyramids but declined the invitation of one of the guides to enter Cheops, preferring instead to stage a camel race between Doctor Tom and myself. In spite of our best efforts, the poor beasts could be urged along only just fast enough to stay ahead of the outraged camel drivers, who ran along behind yelling unintelligibly. We called the race a draw and salved the drivers' ruffled feelings with a little extra baksheesh. The Sphinx, its chin supported by an impressive array of sandbags, looked down on us benignly. Then, suddenly, we were hot and sweaty and had had enough. Back to Shepheard's we went.

The train trip up the Nile to Alexandria was made in darkness, so we saw nothing of the scenery. We said little as we rattled and swayed through the warm Egyptian night, alternately dozing and observing the British soldiers and robed Arabs who were our cotravelers.

Alexandria presented a different appearance, more modern, and cleaner than Cairo—this last was not a particularly difficult feat to achieve. Not too far from the city was a horse-racing track with a fine clubhouse, the whole of which had been taken over by the British Army. There was a golf course within the oval, so Doctor Tom and I tried our hand at nine holes, stopping occasionally to marvel at the cluster of thoroughbreds that went thundering by. It was a delightful place to be in the summer of 1944.

I got sick in Tel Aviv—the pharaoh's revenge. Although I did manage the trip to Jerusalem, I aborted on the side trip to Bethlehem, spending the day in my room convalescing. Later we visited the Mount of Olives and Calvary. The surroundings, with their densely packed buildings, were nothing like the crucifixion pictures I had seen, however, and my preconceptions made connection with the real sites all but impossible. We drove past a police station whose lower floor had been blown out by Jewish nationalists a few days before, killing two constables.

"Is the Irgun on the side of the Germans?" I wondered aloud. Not hardly! "Then why are they killing Brits?"

Doctor Tom started a long rambling discourse on the politics of Palestine that tailed off inconclusively. He didn't know either.

One of the Toms had found a girl and brought her up to the room for a drink. She was of indeterminate origin, but certainly a Middle East-erner—and not bad looking, either, except for a gap between her two front teeth. She proclaimed more than once that "I am more byoothiful than Hedy Lamarr, only my theeth are too far apart." I thought that was stretching things a bit, but I nodded and smiled noncommittally.

Then it was time to pack up. I think all of us, but especially Molland and I, were happy at the prospect of going back home to San Severo.

★

While I was in the Middle East, Claude went off to gunnery school somewhere in Africa. I didn't even know there was such a school until I got back and heard his story. Exactly who did the teaching and what they taught was a mystery to me. I, for one, had found out all I needed to know about gunnery; I was perfectly happy with my combat intuition. If they'd tried sending me to the school, I'd have resisted going for fear that a lot of theory would cause me to start analyzing things, to start thinking too much. Unless they could show me a new way to get a zero-deflection shot, I was not interested. But I don't think Claude had anything to fear from too much desk work. It was an even-money bet that while at school he drank and played poker all night and slept all day.

He took a P-51 down there, so, when the course was over, he fired up his Mustang and took off for San Severo. Not far along the way, while still over some very inhospitable-looking terrain, his engine quit and he was forced to leave the airplane. His chute opened, and he landed without injury in a desert wasteland. While Claude was sitting on a rock, trying to collect his wits, several burnoose-clad Arabs rode up on camels and glared at him fiercely while fingering the hafts of some nasty-looking knives. Claude gave them his most disarming smile, which disarmed them not one bit. Then he tried his "Me American" thing, but that didn't impress them either. Finally he managed, by signs and words like baksheesh to convince them that they would be paid handsomely if they got him to an army unit. That they understood.

Their encampment was not far off. Claude was left to roam about among the tents while they made preparations for the trek to take him out, which they planned for the following day.

Here Claude's narrative digressed a bit to describe the beautiful brown eyes that glanced at him furtively and invitingly over drawn veils. Surely this part of the tale was all BS. Stories about American Romeos being found with their testicles inside their mouths and the lips sewn together were passed around as gospel. True or not, they were enough to give one pause. Still, knowing Claude. . . .

Claude and his guides started early and traveled all day and part of the next before coming to a small U.S. Army outpost. Claude had no idea where he was. After a few preliminary inquiries, arrangements were made to take him to their headquarters and thence to an airfield. He finally caught a ride to Italy and then to San Severo. He was unable to tell us where he went down or what reward his rescuers received. If they were lucky, it was a couple of cartons of cigarettes. But, knowing the Army's propensity for red tape, it was probably nothing at all. And as far as I could tell, Claude's aerial marksmanship was no better than it had been before.

★

One of the replacement pilots came to the squadron from a Fifteenth Air Force B-24 Liberator group right there in Italy. This kind of transfer was unheard of, and no one was quite sure how he pulled it off. Of course there weren't many bomber pilots who, after completing a combat tour, requested a fighter assignment instead of going home, either.

"Libby" was only a so-so fighter pilot, which was to be expected considering the different flying characteristics of fighters and bombers. But all of us respected his heart and his experience, and he was not given the usual new-guy treatment. He must have really wanted to fly the Mustang.

Libby's contribution to the cultural life of the squadron was to teach us a B-24 drinking song that became a favorite at the Officers' Club. It was sung to the tune of an old cowboy ballad, *Strawberry Roan*, and the first verse went:

> Oh that B dash Two Four,
> Oh that four-engined whore,
> The men who fly in it are certain to lose,
> At fifty-five inches she won't even cruise,
> Oh that B dash Two Four.

One evening Libby and I got into a discussion on aerial gunnery, and I was surprised at the simplistic view he had of hitting something in the air. He didn't see anything very complicated about putting the sight pipper on what you wanted to hit and then banging away.

For one thing, I reminded him, the guns were in the wings 12 to 14 feet apart and about 4 feet below the gunsight. For the guns to hit what the sight was pointing at, it was necessary to angle the guns inward and upward so that the gun-bore lines met the sight line at some prescribed range. The effect of gravity was also a factor, since the projectile dropped about 4 feet from the time it left the gun barrel until it reached the range distance. The point at which the guns and sight converged was called the harmonization point and represented the ideal range at which to fire at a target. Beyond the harmonization point the trajectories began to diverge rapidly and to sink more quickly. Whereas the drop during the first half second was only 4 feet, during the next half second it was 12 feet. Even at ideal ranges, the pattern of shots was enlarged by slight inaccuracies in bore-sighting the guns, vibration of the gun mounts, and so on. Much beyond the harmonization point, trying to hit anything was almost hopeless—though that fact didn't keep a lot of people from trying.

Compounding these mechanical and physical factors were others relating to the skill of the pilot. He had to maneuver his aircraft quickly to bring the sight pipper to bear on his aiming point and keep it there. In straight and level flight, this was not difficult. While climbing or diving, however, it was another matter. Except for twin-engine fighters like the P-38, which had counterrotating props, pilots of all single-engine fighters had to contend with torque. On American aircraft, engine and propeller rotation caused the aircraft to veer to the left. A slight offset of the vertical fin was built in at the factory. It generated an aerodynamic force to just balance out the torque. However, this zero-yaw condition was only true at one airspeed and power setting. At a high power setting and low airspeed, as during a steep climb, the torque was greater than the correction; the pilot had to apply heavy right rudder to keep the ball in the center. Conversely, in a high-speed dive, the aerodynamic force was greater than the torque; the pilot had to use left rudder to keep the ball centered and the aircraft flying straight without yawing. The rudder-trim wheel on the left side of the cockpit could be moved right or left to increase or decrease the aerodynamic force. To adjust the trim, the pilot manipulated the cockpit control that moved a small trim tab at the trailing edge of the rudder. The pilot, while looking through the sight, had to feel with the seat of his pants any yaw condition and automatically apply the correct rudder pressure to keep the aircraft flying true. The left hand was continuously on the rudder-trim wheel, feeding in the correct amount of trim to take out the rudder pressure.

Why was yaw important to aerial gunnery? Simply because if the aircraft were allowed to yaw, the line of sight was not pointing in the direction the aircraft was traveling. Any projectile fired while the airplane was yawing would be given a slight shove sideways—just enough to make it miss.

In addition to all this, if the target and the attacker were turning, the attacking aircraft had to be aimed out in front of the target so that the bullets and the target arrived at the same point at the same time. The correct amount of lead, or deflection, depended on the speed and angle-off of the target. Speed and angle-off had to be estimated instantly and converted to lead in terms of radii of the gunsight reticle. An Me-109 traveling at 300 miles per hour would cover over 200 feet while the bullet was in transit. A 90-degree shot at the 109 would require about 4 radii with a 100-mil sight. At 30 degrees angle-off, the correct lead would be half that, or 2 radii.

With few exceptions, all fighter pilots could fly well; only a handful could shoot well. Of these, a smaller number still combined their marksmanship with sharp eyes and aggressiveness. The really successful ones were not necessarily the hot pilots; rather, they were the ones who were always looking for a fight and who confined their shooting to low-deflection angles at very close range.

Libby sat silent for a minute, digesting my pontifications. I waited patiently for his response—a question, argument, rebuttal, something. Then he looked up brightly and said, "Let's have another drink." He would do, I decided. He was a fighter-type already, a true Thirsty Firster.

★

The group had begun replacing the old B models with the P-51D and, about the middle of July, I flew the new model on operations for the first time. The D was a considerably improved airplane. It had a bubble canopy instead of the greenhouse-style enclosure, and the bubble allowed a lot better visibility in the air. Instead of the drab brown paint job, the new planes were NMF—natural metal finish. They fairly glowed in the sky. That we didn't need camouflage any longer testified to the way the air war in Europe was going: We were winning big.

Other changes were less visible to the eye but of equal or greater importance to the pilot. The sight had a 100-mil fixed reticle instead of the smaller 70-mil reticle. The new sight made deflection shots and range estimation somewhat easier. More important, the wing had been thickened slightly so that the armament now consisted of *six* .50-caliber machine guns set upright. Upright guns meant no more jam problem, and, for good measure, the P-51D provided half again as much firepower.

The significance of the increased firepower was driven home to me on July 20, 1944, on my 45th mission. The target was Friedrichshafen, a small town in southern Germany. The original home of the *Graf Zeppelin* and the *Hindenburg*, two famous dirigibles of the '30s, the target was on the north shore of Lake Constanz, through the center of which ran the Swiss-German border. Because the Swiss border extended so far to the east, our planned flight path took us up along the east coast of Italy and the length of the Adriatic before we crossed inland at Venice. We continued northwesterly over the Alps to the vicinity of Innsbruck and then turned almost west to the target. This time we were taking the B-24s of the 47th Bomb Wing.

The flight was uneventful except for the Swiss gunners throwing up a couple of rounds at some heavies that apparently strayed over Swiss airspace. The gunners didn't hit anything, which I suppose was the idea; they were just establishing their sovereignty with a little show of bravado.

On the way home—somewhere around Bolzano, Italy—I spotted a lone Me-109 stooging blithely along between cloud layers. I succeeded in slipping up on him from his six o'clock low, a very vulnerable position on any fighter. As I pressed in I got my gun switch on. When I thought I was in range, I squeezed the trigger. Silence. Nothing happened. I glanced down quickly and saw that I had somehow put the gun switch in the Camera Only position. I knocked the switch into Guns and Camera and, when I looked back up again, the 109 filled the whole windscreen. The first rounds went home, and the flashes on the fuselage and wing roots made a pyrotechnic display the like of which I had not seen before. Pieces were flying off and whipping past me. I held the trigger down until I overran. Then I half-rolled so I was looking down at him through the top of my canopy at very close range. I could see the pilot slumped in his seat, but it was the damage to his aircraft that really shocked me. I expected to see some holes a little larger than the projectiles. What I saw were really huge, gaping tears, and the left half of the stabilizer was almost shot away. The 109 fell off on a wing and disappeared into the undercast. The plane was trailing coolant, oil, and smoke from the flames that appeared to be coming from under the engine.

The rest of the way home was uneventful. Coming down the Adriatic, I relaxed a little and pondered what I had just seen. Surely some of the damage must have been caused by the two additional machine guns, but not all. By accident I had been shown the ideal firing position; zero deflection and so close that you were positive you were going to collide. In a proper fight, that position might be hard to achieve, but shooting from any other position was probably a waste of time and ammunition. Later that afternoon I walked out to the parking area, paced off 200 yards from aircraft in various attitudes, and tried to visualize the sight picture in a combat situation. I realized that, when I thought I had been in range, I had actually been 350 to 450 yards out. I began to wonder how I had gotten one victory, let alone five, which was my current score.

I noticed that on much of the gun-camera film that was shown, the target appeared as a small smudge on the screen, hardly discernible as an enemy aircraft. Small wonder that there were no strikes to be seen; the pilot was firing at over 800 yards! Invariably the unproud owner of the film protested vehemently, "That ain't *my* film. They got it mixed up with somebody else's. I was right on top of the guy." Commenting on someone else's film was not de rigueur, but I couldn't help thinking that the film had obviously been shot by *somebody* and that there was a hell of a lot of it.

The pictures of my last encounter were pretty spectacular—except at the end, when the glycol and oil began to coat the camera lens. The film caused a murmur of comment from officers and enlisted men. Afterward, while the projector was being threaded for the feature film, I caught sight of Langlois standing up near the front, waving to get my attention. He smiled broadly and gave me a thumbs up, I suppose for the benefit of his armament buddies, with whom he was sitting. I felt that I had redeemed him—and myself, too—from the ignominy of the time my guns had jammed.

This victory, my fifth, made me an ace. That was nice, but I didn't feel much different about it than my third or fourth. I'm sure that all combat pilots were aware of the distinction accorded the title, but in our outfit no one put a great deal of stock in it. There was no celebration—not even a handshake or a pat on the back from anyone, and I don't remember ever congratulating anyone else on his fifth victory. It just wasn't that important. Five did make a nice string of crosses on the side of my aircraft, though. With the paint still wet on the latest, I lost no time in having Little Henry take a picture of me in the cockpit.

19

Jim Brooks and I grew closer in the days and months following our arrival in San Severo. He would often come over in the evening to the 308th quarters or some of us would go over to the 307th to visit. I don't remember ever going over to the 309th, and I don't know why. There was never any hard feeling or friction between the squadrons, but who can say what makes up the ingredients for friendship and compatibility? For sure, all eighteen of us who came from Telergma together were friendly to each other, although, in truth, some were less popular than others.

One guy who wound up in the 309th was avoided on the grounds of personal hygiene. On the Liberty ship during the Atlantic crossing, when we were packed twelve to a tiny room, he was observed (how could he not be!) running his socks between his toes at bedtime and then putting the same socks back on in the morning. No one said anything to him about it, but the story made the rounds and he never lived it down.

Another guy carried a not-so-faint air of superiority with him wherever he went. Even before he opened his mouth, you knew that his idea was better, his experiences more interesting, his flying and shooting beyond compare. We all took him with a grain of salt, but his attitude did tend to wear to the point where others just avoided him when they could. He was often reduced to rounding up a few new types, who listened to him in respectful silence. But they were the exceptions.

Harry and Pappy were two of Jim's friends in the 307th who were well liked. Harry had actually been in the class behind us at Moore Field. He had arrived in Panama a month after we did, but somehow he managed to get off the Isthmus by Christmas with the rest of us from Class 43-E. He was from Tidewater, Virginia, but his accent was not the drawl with drawn-out broad sounds so typical of Southerners. His pronunciation of some words sounded more Canadian than anything. We used to kid him about saying "There's a mouse in the house. Get him out," which from him sounded like "There's a moose in the hoose. Get him oot." But he didn't take offense at our bedevilment. He just cussed us out laughingly and went on talking as he would. I gathered he was from one of the old Virginia families and quite well-to-do. He had almost nothing in common with Pappy.

Pappy had been a close friend of Jim's every step of the way through flight training and even in Panama, where they both had been stationed at France Field at Colon. I believe Jim had talked Pappy into volunteering for Spitfires at Telergma, when the assignments were being handed out. Pappy was older than the rest of us; in fact, he had only just sneaked under the maximum age limit of the cadet program, which was twenty-seven. He was also bald, which added to his venerable appearance and clinched the nickname. For him the name Pappy was inevitable, like someone surnamed Rhodes being called Dusty.

He came from Round Rock, Texas, a place I had never heard of before. But as long ago as Pre-flight he had assured us that it was world-renowned as the place where the outlaw Sam Bass met his fate. I had never heard of him, either, but with my usual naïveté, I accepted it all as something I should have known.

Only in military service would two such dissimilar specimens like Pappy and Harry be thrown together. As far as I could tell, their only similarity was their love of cribbage—or, more to the point, their love of beating each other at cribbage. They played at every opportunity and for keeps, asking no quarter and giving none. It was friendly enough, the competition, but with a metallic edge to it. While they played, the drone of their voices sometimes rose heatedly over who had played last or whose crib it was, or whether the count was twenty-four or twenty-five. For the most part, however, the low voices from their corner pronounced the patent phrases of the game itself:

"Fifteen two, fifteen four, and a pair is six."

"Fifteen two, three are five, and nobs is six."

"I got a double double run for sixteen."

"Lucky son of a bitch. I out-peg you all the way around the board, and look what happens."

The other occupants of the room, who knew nothing about the game, picked up the sounds and the phrases—the cant, if not the meaning—just from hearing them so often. One day, when Pappy and Harry had gone to the latrine to drain out some slightly used coffee, Jim and one of his cronies sat down at the deck of cards and cribbage board. When the two returned, they were treated to a mock game in full swing. The jokers never looked up.

"Fifteen for two."

"Twenty-five for two."

"Thirty-five for four."

"Go."

"No, you go."

Harry guffawed at the gibberish that was being exchanged so earnestly. Pappy glared at them and mumbled something under his breath about "stupid bastards." But even he had to smile at the outrageous parody when finally they got their cards and board back.

I don't remember whether Harry or Pappy was winning—they did keep a detailed record—but that didn't seem to matter each time they sat down to play. The game was the thing. I suppose they would have gone on playing forever, or at least until one of them went home. But it was not to be.

Harry didn't come back from a mission one day. Although such things happened and we were geared for them emotionally, this loss was truly tragic. He was shot down by his own flight leader.

Harry was flying wing on one of the more senior members of the squadron who happened to be leading the 307th that day. They had gotten into a fight with some Germans and Harry had surged out in front of his leader while both were firing at an enemy aircraft. As they converged, Harry slid over into his leader's line of fire. He took the full brunt at close range and just blew apart. He had no chance to get out of it. Of course Harry was in the wrong, but I couldn't understand why the flight leader was not able to see in his peripheral vision another P-51 that close and stop firing long before any of his rounds hit Harry.

There was something unsettling about the whole affair. The pilot who had shot Harry down acted as if nothing had happened. I don't know what I expected him to do—he couldn't very well go around in sackcloth and ashes, beating his breast and shouting "Mea culpa." It wouldn't have done poor Harry any good. And maybe the accident was not the leader's fault. We did not hear his side of it at all.

Harry had been grounded for an ear infection when we first went on operations. As a result, he fell way behind the rest of us in missions flown and victories. He naturally had to fly a wing position while the rest of us were leading elements and flights. He was very sensitive about being so far behind. Jim thought he was pressing a little. Perhaps he was. I don't know how else to explain Harry's firing when he should have been watching his leader's tail.

Pappy didn't have much to say, but I don't remember seeing him play cribbage ever again.

★

A few new ground officers were assigned to the squadron as well as a steady stream of new pilots. One of the ground officers was a stocky Pennsylvanian nicknamed Ski. He became the assistant intelligence officer. Ski was a nice-enough chap, but he could not resist the temptation to play the veteran for the benefit of the next bunch of new guys who came in. He swaggered about using expressions that he had picked up since coming into the outfit. He'd say, for example, "Hey, there's beaucoup doughnuts and coffee. Why don't you go over and clobber some?" No one paid much attention to him so long as he confined his posturing to the new guys.

Ski and I had had a run-in not long after his arrival. Lam was trying him out on interrogation. After one particular mission, I was talking to my flight. As I was making some point or other, Ski came up and, in his zeal for doing his job promptly, started tugging on my sleeve. If Lam had done it, I wouldn't have given it a second thought, but I did not suffer new second lieutenants gladly. I turned toward him slowly, put my nose about one inch off his, and said in as even a tone as I could muster, "Shut up and sit down. And don't ever pull on me again." I was a little annoyed, but it was mostly show. The performance had the desired effect, though. Ski usually gave me a wide berth.

One day, Ski fell afoul the humor of my friend George, a tall Texan whose real name was Charles Bushick. Bushick's nickname was a mistaken allusion to the strong but dim-witted character in Steinbeck's *Of Mice and Men;* the Texan had earned it at Aguadulce, Panama, where, under the influence of John Barleycorn, he had wrapped his arms around his instructor and cracked three of the man's ribs.

On the day in question, Ski was sitting at his desk in the operations hut and George was on the other side of the room, not 20 feet away. George picked up the telephone and called Ski. When Ski answered, George identified himself as a fictitious major from wing headquarters. Immediately Ski sat a little straighter in his chair.

"I just called to make sure you got that warning about the new Smolensk dive-bomber," lied "Major" George.

"Oh, yes, Sir," Ski answered. "I brought that up just this morning at a pilots' meeting." He was frantically shuffling through a sheaf of papers on his desk, not exactly sure what he was looking for. "Yes, Sir," he lied. "We're taking that report very seriously here at the 308th."

Everyone in the room had now stopped what they were doing, to watch the fun. The wheels were whirring and the gears were clanking in Ski's head, for all to see. If he could just get that major off his back and off the phone, he would find that bloody memo and get it taken care of. As the conversation continued, he slowly, ever so slowly, began to realize that the "major's" words in the telephone were exactly synchronized with the lip movements of George, sitting across the room. His look of puzzlement turned to one of embarrassment and then outrage. He let the phone slide down into its leather case. To the accompaniment of hooting and laughter, he stood up and stalked from the room, not even bothering to pick up his hat. George had not a bit of malice in his make-up, but Ski didn't talk to him for weeks afterward.

★

Lam and Doc Roth had certain administrative chores that were required on a calendar basis. So, when the group was stood down for two days, they had the opportunity to catch up. Lam read the Articles of War to the assembled enlisted men of the squadron, a semiannual event absolutely without educational merit. He might just as well have been reading the phone book, for all the attention he got. Perhaps the exercise was not intended to educate at all but only to prevent an individual from claiming he did not know a certain act was an offense. I know of no other reason to subject a large group of intelligent men to this torture. The articles weren't easy to read, either; Lam probably went cross-eyed.

Then it was Doc's turn, and his subject, naturally, was the dangers of consorting with women of easy virtue. There were the usual comments from the floor in half whispers: "Easy, hell; it wasn't easy at all" and "Virtue? Is that what you call it?"

The movie the night before had been titled *Dangerous Blondes*, so Doc had a ready-made lead-in for his talk on venereal disease. But it wasn't all talk. After fifteen minutes of discourse, which he considered clinical and the majority of men thought was lurid, he led his audience over to the 307th dispensary.

The 307th flight surgeon, a major, had somehow persuaded three Italian prostitutes to participate in the program. Why they agreed to exhibit themselves to the men filing past, I don't know. Maybe they didn't care, or maybe they had been threatened by the police, or maybe they were promised medical care if they cooperated. What made it all the more impressive was that all three were very shapely and attractive young ladies.

Word went through the quarters like a fire storm. Several of the officers decided that they, too, needed to be educated; they volunteered, unasked, to join the class. By this time, the line alongside the dispensary stretched the equivalent of a city block. Some of us, who weren't very keen on the show anyway, decided to wait until the line went down. However, it wasn't long before those officers who were early goers began filtering back to the quarters with details that quashed any desire the rest of us might have had to be titillated. Titillating it was not. Revolting is what it was. Each of the women was infected with several different kinds of VD and had been placed in a reclining position with legs apart, displaying the ravages of the diseases in living color. It was pretty bad—so bad that the designs of the flight surgeons must have been overwhelmingly successful. *That* was a version of preventive medicine that wasn't taught in medical school.

★

As the spring gave way to summer, the days grew longer and warmer. By July the sun hung every day in a cloudless sky and burned the metal operations hut to discomfort. The sun heated the thick masonry walls and roof of our quarters, too, so that by late afternoon the dim, cool interior had turned warm.

After the evening meal we sat on the steps in the fading light and talked about the day's mission; about what was going on at Group or in the other squadrons; or about home and our other, previous, lives.

As twilight came on, the RAF Wellington bombers—or Whimpeys, as they were familiarly known—began passing overhead at ten-minute intervals, climbing northward. They went out on their night attacks as often as we did in daylight, but theirs was a completely different kind of operation. They went singly, in a steady stream, relying on darkness for protection instead of the fighter escort used in daylight raids. The return must have been in the early morning darkness, when we were sleeping, because I never saw them come back.

One of our squadron pilots had liberated a concertina somewhere and had taught himself to play it. On those nights when he brought it out, I always asked him to play "Lili Marlene," a German song popular with the *Afrika Korps* and the Luftwaffe in Africa. It had a haunting and melancholy melody and invoked feelings in me that I could not name or understand. It brought on a bittersweet sadness—sadness for the young people who grasped, fleetingly, at brief personal encounters or for young lovers who had no chance of ever meeting again. It was sad, too, for all of us who had known the heartache of parting from a loved one in the uncertain hope of seeing and touching again. As the reedy sounds died away, all were invariably silent for a moment, each with his own private thoughts.

Occasionally a songfest would develop and we all joined in, singing lustily the lusty songs of the fighter fraternity. Some songs described unusual sexual encounters. Others were vulgar but funny, like "The Night Watchman":

> The poor old night watchman, he cussed and he swore
> At Mrs. O'Reilly, the dirty old whore,
> For having to shit, she said all things must pass,
> So she flung up the window and put out her ass.

> The poor old night watchman was just passing by
> When a piece of that stuff hit him right in the eye.
> He threw up his hand to see where he'd been hit,
> "Gaw blimey!" he cried, "I bin clobbered by shit."

> Refrain: Tallyho, Tallyho,
>   It's a mighty fine song and it's all about shit.

And on and on it went. Another song, "The Dying Aviator," dated from World War I and was on the gruesome side:

> The young aviator lay dying,
> And, as neath the wreckage he lay,
> To the mechanics assembled around him,
> These last parting words he did say:

> "Two valve springs you'll find in my stomach,
> Three spark plugs are safe in my lung,
> The prop is in splinters inside me,
> To my fingers the joystick has clung.

> "Take the cylinders out of my kidneys,
> The connecting rods out of my brain,
> From the small of my back get the crankshaft,
> And assemble the engine again."

Sometimes we would build a fire beside the squadron street and put on the kettle, an inverted steel helmet, to boil eggs. George had a ready source of fresh eggs, which he purchased from the local Italian farmers with the universal medium of international wartime trade— cartons of cigarettes. The eggs were a treat. What a switch the fresh eggs were from the powdered eggs we usually had for breakfast. Reconstituted with water, the breakfast eggs were cooked into a shapeless, tasteless mess. But the fresh-egg pleasure was short-lived. The British Army, which had jurisdiction over the eastern half of Italy, ordered the farmers to stop selling eggs to Americans. Either the Brits didn't have the money or the quantities of cheap cigarettes we Yanks had to compete for the limited supply.

The only other contact I had with the Brits was equally unsatisfactory. On a stand-down in July, a bunch of us jumped into an open command car commandeered from the motor pool and drove over to the northern shore of the Italian spur, just east of Lake Lesina.

It was a beautiful beach. Back away from the water's edge it was hummocky but it flattened as it sloped down toward the wavelets that lapped softly against the wet sand. The last hundred feet to the shore, the sand was fine and dry, so fine that it flowed like sand in an hourglass. Our footsteps barely remained; they filled back in as we walked, leaving only faint depressions that didn't look like footprints at all. As far as the eye could see in either direction, the beach was ecru, almost white, and so virginal that it was unmarred by anything cast off by man or cast up by the sea.

The azure Adriatic stretched to the horizon with no swell to disturb its placid surface. Only ripples sparkled, like a million diamonds in the bright sunlight. And it was empty of any human beings except ourselves. We stood spellbound, drinking in this incredibly peaceful scene.

Then a jeep drove up and a lone British Army officer got out and strode over. He looked very smart in his Sam Browne belt, polished shoes, and swagger stick. I put him down as a rear-echelon, headquarters type. He was very businesslike as he informed us, in clipped tones, that this particular beach was for the sole use of His Majesty's Forces and would we please leave the area immediately. We probably should have knocked him on his ass, but I guessed that he had armed reinforcements nearby. Anyway, who needed strife and conflict? We had come over here to get away from that. So we packed up and left, but not without some well-chosen words to our "host" about the behavior of Allies. I forget who gave him the parting shot: "With friends like you, who needs enemas?"

20

The pilot strength of the squadron had hit its low about May 1, 1944. Replacement pilots began to arrive, slowly at first, and then with increasing regularity. They came at about two-week intervals, sometimes in groups of two or three, sometimes five or six. By the middle of July, nineteen pilots had been added to the 308th's roster. As each new group came in, it had to suffer through the new-guy treatment of pulling lousy administrative jobs, living in crowded quarters, and being socially ignored by the veteran pilots. To begin with they were overawed at the prospect of flying combat, and everything they saw and heard was strange and different. All were eager to check out in the P-51 and start their operational flying, but they were touched by anxiety. With a couple of missions under their belts and another group of replacements below them in the squadron pecking order, they were finally accepted.

As I observed each successive new group on arrival, I couldn't believe that our group had ever been that green. Had we really changed that much in a couple of months and forty-odd missions? Of course we hadn't come straight from the States with 50 hours total fighter time, as most of them did now. I had 240 fighter hours when I arrived at the 31st, and that was typical of our group from Panama. We were already accomplished fighter types and, although we had no combat experience, I think we flew as well as anyone in the group— at least we thought we did, and that was half the battle. A few weeks after joining the group, while we were still in the "be seen and not heard" category, several of us marched into the Officers' Club one evening, called for everyone's attention, and proceeded to put on an impromptu minstrel show. We were brash young men. If we were not welcomed with open arms, at least we were quickly but grudgingly accepted.

When it was Stick Thorsen's turn to leave, I was genuinely sorry to see him go. His replacement, Major Harry Dorris, came over from an A-36 squadron. He was a nice-enough chap, but he knew nothing about the kind of flying we were doing. He hadn't acquired the gift, the ability to pick out the distant tiny dots at the horizon. In fact, he had trouble finding them even after they were called out. Lieutenant Joseph Sheehan, one of the fun-loving oldsters in the squadron, liked to imitate him. Sheehan came from Boston and was as Irish as Paddy's pig; therefore, loved a drink and a joke. He used to have fun playing both sides of a mock conversation on the R/T with the rest of us sitting around, egging him on.

"Border Leader, Border Blue here. Bogies eleven o'clock, slightly high."

Pause.

"Ah, I ah, I don't have 'em, Border Blue. Keep your eye on 'em."

We all roared because that was invariably how our new CO answered. But you had to give the new CO credit. In the two months that he was with us, he scored a number of victories. He was one of several high-ranking pilots who joined the group about this time.

One high-ranking novice had a lot of fighter time but no combat experience. He had the notion that he was above serving a combat apprenticeship but could step right into the thick of it. Worse still, he convinced the right people that his rank and flying time qualified him to start off with a flight lead on his first mission. The result was a disaster.

The group had formed up and was climbing out on course. Over the Yugoslavian coast an RAF reconnaissance Mosquito appeared, heading in the opposite direction, returning to our base. This was a common occurrence; I believe they went out to the target a couple of hours ahead of us to report on the weather. Before anyone knew what the novice was doing and could say nay, he called for his flight to jettison tanks. He went barreling after the Mosquito, thinking it was an Me-210, which it vaguely resembled. The Mossy fired the colors of the day, a recognition signal consisting of three closely spaced colored flares.

"Watch out, he's firing rockets!" the tyro warned as he made a firing pass. When he got in close, however, he must have seen the RAF roundels, because he quietly re-formed the flight and went home. There was nothing else he could do; his external tanks were gone, and the mission had hardly started. I heard later that a British squadron leader came by the bivouac area that evening and asked to meet the chap who had fired on him. When he was introduced to the embarrassed senior officer, he said with the reserve so typically British, "I say, your line of flight was all right but your deflection was a bit off." Quite a put-down, having your gunnery criticized under those circumstances. To the officer's credit he subsequently became a fine combat pilot. There isn't—there never has been—a substitute for experience.

A stranger thing happened to George, one of our Panama buddies, on a flight to northern Italy. He called his flight leader, said he was going home, and abruptly left the formation. I heard the exchange on the R/T, so when I got back, I asked Lam what the trouble was with George.

"He's quit flying," he said.

"Quit flying? What the hell are you talking about?" I asked incredulously.

"He's packed it in. He's not going to fly anymore," Lam answered.

I couldn't believe it. George didn't have an abort history, and his combat flying seemed to be coming along as well as anyone else's. But it was true. He gave it one more try with a local flight out of San Severo, but it was no good. He told me he was so shook and lacking in confidence that he even considered bailing out. Although George denied it, I thought his problem went back to an accident in Panama.

As part of a war game with the Navy, George was flying wing on his flight leader, who was chasing a Navy fighter in a steep dive toward the deck. George was in especially tight because moments before he had been chewed out over the radio by his flight leader for not keeping it tucked in. Right on the wave tops the Navy fighter and his pursuer made a sharp pull-up to the right. George had no chance to follow. His propeller went into the tail section of the flight leader, who snap-rolled right into the water. George's prop must have looked like a pretzel, but somehow he managed to make it back to the field and land, although he took several passes before he spiked it down. They said he made the first pass with gear down at 200 miles per hour.

The dead flight leader had celebrated the birth of his first child a few weeks earlier, which made the onus for the accident doubly hard on George. George seemed to get over the tragedy, and he went back on operational flying after a few days. Soon, the incident was all but forgotten—by everyone except George. I believe something connected with the accident was the reason George stopped flying. He remained in the squadron as a ground officer and no one thought the less of him for his trouble. We all knew he had given it his best shot but had lost the battle with whatever demon was tormenting him. George was an honest man whose time had run out.

★

Attrition from combat losses and older pilots going home continued to create vacancies in the squadron, so several of us began to move up. I had made first lieutenant on June 15, 1944, along with most of my buddies. Little Henry Goehausen had become squadron operations officer earlier, after Twig Byrnes had been shot down; Jim Brooks had been given the same position in the 307th Squadron.

Now I was made a flight commander like Sheehan, who was our senior in the group by a few months. All the pilots were administratively divided into two groups: half were under Sheehan and the other half were assigned to me. Goehausen, together with Sheehan and I, made up the schedule for the next day's mission. We decided who was to go and what position each was to fly. When we were satisfied with the lineup, we took it over to the squadron CO for his approval and then posted it on the board in the quarters that evening. I found scheduling a trying task. We tried to give everyone a fair chance, balancing the need for putting up the best pilots in the key slots against letting some of the newer pilots get lead experience. Not everyone was satisfied with the result; indeed, we often disagreed among ourselves as to who was ready and able. Occasionally the CO had to make a change. But once the schedule went up on the board, there was no more discussion and the three of us united: We brooked no complaint from the disgruntled ones who thought they should be leading elements or flights but were again relegated to the wings.

One evening, just after the schedule was posted, I was vegetating on my cot and overheard a small group of pilots. They stood out in the foyer, scrutinizing the list. They were not happy and were making that known in hushed comments among themselves.

"Look who the hell they got leading Yellow Flight!"

"Yeah, I got more missions than he does."

"Where am I? I knew it! Flying a damn wing again."

"Who the hell made up *that* schedule?"

Without getting up, I shouted through the doorway, "I did. Who wants to know?"

I hadn't recognized their voices, but they sure recognized mine. There was no reply—only quiet footsteps shuffling away.

★

As a pilot gained seniority, he moved up to four-to-a-room quarters. Better still, he got an aircraft permanently assigned to him. The plane could be emblazoned with a name on the nose, and the pilot's name could be painted on the left side, beneath the cockpit. Having an airplane of your own was an ego trip, to be sure, and most pilots wasted no time having their pictures taken alongside the machine that had been personalized for them. But it was more than that. From flying the same plane so often, I knew exactly how the engine of HL-N sounded, knew all its idiosyncrasies, knew where I had left the trim tabs set, and knew where I wanted the seat positioned. In short, I knew the plane thoroughly, and it was mine. I took care of it as if it belonged to me, saving the airplane and engine from abuse whenever I could and at least knowing about it when I couldn't. I didn't want anyone else flying my plane—certainly not any new replacement.

Each pilot tried to find a name for his aircraft that had some personal significance. Oftentimes, the name had some esoteric meaning; it was a sort of inside joke, like Thorsen's *Nightshade*. Most frequently used were names of wives or girlfriends. Walt Goehausen's *Miss Mimi II* obviously referred to Miriam, his wife. I think the name of Tom Molland's plane, *O Kaye*, was a play on the name his girlfriend back home in Fargo, North Dakota. Doctor Tom's *Queen Jean* was named after a girl he had met in Oklahoma while in Basic flying school. He had made plans to marry her, but she sent him a Dear John letter not long after he had the name put on. He didn't bother to take it off.

Someone suggested I name my plane *Racine Reaper* and make the *e* in the second word so small that it would be left out in pronunciation. I rejected that suggestion out of hand. How in the world could I show a picture with that name on it to my wife, my folks, or anyone else back home? I also rejected the thought of using a feminine name. To my mind that motif had been overworked.

I can't remember when I came up with *Flying Dutchman*. I wasn't at all clear on the story the name came from, but I knew the *Flying Dutchman* was a phantom ship. And back in Wisconsin, when I was a lad, Germans were often referred to as Dutchmen. My surname qualified me as Dutch, so *Flying Dutchman* my plane became.

As a flight commander, I shared a room with Sheehan, a privilege of dubious worth. He was one of the few genuine characters I have ever met. Sheehan was to be at the center of the most bizarre and/or outrageously funny occurrence that could be imagined. He somehow had the knack for meeting and befriending equally improbable characters, one of whom was a British major, the civil governor of San Severo. On one occasion, when I had gone to town with Sheehan to the major's house for dinner, the major clambered up onto the table midway through the meal. Standing among the dishes and flinging his arms about, he told of a time in North Africa when Winston Churchill had visited his battery. Apparently the major had taken issue with something the prime minister had said about the guns and, to the great discomfort of the accompanying general officers, had spoken up in a most unseemly fashion. I suspected I knew how the major came to be at San Severo. During the rather lengthy recitation, Sheehan kept yelling for Faulkner, the major's batman, to bring him another drink. Later the major told about how he and Sheehan had entered Faulkner in a British Army boxing tournament. The results for poor Faulkner were disastrous. Of course, neither of the masterminds had a mark on him from Faulkner's bout. But that didn't keep the major from complaining disgustedly about Faulkner's stupidity in the ring. Smiling, Faulkner waited in the background.

Both Sheehan and the major drank a little more than excessively. To ward off a hangover and other evil-spirit infestations, my roommate used to get small tins of Liver Salts from the major, and Sheehan would take a generous dose before going to bed. One evening he came home in his cups and took his dose of Liver Salts. But, being a bit foggy, he forgot about that dose and took another—possibly more—before piling in. I woke up in the middle of the night to hear him in his bunk thrashing around yelling, "Stick a pin in me quick, before I explode."

He kept hollering that he was going to blow up and, in the dim light, I thought he did look a little bloated. Perhaps I should have stuck him; I was mad enough. But my most sympathetic response was to tell him to shut up. After that, I turned over and went back to sleep. In the morning, he didn't seem any the worse for his nightmare and could only vaguely remember waking up.

★

A real benefit of being a flight commander was having a jeep to run around in. Not only did this make getting from the housing area to the airdrome easier, but it also allowed some of us to get in to San Severo or Foggia. The run in to San Severo was especially popular because there was a small PX of sorts there and also a shower with hot water. On those rare occasions when the group was stood down, it was no trick to fill the jeep with willing warriors who wanted to loll about on the beach in the warm summer sun.

Once, when I couldn't or didn't want to go to the beach, I let Shelton take the jeep. His claim to fame was as joker, first class. On the way home he passed a two-wheeled, horse-drawn cart presided over by a snoring Italian driver. He stopped the jeep quietly. Without waking the driver, he took the bridle and carefully led the horse in a wide 180-degree turn. He started the horse safely on course back into town, then returned to the jeep and drove off. That must have been one surprised farmer when he woke up back where he started from. He probably beat the hell out of the horse.

An example of the darker side of combat humor began back at Moore Field, with a newly commissioned lieutenant named Johnnie. Johnnie had married a cute little girl from back home in Georgia. One day in Panama he had engine trouble with his P-39 and had to bail out over the water. His chute opened fine and he landed about three miles from shore. Some natives recovered his parachute, but, he was never found. Since the harness straps were still fastened, it was assumed that a shark or barracuda got him, probably while he was unconscious in the water.

After we returned to the States, one of the pilots stopped to visit Johnnie's widow and brought her along with him when he reported to Dale Mabry Field, at Tallahassee, Florida. She quickly forgot Johnnie and took up with two others in our group, a handsome fellow named Jackson and another named Carl. Both were posted to the 307th Squadron when we joined the 31st. On one of the very early missions, Jackson was shot down and killed over Ploesti. I think Jim Brooks was the first to put together the coincidences and to begin referring to the Georgia girl as Jinx Woman. First Johnnie and then Jackson. We all thought it was a great joke—all except Carl. His discomfort was our cue, and we showed him no mercy. We reminded him with mock seriousness that his contact with the Jinx Woman had been a fatal mistake; he would surely be the next to die. Carl would become visibly shaken and agitated.

"What do you keep saying that for?" he would blurt out. "I don't want to hear it. That's all bullshit and you know it. I don't want to hear it. And anyway, I never slept with her." This announcement produced such a chorus of incredulous hooting and jeering that poor Carl would go off muttering, his face a few shades whiter. I suppose it was a cruel trick—perhaps it even affected his flying—but we all were in on it and thought nothing of it. Humor in an operational outfit could get macabre at times.

Fred Trafton was another squadron character, although in quite a different manner than Sheehan and his peccadilloes. Fred had spent

some time in the RAF and had transferred over to the U.S. Army Air
Force as a flying sergeant. Somehow he found his way into the 31st
Fighter Group and had worked his way up to second lieutenant by the
time I first met him at Castel Volturno. From the start, he treated us
replacement pilots as equals. It was just his way. I soon discovered
that he showed the same easy familiarity to colonels and corporals
alike, and, as far as I could tell, no one seemed to take umbrage with
him for it.

Freddie failed to return one day in April from a mission to Austria.
After a decent interval during which no news was forthcoming, we all
assumed that he had had it and proceeded to dispose of his things even
though he was still officially listed as MIA. A couple of months later
he showed up at San Severo with some very interesting stories to tell.

On his last flight he had gotten into a fracas with several Me-109s
over Yugoslavia. He shot two of them down but took a couple of 20mm
cannon shells in his own cockpit. The shells carried away his instrument
panel and part of his thigh. Fred hastily abandoned his stricken machine
and had the great good fortune to float down near a band of Partisan
guerrillas, who rushed him to a clandestine field hospital within fifteen
minutes. He most certainly would have bled to death otherwise. During
the next few days, they moved often, sometimes on the run from the
Germans and sometimes from the Chetniks, a rival political faction
fighting both the Germans and the Communist Partisans.

In several weeks Freddie was up and about, well enough to go out
with his new comrades on several raids against the Germans. The high
point of his career as a guerrilla was taking part in the demolition of
a bridge. This life seemed to suit Fred quite well—too well, in fact.
Word was sent through to him several times to make himself available
for repatriation, but he ignored the orders. Finally, he was threatened
with court-martial, which convinced him to say good-bye to his
newfound friends and return to Italy. He was very close-mouthed
about the details of the route and the method by which he was brought
out. In spite of our plying him with liberal quantities of Old Overshoe,
which he downed with ease, he never did tell us how he got back.
Being in possession of sensitive information about the Partisans
virtually ensured that he would never fly over enemy territory again.
He putzed around the squadron for a few days, waiting for orders to
send him home. Once or twice he went down to the flight line to feel
the fire in his belly again and to see the massed aircraft head out,
climbing toward the Adriatic.

Before Fred's plane was downed, he had not had the chance to
have a picture taken of himself with it. Now the plane was a pile of

junk somewhere in Yugoslavia, where it had crashed almost three months earlier. With the victories that he'd gotten on that last mission, he now was an ace, and he wanted to record the fact for posterity. Mine was the only 308th plane that had five crosses on it at that particular moment, so he asked if he could use it for a backdrop. I thought that was a great idea and went along with him and Little Henry, who was going to do the honors. Fred, looking aft, sat on the wing up close to the fuselage. His left arm and shoulder blocked out my name, but the five crosses showed up nicely beside him. Goehausen developed the film in his own cobbled-up darkroom, using helmets as developer, hypo, and wash trays. The picture came out as fine as all the others he had processed like that. I never did figure out from where he requisitioned the chemicals and paper, but he sure made good pictures.

Finally, Trafton's orders arrived. We threw a bash for him the night before he left, and the subject of his battle scars came up. Fred stood up, dropped his britches, and began to count the holes in his legs. Everyone pitched in to help and I believe we got up into the forties—about as high as a bunch of fighter types could count under the circumstances.

Not all the group pilots were stereotypical fighter pilots, however. Doris Boyd was our Quiet Man. Although he had been with us through flying school and Panama, I don't think any of us knew him well or much about him. He was not a man of action; he was more of a poet or, like his father, a man of the cloth. Even his given name was different. Because Boyd's refusal to participate in the usual carousing was so adamant and so obviously sincere, no one badgered him and he was pretty much left alone.

On the Liberty ship while crossing the Atlantic, Boyd exercised and ran on deck to maintain his physical fitness—not in preparation for combat but because he felt that his body should be maintained as befitted a Divine gift. Mansberger, who was as close as anyone came to being his friend and who was blessed with a near-perfect physique, was more the conventional fighter pilot. Mansberger's habits caused Boyd no end of discomfort. More than once he upbraided Mansberger in his own gentle way, urging him to stop abusing his body. But Boyd met with little success.

Boyd was killed one bright summer day over southern France. It was an odd, almost bizarre mission, hardly worth the cost.

Somehow, headquarters had gotten wind of the fact that a very large number of German aircraft—something like thirty-plus—were temporarily on an airdrome in southern France. A mission was laid on to attack it. To stay under the enemy radar, we flew on the deck all the way from Italy to the French coast. The group was going to strafe the airdrome. With the element of surprise, the defensive ground fire was expected to be light. That would allow us to work our will on the parked aircraft. Of course, it would be no small feat to keep forty-eight Mustangs in the same piece of sky below 50 feet altitude, and there was always the fear of someone getting vertigo from the long periods of staring at the formation lead while the blue Mediterranean whizzed past. All went reasonably well until the dark line of the coast appeared. For reasons that were never satisfactorily explained, the 308th squadron leader pulled up a few thousand feet after making this landfall. Perhaps he was uncertain of his navigation and wanted to get a better look—whatever, we were still twenty minutes from the target and the proverbial cat was out of the bag. By the time we found the 'drome, it was clear that the planning had come unraveled. Instead of the gaggle of planes promised by Intelligence, only three lonely aircraft squatted there. Worse still, the ack-ack was already lacing the sky in an alarming fashion. There was nothing for it now but to go in and get what we could: fuel storage, maintenance sheds, anything anyone could get his pipper on. Boyd was hit on the first pass and bought it right in the middle of the enemy airdrome. He had no chance to bail out, if indeed he was alive; one great ball of fire, his plane augered right in.

After we got back, I went over to the 307th. A few friends and I sat around and had a quiet talk about the day and our loss. Everyone agreed that the mission was an absolute shambles from beginning to end, but the loss of Boyd was accepted as "one of those things"—not the first and most assuredly not the last.

Mansberger did not fare much better. He was killed a few weeks later over Ploesti.

★

With all the airmen going down over southern Europe, it was inevitable that some crew members would succeed in avoiding capture and make it back to Italy. After their return the Fifteenth Air Force would shuttle them around to the various bases and let the active air crews profit from the episodes they related.

Someone got the bright idea that on each flight we should carry photos that could be used by the underground to prepare false identity papers. No one seemed to know whether this was a harebrained scheme cooked up by Intelligence or whether it had come from someone who had made it back and knew what he was talking about.

On the appointed day, all the pilots had to repair to the group headquarters building where a photographer had his camera set up to take passport-type photos of each of us. It turned out that only one shirt, one tie (very loud), and one jacket were available. So, each of us in turn had to don this ensemble to have front and profile pictures taken. They were made outdoors in the sunlight, with the wall of the building for a backdrop.

We all laughed about the possibility of the identical coat and tie showing up on many different sets of identity papers. Ah, well—it was good thing none of us was going to get shot down. The prints were made up and given to us before each mission, along with our escape/ evasion kits and money packets.

★

When the news went through the group that some Mustangs from the Eighth Air Force were going to stop over at San Severo on their way back to the United Kingdom from Russia, everyone looked forward to their arrival—anything out of the ordinary that promised a change from the daily routine was welcomed. The fact that the visitors were from the Eighth Air Force piqued our curiosity. The letters from home, the Hollywood war pictures, the newsreels and newspapers, all reminded us constantly that the bombers and fighters of the Eighth Air Force were daily battling the fierce hordes of Nazi planes and winning the air war over Europe. It rankled a little, but it was no big deal—we had come to terms long ago with our "Other Theater" role. The coverage rated by the Eighth probably boiled down to the simple fact that the media people preferred to live in London hotels with all the trimmings rather than in Italian tents. Who could blame them? If nothing else, they were pragmatic. And I think Eighth Air Force Headquarters was well aware of the value of publicity and cultivated it. No one in Italy seemed to know what *public relations* meant, thinking perhaps that it was something that went on behind closed doors at the rest areas like Capri and Manfredonia. Of the photos I have of the planes and pilots of the 31st, not one is an official Air Force photo—all were taken by Goehausen or me.

When the Eighth Air Force types finally arrived, the intercommunication was strained, like that at a dance in the high school gym with the girls on one side and the boys on the other, except now it was

Them and Us. These guys were no Jim Goodsons, our early mentor from the Eighth Air Force's 4th Fighter Group. From the outset, one thing became clear: They had come down to Sticksville to show us how the game was played at the pro level.

"Did you see those white scarves? They looked like Hollywood extras, for God's sake," someone commented disgustedly. Brooks said he had been down to the flight line to look at the new K-14 gunsight that they had in their 51s and had seen some aircraft decorated with odd victory symbols, motorcycles, haystacks, outhouses, and the like. Perhaps he was kidding—somebody sure was.

The visitors flew one mission from Italy with us, to Wiener Neustadt, I think, and got the living shit kicked out of them. One came back with a serious wound. They lost several, having scored only one or two kills in the process. I am ashamed to admit that the locals, myself included, took some small measure of satisfaction at their misfortune. They were a chastened lot when they left for England, and I think that everyone from both camps learned a few things.

21

I was on my way to turn in one evening when I ran into Lam, a perplexed look on his face.

"What's up?" I asked him.

"I wish I knew," he answered. "That stupid ass Levy has got the operations order for tomorrow's mission and is working on it." Levy was the group intelligence officer.

"So?"

"He's locked himself in the briefing room and won't let me in. Won't let anyone in." Lam was really exasperated. I could see why, but I still had to laugh at the picture of him pounding on the door like a betrayed husband, demanding to be let in while Levy barricaded himself inside. But erratic behavior was nothing new and someone obviously had scared hell out of Levy about keeping the mission a secret.

I started on my way again, taking my leave with an over-the-shoulder comment, "See you in the morning, Lam; maybe then we'll get the poop from the group."

At 0330 on July 22, 1944, we assembled in the briefing room and found out what was up. The mission was a shuttle flight to Russia. The 31st had been picked to escort one of the P-38 groups, which was to strafe in the Ploesti area. Then, instead of returning to Italy, we were going to continue to the east, landing at Pyriatin, Russia. The wing commander, Brigadier General Strother, was going along, flying with the 307th Squadron. Jim Brooks told me later that the group CO took him aside and told him to keep a sharp eye out for the general and not let anything happen to him. Poor Jim.

The group was off on time and, to no one's surprise, there were no aborts. The rendezvous with the 82d Fighter Group was effected, and the two groups continued on to Zilestia, near Ploesti, where the P-38s went down to the deck and did their thing. After the show was over, we set course for Russia. It seemed strange indeed, exiting the Ploesti-Bucharest area in the "wrong" direction. The Black Sea appeared in the distance, just at the horizon over on the right. As we flew across that strange countryside, I wondered how this bunch of fighter pilots—traditionally not among the world's great navigators—would manage this wandering so many hundred miles from home.

As we neared our destination, dropping down to 8,000 to 10,000 feet, the countryside was plainly visible. I had never seen such country before. Flat it was, stretching away without the hint of a hill or dale. A copse appeared here or there, and sometimes two or three trees stood together, but basically it was a treeless plain across whose surface, single-track dirt roads led from one tiny village to another. Occasionally a river meandered southward toward the Black Sea. How every pilot managed to find that tiny grass field in that great, flat, monotonous landscape is a mystery to me, but we did.

After landing we were met by some of our maintenance personnel, who had left Italy about ten days earlier with no explanation. They had been flown to Teheran via Cairo and then through the back door into Russia. There was a little welcoming ceremony and speech by the ranking Russian officer, who remarked through an interpreter about the extreme youth of the American pilots. My eyes were riveted on his mouth, watching his steel false teeth moving up and down. I was scarcely aware of what he was saying. I looked around and, though no one appeared to be all that young to me, we were for the most part in our early twenties and quite a bit younger than the few Russian pilots there.

We were then briefed by an American major, who informed us that the field security was provided by noncombatants, mostly old men who could not understand any English. If we were out after dark and heard the challenge "*Stoi,*" we were to shout out at the top of our lungs, "*Amerikansky pee-lote!*" I had seen some of the sentries, and the rifles with which they were armed were positively ancient; I didn't want to be anywhere near if one of them was fired. I believe the sentries would have fired, too, if the reply was not promptly given. The Russians did not take breaches of military discipline lightly.

One of our mechanics who had been there a couple of weeks before our arrival told me about a Russian truck driver who had been cutting across the temporary runway, causing the PSP to start curling at the edges. His lieutenant stopped him and reminded him that all vehicles were required to go around the end of the runway. When he cut across again, his officer pulled him out of the cab and shot him. I don't know if the story was true or not, but, from what little I had seen, it certainly was not inconsistent with the way things were done on the Russian Front.

We were to disperse the aircraft farther from and out of range of German bombers, which had attacked and destroyed a number of B-17s from England at a neighboring base a month earlier. We took off for a field near Kharkov, about forty-five minutes to the east. The plan was for us to stay overnight and return in the morning, but the weather did not cooperate; we were stuck in Kharkov. There were no American support facilities or personnel there, so our breakfast consisted of the local fare, something that resembled cold cucumber soup with bits of greenery and little pieces of something doughy floating in it. I was hungry, but I couldn't manage more than a few spoonfuls.

When it became apparent that we weren't going to get off the ground, a delegation of us immediately began to badger the Russian lieutenant in sign language for permission and the necessary transport to visit the city of Kharkov. His enthusiasm for this venture was underwhelming, and I held out little hope for approval. However, I had underestimated the persistence and eloquence of our delegation. After a seeming endless succession of phone calls, the lieutenant finally found someone with the authority to say *da*, so we all piled into an old truck and were off to town. The lieutenant didn't know a word of English, which made it pretty tough to ask anything and harder still to figure out his answer—assuming he had understood the question. On the way we passed a huge tank on its side beside the road and could see several others in the distant fields, mute testimony to the terrific armored battle that had taken place here the previous year.

Once in the city we drove around ogling the buildings and people as if we were in the Forbidden City, which I guess we were. We stopped at last by a small park and got down to stretch our legs. It was noontime and a small crowd of older people soon gathered. On our upper arms, each of us had an armband with the Stars and Stripes on it, a signal for some of the more venturesome of the locals to try a few words of English or German or anything else they thought we might understand.

I was suffering from that dreaded malady called—in this part of the world, I suppose—czar's revenge. Communicating my problem to the lieutenant turned out to be a poser, and I finally had to resort to sign language to make known to him the nature of my predicament. An Oscar-winning performance it was not, but it had the desired effect. My face must have been very red, but my pantomime did not cause the least stir or laughter among the good Russian folk. The lieutenant got some directions from a helpful old man. The officer, Sheehan, and I went a couple of blocks, turned in between some buildings, and found a smallish shed at the rear of one of them. He must have got his directions wrong, though. Whatever the shed was, it was *not* a latrine. However, I was past the point of no return, and he knew it. So, after wringing his hands and making a few clucking noises with his tongue, he went off to tend his other charges. He left Sheehan, who had come with us, to accompany me back. This was a poor choice, considering Sheehan's nose for mischief, but of course the Russian couldn't have known. As we emerged from between the buildings, I distinctly heard a woman's voice say, "Excuse me, American officers."

I turned to face an older lady of perhaps fifty years, obviously addressing Sheehan and me. She was a professor of languages at the university, she explained, and wanted to know if we would come with her to speak to her English-language students.

I was a little leery of getting separated from the group, but I never got to vote. "Why certainly, dear lady," Sheehan replied. "We'd be delighted to speak with your students." With that, he offered his arm, which she happily took. Off they went, with me trailing behind casting worried looks over my shoulder. It was only a short walk to an old brick building with wooden floors that had obviously been pressed into temporary service by the university. We stood out in the hallway with a half dozen young adults, talking slowly in simple declarative sentences and answering their questions. One girl wanted to know if I knew her uncle, who lived in "Pennsylvania, Philadelphia." I answered apologetically that I didn't think so. After ten minutes, the professor thanked us and herded her class into the room. We were once again on the street.

We started back the way we had come, but at the first corner, a fairly large intersection, a crowd—composed, I thought, of students—congregated. They were chattering away in Russian to each other and to us, too. Sheehan had singled out two rather pretty girls and stood conversing with them, he in English and they in Russian. I swear they understood each other. I was to the point of asking him what they were saying when our truck came tearing up the street. Sheehan was for bolting, but I vetoed that suggestion in no uncertain terms. As the truck ground to a halt, the Russian lieutenant's grim look told us our adventure was over. He motioned for us to come and get in and, once we were aboard, the truck headed straight back to the air base. Our fellow passengers told us that, after leaving the park, the lieutenant had counted noses and, when he'd came up two short, he'd gone white as a sheet. They had been speeding up and down the streets ever since, looking for us. Sheehan and I were not very popular on that truck since we were blamed, with some justification, for curtailing the excursion to the city. The best-laid plans *gang aft a glae.*

The weather cleared that night, and we went back to Pyriatin the next day. One mission, a kind of Allied cooperation showpiece, was laid on to be flown from our temporary Russian base. The target was near Mielec, Poland, and was purportedly aimed at supporting the Russian Front, which was near Lvov at the time. Our squadron dutifully patrolled an airfield in the target area. When I called out a small group of enemy fighters, the CO acknowledged the call ("Ah, I don't see 'em. Keep your eye on 'em") and ordered everyone to stay in formation.

I'm sure he wanted to keep the squadron intact for the flight back to Pyriatin, but passing up such an opportunity did not sit well with me. I liked it even less when the other two squadrons got into a great gaggle of Ju-87 Stuka dive-bombers. The encounter must have been like shooting fish in a barrel; we could hear our two squadrons on the R/T, fighting over the slow Stukas and getting in each other's way in their zeal for victories. I listened in helpless fury at the goings-on and I don't think I was alone in the squadron. Scoring two and three Stukas was common on that mission. In all, twenty-seven of the dive-bombers were destroyed, not counting three probables. In the long cockpit enclosure, the Stukas had a rear gunner facing aft who was armed with a 7.9mm machine gun, about the size of a .30-caliber. It was a pitiful thing to put up against six .50-caliber machine guns. The Stuka was hopelessly out-classed by the Mustang and outgunned, too. But some of the Stukas did not go quietly. Major Sam Brown, the 307th Squadron CO, took a 7.9mm round through the canopy that left a long mark on the top of his helmet, just creasing it. Death doesn't pass any closer than that. The virtual annihilation of the Stukas was not exactly a fair fight, but whoever said war was fair? I'm sure that the Russian troops, who had borne the brunt of the Stuka attacks, thought it was more than fair.

On July 26 we headed for home, making a fighter sweep in the Ploesti area on the way. I spotted a lone Me-109 east of Ploesti, but he was at a much lower altitude and his camouflage paint just matched the tan, brown, and green patches of the ground. I lost him. Old "I don't see 'em" was leading, and he nixed any screwing around for one 109. I think he was right. And I didn't have anything to bitch about—I didn't see 'em either.

The group was met at the airdrome by a group of VIPs that included Major General Nathan Twining, commanding general of the Fifteenth Air Force; so a kind of carnival atmosphere prevailed at the debriefing and interrogation. Everyone wanted to share in what turned out to be a remarkably successful operation: thirty-seven enemy aircraft destroyed in the air and nineteen vehicles on the ground, without the loss of a single aircraft or pilot. What I thought was equally impressive, in spite of the usual maintenance problems in piston-engine planes, was that the 31st had left no aircraft behind but brought them all out when we left. Of the 31,433 rounds fired, there were only five gun stoppages. It was a truly remarkable achievement by pilots, mechanics, armorers, and everyone else connected with the mission.

The group received a second Presidential Unit Citation in recognition of the operation. However, Stateside newspapers made no mention of this. Everyone in the group had come to expect and accept being ignored. The air war in Italy just wasn't news.

22

During and after the Russian mission, the pilots who had made the flight were fond of using the few expressions in Russian we had learned. In the morning, we greeted each other with something that sounded like "*dobro utro*" and in the evening, "*dobro noch.*" It was a form of elitism, a badge or password that separated those who had gone on the great adventure from those who had not.

On July 28, after the morning round of *dobro utro*'s and breakfast, everyone filed into the briefing room. We learned that this was to be the group's twelfth mission to the Ploesti-Bucharest area. I was not scheduled to fly.

Ordinarily, when I didn't fly, I went off somewhere. I'd take my laundry to my washwoman in San Severo, go for a hike up the mountain, anything. Perhaps I subconsciously avoided the stress of sitting around squadron operations, waiting for the guys to come back, expecting the worst. People like Lam did the waiting every day and had done it for years. At thirty years of age, or close to it, maybe he had learned to cope with such things. It was different for me because I had been on both sides of the fence; I had been a part of those who had gone and also of those who had stayed behind. Going was easier. You had something to do every second of the time. Even if you were not in complete control of the unfolding events, at least you were a party to them. You were there as things were happening.

To stay behind was to wait, and wait some more, to smoke too many cigarettes, to wonder, and to imagine. You kept the vigil, watching toward the horizon for the first specks to appear. Or you waited inside the Quonset hut, hearing the first distant hum and then the full, deep-throated roar of Merlin engines as the Mustangs pitched out over the runway to make their landing pattern.

Today I had nothing else to do and decided to participate in the pre-flight activities and sweat it out down at the airdrome while they were gone. Lam and I stood outside and watched the planes form up and set course, gradually melting into a large dark blur in the sky and then disappearing altogether.

We fiddled around, talked quite a lot, argued a little about nothing, and then started checking our watches more and more frequently. The nervousness was contagious and someone wondered aloud every five minutes, "Where the hell could they be?"

If no enemy fighters were encountered, the group aircraft would come back in batches of eight or even in squadron strength, their drop tanks still on. If this is what the waiting operations personnel, mechanics, and armorers saw, even before the first aircraft touched down, they had a pretty good indication of what had happened. Today it was five hours before the first returnee showed up, and he was alone. More arrived by twos and threes, then a steady stream of aircraft from all three squadrons entered the initial, pitching or rolling out and taxiing in. Not one had its tanks on. The black streaks under the wings aft of each gun and the missing muzzle covers on most aircraft confirmed that there had been a hell of a battle.

The energy level in the squadron operations hut had been building steadily since the first plane had appeared. I was caught up in the excitement. When I saw Tommy Molland's plane—HL-C, *O Kaye*—taxiing in, I ran out into the dispersal area to greet Tommy, who had led the 308th that day. After he pulled off his helmet and ran his fingers through his hair, he confirmed what we already knew: The Luftwaffe had come up in strength and put up a tough fight. He had gotten two Me-109s himself, and he sketched in the details as we walked in to operations together.

When everyone had finished reporting to Lam, the whole picture was clearer. Forty to fifty German fighters had shown up and aggressively attacked our bombers and fighters. The squadron claimed five victories and two damaged while suffering no losses. Besides Molland's two, Doctor Tom got one and a damage, Edge got one, and two other pilotss each shared credit for a 109 destroyed and one damaged.

I hadn't got a damned thing except a nervous stomach. While sitting around the ops hut, I had missed the whole show, and I didn't like that one bit. I was happy for the guys who had scored, but today I wasn't among them. I was an outsider, a bystander.

"Well," I told myself, as I joined the general exodus from operations, "I'm not missing any more missions to Ploesti if I can help it. Or Wiener Neustadt, either."

★

Three Red Cross girls lived in the town of San Severo and split their time between the fighter groups in the area, meeting the returning pilots at the flight line and serving doughnuts and coffee. All the pilots and enlisted men admired the girls from afar and coveted their companionship, even in the face of impossible odds. Jean was the youngest and prettiest of the three, and she and Jim Brooks hit it off instantly. I don't know if *love* is the right word, but they certainly were very fond of each other. And, as far as I could tell, it was on the up and up. He usually asked me and several others to come along when he went into town to call on her. I don't know whether Jim didn't trust himself to be alone with her or whether he was being magnanimous to the have-nots. Whatever the reason, we tagalongs were grateful and happy to have somewhere to go and something to do to break the monotony of our all-male existence.

Doctor Tom staked out one of the other two girls, a pretty blonde a little older and wiser than he. He did manage one or two dates with her, but she was only mildly interested. When he finally made his move, her only comment was, "How crude." Tom went down in flames. That was the end of that budding romance, and she soon showed a marked preference for one of the other pilots in our squadron. He was certainly not handsome, not nearly as good looking as Tom, but he was more mature; had an easy, charming manner; and was totally unpredictable. Apparently his style was more to her liking. As far as she was concerned, he was her man. I think we were all proud that, of the hundreds and hundreds of eager candidates available, the 31st had two of its own in such a favored status.

The evenings didn't amount to much. If the other girls were not occupied, they also joined the four or five of us from the 31st. We shared our weekly beer ration, sang, or just talked. We didn't have all that much to say, but, without the distraction of television or even radio, conversation was still a practiced art and we were all artists, more or less.

Sometimes we all went to the movies, either at the San Severo Opera House, which had been taken over by Special Services, or out at our base. Since most of the Hollywood stars were in uniform or on bond-selling tours and the need for pictures was undiminished, a lot of movies were cranked out without regard to quality. But, with a captive audience, they didn't have to be very good to hold attention. Most of the movies were merely watchable. The war pictures, especially the flying ones, were terrible.

Invariably, our celluloid hero goes aloft alone to avenge the death of his friend. He runs afoul of Tokyo Joe, the scourge of the skies. Joe flies an AT-6 painted to look like a Zero. Joe wastes no time getting on the tail of our hero and stitching a neat row of holes across his wing. But, with true American cunning and grit, our hero does a loop, confounding Joe, who is left frantically searching the skies for his intended victim. Too late he realizes the tables have turned; the Yank, in his shark-nosed fighter, is now sitting squarely on his tail.

"I've got you now, Tokyo Joe," says our hero through clenched teeth as his machine guns belch death and destruction. Tokyo Joe is last seen slumped in his cockpit, blood oozing from his mouth, the clouds whizzing past on the rear-projection screen as he begins his final dive. It was probably great stuff back home and made everyone cheer and clap and feel good. We laughed until our sides ached. Sometimes we cheered for Tokyo Joe or Herman the Heinie, but it didn't do any good—they were doomed even before the picture started.

Not all the entertainment was black-and-white flicks. Live USO shows were a great treat, even if they did not feature the big-name stars who seemed to favor the more urbane theaters and bases. A USO show starring Helen Young, reputedly a Big Band singer, played at San Severo and got a rousing reception. Patsy Morgan, a Hollywood actress, was featured in another show and had everyone on the edge of his seat. Perhaps we were all starved for some flesh-and-blood professional attention. Patsy Morgan was treated royally, like a headliner, and she loved it.

An Italian stage show was presented, too, and the performers were greeted with much laughter and applause, the same as with American troupes. The accompanying orchestra played American hit tunes and a good many of them went unrecognized until the titles were announced. No matter. The show was a change from routine, and everyone went along in the spirit of the thing. The Italian cast loved it, too, returning again and again to do encores.

★

The spur of the boot of Italy—to the east of Foggia, where Italy jutted out into the Adriatic—was a desolate, wild place. It was a promontory, the Gargano Promontory, which rose to a height of several thousand feet. A few roads led into towns on its rim, but no road traversed its length or breadth. The spur was inhabited by herdsmen and, it was whispered, by some Germans who had been left behind by their retreating army to spy on the fighter and bomber bases scattered below in a semicircle to the west and south.

Our housing area backed up against the steep slope, where it rose up on the western side. Perched high above us were the stone ruins of a castle. A narrow dirt road led from our buildings around the base of the promontory and finally connected with a larger road leading into Manfredonia. If the destination was the beach, it was shorter to take this route than the highway from San Severo to Foggia and then back out to Manfredonia.

Manfredonia had been a sleepy little fishing village, caught between the high bluffs to the north and the sea to the south. With the advent of the Fifteenth Air Force, it was a sleepy little village no longer. It wasn't even a fishing village anymore. The Americans who populated the rest camp there hired the boats and fishermen to go out sailing daily, so the fishing industry collapsed. The locals were left with fistfuls of money but no fish to eat.

On one stand-down at the very end of July, several of us from the old bunch secured a cottage at the Manfredonia rest camp and planned to lay on a party, gathering all the booze, beer, and other goodies we could muster. The Red Cross girls were coming, too, and we looked forward to a great time, adding our little bit to the disruption of the Manfredonian economy.

The girls had gone down the day before, since they had a cottage reserved at the rest camp. Jim Brooks and several others had gotten away early in the morning, but George and I were delayed by some duty or other. It was late in the morning before we started down the shortcut road in our jeep, kicking up a plume of dust. It was another in a seemingly endless string of beautiful summer days. We were in high spirits.

Suddenly, in the road ahead, was a knot of Italian peasants, waving frantically for us to stop. Some were weeping; all were talking excitedly, none in English. George, who had grown up in San Antonio, Texas, could get by in Spanish, and he recognized some words like "*pobrecito*," which he said meant "poor little one." By their gestures, the people clearly wanted us to follow them, so we parked the jeep, took the rotor out of the distributor to immobilize it, and followed their lead up into the hills. We climbed steadily through brush-covered knobs and gullies for ten minutes. Then, following the pointed fingers of our constantly chattering escort, we could see a large white cloth on the ground ahead. It was a parachute. As we came up to it, I could see a still form beneath it. George lifted a corner of the chute and verified that it was an American pilot, and he was dead. We were shocked and just stood there looking at each other, trying to collect our wits. But our guides were not finished with us yet. They indicated that there was a crash site nearby. Two P-51s from a sister group had obviously had a midair collision. When George returned from the crash site, he said it was pretty bad. The second pilot had ridden his aircraft in, and there wasn't much left of plane or pilot. The collision had occurred at such a low altitude that the pilot of one plane didn't get out at all and the pilot of the other had jumped too low for his chute to open fully.

George and I put our heads together and decided that there was nothing we could do other than to get some medical people out there to remove the remains of the two pilots. He volunteered to stay while I went back to the jeep, all the while using gestures to reassure the still-excited Italians that we were not going off but would, in fact, take care of things. I can't remember where I finally found a field telephone out there, or how I managed to get in touch with anyone, but eventually I got through to a medical officer on duty at one of the nearby bomber bases. He was not very cooperative, asking why the parent fighter group couldn't do it, how he didn't have the personnel, wasn't supposed to leave the base, and besides and so on. But I had heard enough; I was getting mad.

"Listen carefully," I told him, "'Cause I'm only going to tell you once. I can't contact any fighter group on this phone. You're the only one I can get. And if you're telling me that you want to leave those poor bastards lying out there on the ground because getting them doesn't fit your plans, I'm perfectly willing to drive all the way to Fifteenth Air Force Headquarters and tell them what you said. Now, what is your name, Doctor?"

I was really pissed by now, mad enough to have made good on my threat, but my tirade had a salutary effect. He immediately relented, asking for detailed directions to the site. I went back to pick up George, and finally we were back on the road again. But our gaiety was gone—and most of the day was, too. It was late in the afternoon before we found what was left of the party. Most of the people had already gone and the rest were leaving.

"Where the hell have you been?" Jim asked.

George and I, each chiming in alternately, told our sad story to the last few, who stopped their packing up to listen.

"We really had a great time today. How do you get into these messes?" someone wondered aloud.

George and I looked at each other for a moment before he answered, "Just lucky, I guess."

23

Major Harry Dorris, the squadron CO, left for the States on August 1, 1944. He was succeeded by Tommy Molland. Every pilot in the squadron received the news with great enthusiasm, especially us veterans. Tommy was our kind of guy, and we would have followed him anywhere he saw fit to lead. Shortly after the selection was announced, Lam buttonholed Little Henry and me and said he thought that it would be a good idea henceforth to address Tommy as Captain Molland, at least in front of the rest of the officers. We instantly concurred. He could still be "Tommy" in private, back in our rooms, but it was important to show by example that officially he was no longer to be treated as a buddy. He was the Old Man now. The first time I spoke to him in that fashion, in the operations hut before a mission, he looked at me squarely with those bright blue eyes and a half smile at the corner of his lips, and I knew he understood.

I got another Me-109, my sixth, on August 3. It was on a return trip to Friedrichshafen with B-24s, and the weatherman had promised broken cloud buildups at all altitudes from Venice all the way to the target. Molland was leading the squadron and the group, and I was leading Blue Flight. The rendezvous point was at Bressanone, Italy, which we made on time at 1030. As Tommy had established at the pre-flight briefing, we were the low squadron, at 25,000 feet. The other two were stepped up: the 307th at 26,000 feet and the 309th at 27,000. Ten minutes after rendezvous, hardly before we had settled into our escort pattern, Tommy got a call from the lead bomber: His rear element was under attack from below at 20,000 feet. Blue Flight was closest. I turned back toward the enemy. After careful and intense scrutiny, I saw six Me-109s down there. When I called them out, Tommy acknowledged my call with a terse, "Roger, Blue. Take 'em."

That was all I needed. A half second later our tanks were off and we were tearing down at full throttle. The 109s scattered quickly, apparently wanting no part of Mustangs. I managed to focus on one of them and kept him in sight as we closed rapidly on him. I tried to slow the excessive rate of closure by jerking the throttle off at about 500 to 600 yards. Even so, the distance to 250 yards narrowed quickly; I was fighting the change in rudder trim even as I began firing. It was a zero-deflection shot, and the first rounds went home. As soon as I saw strikes, I pulled the trigger again and held it down for three or four seconds. Most of the hits were in the fuselage, and a good part of the empennage was shot away. The German plane started its final dive from 10,000 feet—streaming oil, glycol, and smoke—crashing about fifteen seconds later. The pilot didn't get out.

While the flight was re-forming, I gave the area a good visual check. There was no doubt about it; the rest of the 109s had made good their escape. We were about halfway between Innsbruck and the target. My flight was more or less intact, so I decided to climb up toward the target-bound bombers and finish the escort job. Later on the mission, five FW-190s were called out but not engaged. After I landed, I found out that I had the distinction of scoring the only victory chalked up by the group that day.

I had gained tremendous confidence in the Mustang and in my ability to fight with it. Experience had gradually cooled my hyperexcitement; I could now keep a detached calm in a fight, in spite of all the screaming on the R/T, and the physical and mental exertion. My senses had been honed to a razor-sharp edge and my reflexes were lightning quick. At least that was how I felt, and it was a good feeling.

The sensation I felt at encountering a Me-109—of recognizing the rounded, blunt nose; the short wings; the long, thin fuselage; and small rounded tail—was like a stab in the chest. The mottled camouflage paint, the large crosses, the greenhouse cockpit enclosure all screamed it out: 109! With the realization came a rush of adrenaline, and my mind and body leaped to a new level of awareness and intensity. I know my pulse rate shot up, not from fear but from excitement and keenness.

The physical actions that followed were automatic: hitting all the right switches and getting the power up while simultaneously and instinctively beginning a maneuver, whatever it might be, that would put me in a firing position in the shortest possible time. If there were more than one 109, I didn't try to scatter my shots here and there. I picked my target, usually the closest; closed as fast as possible; and loaded him up in one firing pass from 300 yards down to 50. I didn't like to overrun—there was always the chance that the plane and pilot would survive my charge, and I didn't want to get out in front of him. Instead of overrunning, I'd break off violently to one side or the other. But I didn't want to close slowly, either, or sit behind him for ten to fifteen seconds. I knew from my own reactions under similar circumstances that any German pilot who saw one of his own in trouble was going to give me his undivided attention. I always assumed, when making a firing pass, that someone saw and was coming. True or not, all maneuvers before and after a firing pass—sometimes during—were violent, gut-wrenching, blood-draining turns. Combat was hard work, physically as well as mentally.

Sometimes I violated my own instincts. More than once I pulled the power back to stay behind a German longer if I was having trouble hitting, unwilling to break off without destroying him. But I was not comfortable going against my instincts. Sometimes I half flinched in anticipation of the first 20mm impacts, even as I concentrated on holding the orange ring and pipper of my sight on my quarry.

★

Right after the briefing, the mission scheduled for August 4, 1944, was canceled because of bad weather in the target area. This proved to be just one of four such cancelations during the first two weeks of August. In between the weather systems moving across Europe, we did manage to get off a couple of times. On August 7 our group was tagged to fly close escort for a force of B-17s and B-24s attacking Blechhammer. The group also put up an "outlaw squadron" of twelve additional planes, one flight being contributed by each of the squadrons. Doctor Tom was leading the four ships that made up the 308th flight. Since they had no close-escort responsibility, I would gladly have swapped my position as squadron leader for his, if I could have.

On the way up toward the target, Outlaw Squadron was 3,000 to 4,000 feet above the group and behind by four to five miles. Forty minutes before rendezvous, while still over the northeast tip of Lake Balaton, the squadron encountered twenty to thirty Me-109s trailing the main formation. Captain George Loving, from the 309th Squadron, was leading the group that day. He told Outlaw Squadron to have at the German fighters while the rest of the group stayed together and pressed on to meet the bombers. It was a battle royal, a real eye-gouger that lasted twenty-five minutes. Doctor Tom got three confirmed and one damaged, and another of the 308th pilots also got a victory. The group met some scattered fighter opposition in the target area, but I drew a blank. That was an awfully long way to go into southern Poland just to listen on the R/T to other engagements. But I was getting more philosophical about the fickleness of the gods of war. There would still be plenty of fighting to go around.

Ploesti got the call again on August 10, but the Luftwaffe failed to show. I was glad I didn't go.

Then, beginning on August 12 and continuing on August 13, we started softening up southern France in the Toulon area, the heavies attacking harbors, docks, and bridges. Although we did not know it at the time, this was the opening phase of the preparation for the landing of the U.S. Seventh Army on the Mediterranean coast of France.

The missions were pretty routine, but the one on August 13 only started out that way. We saw no enemy fighters. Even though we had plenty of fuel to make it back to base, I decided to take the flight into Ghisonaccia, a small field on the east side of Corsica, just to break the monotony on the leg home. Sitting in one position, strapped to the seat, for five and a half hours got to be a little hard on the hinder, not to mention the bladder. We didn't often have the opportunity to take such a break; when the chance presented itself, it was not to be ignored.

While waiting for the fuel trucks to finish topping us up, a P-51 from another group made an erratic approach and an even worse landing. He shut down near us, so I walked over to pass a little time with him. As I came up, the pilot had the canopy open and was talking rapidly, almost shouting, to no one in particular. After he unbuckled and climbed down, he calmed down and told his story.

He and his wingman had left the French coast and were just nearing Corsica when he glanced idly over at his wingman. To his shock and horror, his wingman's machine was disintegrating under a hail of 20mm fire. He broke wildly, but it was too late to do anything. The enemy aircraft were gone. His wingman, burning fiercely, fell into the sea.

What could I say? I mumbled some words of condolence and got my flight out of there as quickly as I was able. A small mistake or a momentary lapse was all it took to invite disaster, and then the bill had to be paid. Sometimes, unfortunately, the paying had to be done by a wingman for his element leader's inattention.

On August 14, all three squadrons flew to a temporary field on the west coast of Italy, near Tarquinia, north of Rome. It didn't take a mental giant to figure out that something big was in the offing. By the time we landed at Voltone Airdrome, everything was pretty well laid on; two rows of tents were already up and waiting, field kitchens were in operation, and there was a cheerful, lighthearted tone to the whole thing. It was almost like a vacation.

At a preliminary briefing by Lieutenant Colonel Tarrant, we learned that the "something big" was the invasion of southern France: Operation Anvil. Our job was to provide top cover for the transport planes carrying paratroops or towing gliders.

For us the operation got under way the next day, late in the afternoon, and once we were airborne, we could see the extent of the air armada. It was quite a sight. The C-47 was no ball of fire under the best flight conditions; with multiple gliders in tow it was an absolute sloth. Staying with a pack of C-47s was hard work, even with the throttle pulled way back. They seemed to be standing still in the air as we scissored back and forth over them.

There was no air opposition as we approached the south coast of France in the Cannes-Toulon area, which was a lucky thing; we were spending a lot more time gawking at the ground activity than tending to business. I was especially fascinated by the gliders. Once they were released, they didn't have much time to pick a landing spot. From what I could see, some of them, after they were committed, wished they could have "overs," the chance to do it again. Those postage stamp–sized fields must have been a whole lot smaller and rougher than they looked from our altitude. Many of the gliders began shedding parts as soon as they touched down, slewing sideways to a stop or nosing up. The larger fields seemed to attract the most traffic, and it was not uncommon to see several gliders approaching these fields simultaneously from different directions. I saw two gliders run together, trying for the same field at the same time. The action, from the air, looked positively chaotic. I couldn't see how the troops could come out of that mess sufficiently well organized to fight.

No enemy trucks or armor were to be seen behind the landing zones, so we stooged around until our scheduled departure time. Then we headed out over the Mediterranean, back to Voltone. By this time it was past 2000; though it was not dark yet, the light was fading fast. Voltone did not have lights on the field, so there was quite a competition—more like a mad scramble, actually—to get down onto the ground while it could still be seen. Everyone was finally down by 2030. The only casualties were two pilots from a sister squadron; they had collided in the gloom while taxiing.

At 0600 the next day, August 16, we learned that our next job was to cover C-47s carrying out resupply parachute drops. Again we saw no flak and no enemy fighters on the mission. So, as soon as the transports were well out of harm's way, we headed back to Voltone. After landing at noon, we were told that Operation Anvil was all over as far as our participation went. We were going back to San Severo as soon as we were refueled. A long bomber-escort mission had been laid on for tomorrow, we learned, and Maintenance needed the airplanes to get them ready. So we dragged our tired asses back out and hopped over to San Severo. The mechanics didn't get any bargain—they worked long into the night, getting the machines ready. No one said who was going to work on the pilots to get us ready. Our wake-up call was scheduled for 0600.

24

One evening, in late July or early August, Tommy Molland had come over to my quarters and we had talked flying, as usual. I could tell he had something on his mind, but with Tommy you had to be patient, assured that, whatever it was, it would come out in time. Even though enemy fighters were getting scarcer, it was his opinion that the shortage was only apparent rather than real. He believed the change resulted from a switch in tactics, not from attrition of the German fighter forces. Looking at the air battle from the Luftwaffe's point of view, their pilots were not doing well against the Mustangs and, any way you sliced it, knocking down heavy bombers had to have a higher priority than fighter-on-fighter engagements. We agreed that the best tactic for German fighters would be to get off the ground at the approach of the bomber stream, avoid the covering fighter escort, and watch for bare bomber groups or stragglers to pick off. We concluded that our best chance to meet enemy fighters was to loiter in the target area after most of the attacking force had left for home. The logical thing for us to do was to pull back the power as much as possible, thereby saving fuel and increasing our time over the target vicinity.

Another way to extend the time aloft was to cheat a little on the fuselage tank. Two months before I had tried that ploy and had achieved a dismal failure. But two months past was a long time ago. I was sharper now. On recent missions I had been changing off the fuselage tank early, keeping in it a few more gallons than the recommended thirty. I thought I could get away with burning off only thirty-five gallons before going to the drop tanks. Leaving fifty gallons in the fuselage tank involved some risk, but my confidence was equal to it.

On August 13, Tommy came over with great news. He had gotten permission to put up four extra aircraft—he called it Black Flight—whose sole responsibility would be to flog around the sky, looking for enemy aircraft. He intended to lead Black Flight, and he offered me the opportunity to fly his element lead. I eagerly accepted the proposition. The plan was to join on the squadron after takeoff. But, once in the target area, we would range far out to either side of the bomber stream, free-lancing. It was an ideal set up for testing our ideas.

Our chance came on another scheduled attack on Ploesti, on August 18. Tommy assigned one of the other senior pilots to lead the squadron. He and I, with our wingmen, tagged along as a fifth flight, using the call sign Border Black Flight.

As we neared the oil fields, I called out some tiny dark specks just above the horizon, away to the east. Off we went. However, I failed to keep the bogies in sight. After stooging around for a few minutes, Tommy turned back toward Ploesti. I was stacked down on his left. We hadn't been straight and level for thirty seconds when I happened to look back and upward. My blood froze. There were 109s up there—a whole lot of them—and they were close! I could see the leader's painted spinner turning in what seemed to be slow motion; he was that near. I was dumbfounded. I couldn't believe they had gotten so close undetected, and I sure as hell didn't understand why they hadn't bounced us—unless they were as surprised as we were.

"Black Leader, break left!" I snapped out.

Instantly Tommy was in a vertical turn to the left. I broke to the right, underneath him. I saw about half the 109s turn away from us, but the rest followed Tommy and his wingman. As I got partway around, I caught sight of them again. I could see they hadn't closed on Tommy and didn't seem to be turning hard. I whipped up into a wingover and came barreling down in the opposite direction, picking out the nearest one. I waited until I couldn't miss and then cut loose with the six .50s. My guns poured a steady hail into the German plane at very close range. The 109 pilot bailed out immediately. As soon as he and his jettisoned canopy were clear of his aircraft and out of my vision, I forgot about him and got back to business.

While I pulled up slightly, I made a quick check around me. I spotted another 109 low and ahead on the left. I was still at max throttle and had come down below 10,000 feet, so I was really moving. I closed on him very fast—almost on the deck—and again got strikes all over him from the first burst. I held the trigger down for another second. Suddenly his cockpit canopy whipped off, and he came hurtling out. I let up on the trigger as quickly as I could, but some of my rounds were still on their way as he separated from his machine. I turned tightly to keep him in sight and watched him tumble end over end. I waited for his chute to blossom, but it never opened. He hit in a ploughed field not far from where a Rumanian farmer was working with his horse. I had never seen the actual death of one of my adversaries before; it was unnerving. It had not been deliberate, but I must have hit him as he came out, and I wondered if I could have been a split second faster in releasing the trigger. But there was no time to worry about that now, unless I wanted to join him.

I looked around and found I was alone in the sky. I had no idea where my wingman was and only a vague idea where *I* was. Some 40 miles east of the target area, I judged, and I would have to recross Ploesti alone on my way home. This prospect did not enthrall me. As I reduced the throttle and prop settings and checked my fuel, I tried raising Tommy on the R/T. No joy. Ruefully I recalled how I had hoped to remain in the target area until everyone had left. Well, I was getting my wish, but the prospect looked a little different from where I was sitting now. I had seen enough 109s for one day, thank you.

There was no on-board round counter, but I estimated that I had a couple of seconds of firing time left, and I knew that I had enough fuel to make it back. Briefly I considered staying down on the deck but decided that any advantage in being able to escape detection was outweighed by the disadvantage, possibly fatal, of not being able to dive away if attacked and cornered. I set up power for a climb back to altitude and began making sharp turns every ten seconds or so to clear my tail as I climbed.

Bang! The aircraft shuddered. I broke right by reflex. After I went to full power, I sneaked a peek back. Sure enough, there were two 109s coming hard, the typical black smoke from the 109's water-injection system pouring out of their exhaust stacks. I continued my max-rate turn, and then we went through some violent gyrations. They didn't seem to press the attack, however, and I suspected that they were low on fuel. They broke off the engagement, no doubt assuming that I would be more than a little relieved and willing to do the same. Logic was all on their side; low on fuel and ammo, on the deck and outnumbered, I should have jumped at the opportunity to break off a fight 600 miles from home. No chance. My adrenaline was really flowing now, and I was determined to have a go at them.

I latched on behind them easily, since they were taking no evasive action. I closed steadily, all the while being led away to the northeast at treetop level. They were flying line abreast about 300 yards apart. I began to move in on the one on the left, but, as I approached firing range, he started a turn away from the other. That didn't appeal to me, since it would have put his friend in behind me. I rolled out and they did too, putting everyone back in his original position. North was the wrong way for me; I couldn't afford the gas, so I was going to have to do something soon. I moved in again on the left one, but this time his buddy turned too quickly and steeply. He passed over me at a 90-degree angle. There was no way he could reverse his turn in time to get a shot at me, so I forgot about him and pressed in boldly on my quarry. As I began banging away, I saw tracers. That meant that I was almost out of ammo—the armorers put in a tracer every so often in the last fifty rounds as a warning. Well, it was too late to play timid now. I was down to two guns firing when he must have looked back at me at just the wrong instant. I don't think I scored any hits on him, but he flew right into the ground, hitting on a slight rise in the middle of a wheat field. I broke off sharply by reflex, just missing what looked to be his ricocheting aircraft. I stayed down and kept going.

I could see no sign of the other 109, thank God, for I was in serious trouble. I had no ammunition, marginal fuel, and an engine that was running, but not very well from being tortured beyond its design limits. I left the throttle at takeoff power and started to climb again. Twice in the space of fifteen minutes, enemy aircraft had materialized as if by magic. That had never happened to me before, even once, and it really shook me.

The engine smoothed out and ran surprisingly well. I was soon at 20,000 feet, homeward bound. Great black clouds of smoke rose from the oil refineries. Higher up, close to my level, a cloud of dark dissipating flak bursts was still hovering over the target. I didn't spend much time sightseeing; my head was really on a swivel now. I transmitted in the blind and succeeded in raising Jim Brooks, of all people. He said he had already departed the target area with his flight but would turn back to try to find me. Even though the link via the ether waves was a tenuous thread indeed, it was enough to assure me that I was not alone. My spirits rose a little. Jim tried to spot me, but I must have been too far out—a little tiny airplane in a great big sky—and, when his flight declared minimum fuel, he had to start for home.

That flight back was the longest of my life. My flight suit was soaked with sweat, the parachute harness and lap belt felt tight, and the rubber oxygen mask made my face itch continuously. The high tension of combat had given way to nervous anxiety and a touch of nausea. With nothing better to do, I found myself checking the fuel tanks every minute or two, even though the needles couldn't possibly have moved and I knew it. Making it home was going to be close. As I droned across Yugoslavia and the Adriatic Sea, I had everything pulled back as far as I dared, to conserve fuel. When I caught sight of the PSP strip at San Severo, I was running on fumes. I made a close-in approach, pitched into a tight pattern, and drove it down on the wheels. It was the worst landing I ever made. Langlois and Carpenter, my crew, were still waiting, with one other twosome, at the end of the runway. When I turned to clear the PSP and they could see my markings, Langlois and Carpenter were visibly relieved. Langlois raised his arms above his head with clenched fists, and both men got up on the wing for the ride into the parking area. We left the other crew still standing there, searching the eastern sky for one more Mustang. They looked disheartened, and I felt sorry for them; I was sure that their vigil was in vain.

As I taxied, I glanced over at my passengers and held up three fingers, which set them to laughing and slapping each other on the back. After I shut down, we scrutinized every inch of my machine from nose to tail and could find no damage of any kind, not even a scratch. Two exhaust stacks were gone, but that was from running at too high a power setting for too long. The crew chief, Carpenter, first gave voice to a suspicion that had been lurking in the back of my mind.

"Do you suppose," he asked, "that you weren't hit at all but that the engine just detonated?"

I wasn't sure. How could I be? But I was sure of one thing: If it was a detonation, a sort of backfire, the timing was perfect. Two or three seconds later, and it would have been lights out for me. I thought about Colonel Robert L. Scott's book *God Is My Co-Pilot*. I think that I had borrowed his copilot on that mission.

The rest of Black Flight was already down. Tommy had gotten one but in the process lost contact with me as well as the other enemy aircraft. My wingman had gotten lost on the first break but managed to join up and come home with Tommy. No one had witnessed my last two claims, but luckily my film of all three encounters was some of the best that had ever been shot in the group. The last film plainly showed the 109 hitting the ground. This caused quite a stir as the audience applauded and commented loudly and appreciatively. Mechanics, armorers, and clerks were connected to the aerial battlefield only through their work on the ground, and they participated vicariously in the fighting through the gun-camera films. Small wonder they were appreciative!

25

Group Headquarters had recently begun to talk up the idea of social interchange with bomber groups, and I suspect that the policy actually originated at Fifteenth Air Force Headquarters. Cultivating a closer understanding between bomber and fighter pilots was undoubtedly a good idea, but on the basis of sheer numbers, I wasn't sure that anything more than a token effort was practical. Nevertheless, I was more than willing to do my part.

I had, in fact, already done a bit. Months earlier, during the first weeks at San Severo, our base had had no shower. We had to go to the city to use one that had been set up for bomber and fighter groups in like circumstances. During this period, when we went in to San Severo at every opportunity to luxuriate in the hot water, I spied someone who looked an awful lot like a fellow I had known in Racine. I didn't know him well; he was several years ahead of me in school, but the high school wasn't that big. I thought I caught a glimmer of recognition from him, too.

When we were out in a small anteroom, dressing, I asked him if he was from Racine. With a slowly spreading smile, he acknowledged that he was. His name was Bob Schliesmann, and he was a navigator assigned to one of the nearby B-17 groups. We chatted for a bit, going through a round of "Do you know so-and-so?" and "Whatever happened to so-and-so?" He gave me the name of his base and his unit, and I promised to visit him as soon as I could.

I was still a new guy then, and new guys couldn't get vehicles very easily to go gadding about—or airplanes either. So it was during a stand-down in the first part of August before I could get permission to go.

It wasn't a long flight to Foggia Main—no more than twenty minutes, chock to chock—so I had hardly got my gear up when it was time to put it down again. I landed and taxied over to what appeared to be a small transient ramp among the four-engine monsters scattered about on both sides of the PSP runway.

Several mechanics and a few air-crew officers began to gather as soon as I shut it down. I draped my helmet over the top of the stick, left my chute in the bucket seat, closed the canopy, and hopped down. Looking back at the *Flying Dutchman*, I felt a glow of pride. It was a very nice-looking piece of machinery indeed. It was a brand-new D model, and the natural-metal finish still gleamed as if it had been burnished. The red paint on the spinner and striped tail surfaces was new also, shiny and unchipped, and the row of six crosses and "Lieutenant Goebel," in script on the side beneath the cockpit, just set it off.

I tried to act casual in front of its admirers. Some of them, the air crews, had seen Mustangs from a distance, criss-crossing over their formations at 25,000 feet. But few had ever seen one up close before. And the crosses did not go unnoticed, either. The onlookers liked fighters a lot; when airborne, and they liked *a lot* of fighters.

When I asked directions, everyone was helpful. In a short time I found Bob Schliesmann's tent, and by coincidence he was at home. We greeted each other warmly—far more congenially than our prior relationship would have warranted, had we not been standing 5,000 miles from Racine. We didn't have all that much to talk about, but his tent mates were as interested in P-51s and fighters as I was about their operations, so we spent most of the time exchanging horror stories and tales of derring-do.

Then it was time for me to head out, and Bob walked back to the flight line with me. A knot of people still stood around my plane. As I was saying good-bye to Bob, a captain asked me if it was my aircraft, obviously referring to the six victory crosses. When I told him it was, he raised his eyebrows slightly and nodded approvingly, as if to say, "Not bad. Not bad at all."

Bob asked me to give the field a buzz job, but I answered lamely that we were under orders to fly no lower than 200 feet, and I didn't want to get into trouble. I would have dearly loved to have torn up that field at 8 or 10 feet. But when it came to disobeying orders, I didn't have the balls that Little Henry had.

After I was off the ground, I left the throttle at full power, held it down to the end of the runway, and pulled up into a near-vertical climb. Since the *Flying Dutchman* was clean, without external tanks, she went up pretty smartly. When she began to slow near stalling, I walked it around with rudder and aimed it for the end of the runway, leveling off and charging down the runway at about 350 miles per hour. I did let it get down to 100 feet, but I'm sure Bob was disappointed. One hundred feet was no buzz job—it was pretty tame stuff—but I remembered the aftermath of Little Henry's victory roll, and I didn't need that.

Bob had reminded me to look at the tail markings of his group so I could be on the lookout for them in the air. A couple of weeks later, I did spot the group's marking: a "Y" on the large B-17 tail, with a distinctively painted rudder. No enemy fighters were up that day. We were just stooging around the target area, so I thought I'd have some fun. I took my flight up level with and abreast of the group lead bomber, pulled the throttle back, and put half flaps down. They were doing something like 150 miles per hour. I sat out there for a minute, wanting all the gunners—and pilots, too—to get a good look at the aircraft profile and the U.S. markings; I wanted no mistaking us for 109s. Slowly I began to slide in closer until I was almost in formation. Then I hand-signaled a copilot, who was looking at me out of his side window, to change to the common channel.

I switched over too, and immediately caught his transmission.

"Hey, little friend, what're you up to? Over."

"We're fearless Thirty-firsters, out to stalk the wily Hun and keep the world safe for democracy," I told him. "One of your navigators, Bob Schliesmann, is a friend of mine. Would you like our undivided attention for a bit?" There was no harm in putting in a plug for Bob.

"That'd be great Goebel, thanks a lot," came the reply.

That surprised me until I remembered that I had come in on his right side, presenting my left side to him; he could see my row of crosses, which now stretched to nine, and he could also read my name. I changed back to our working channel, told the flight to raise flaps, and pushed the throttle back up where it belonged. Away we went as if the bombers were standing still.

We had plenty of fuel, so we made a big show of sticking close to that group and its neighbors, the rest of the wing. My path and Bob's did not cross again, so I never did get his reaction to this episode. But at least it gave me a chance to play the hot shot and it gave the bomb group something to talk about for a couple of days.

★

August 22, 1944, proved to be another milestone in my combat career—I got my chance to lead the entire group. The mission was to escort a mixed force of B-24s and B-17s to Blechhammer, Germany (in what is today Upper Silesia, in southwestern Poland). To get there, we would cross Yugoslavia, Hungary, and Czechoslovakia. It was a long haul—over 650 miles.

I wasn't overawed at the prospect of leading forty-eight aircraft on such a flight. But I was a little nervous at the pre-flight briefing, when I rose to give my pitch before that sea of upturned faces. Many of the pilots were my contemporaries; some had been in the group longer, but most were new guys at varying levels of experience. Some of the attentive faces, members of the 307th and 309th Squadrons, I did not even recognize, although all looked familiar to me. I reminded myself that I had sat out there fifty-six times, listening to the instructions of the group leader, so I knew the drill. I knew what I was talking about, and I hoped I projected the confidence I felt as I outlined the mission.

We were to rendezvous with the bombers north of Lake Balaton, in Hungary, an unmistakable checkpoint fully 35 miles long. From there we were to take them to the target, an awfully long way to be zigzagging over the heavies. A sister P-51 group would relieve us at the target and provide the withdrawal cover for the 24s and 17s. The distance was just too far for us to take the bombers all the way in and back out again, scissoring all the way.

The takeoff and join-up went as planned, and I admit to a great thrill and some small butterflies in the pit of my stomach as I surveyed the scene around me. The sixteen aircraft and spares of the 307th were above and back a little on my left side; those of the 309th were above them to my right; and my squadron, the 308th, was tucked in behind me. No one was out in front of me. I was it.

Trouble, never far off, was waiting for me as we neared the rendezvous point. Visibility was very good—good enough to see 40 to 50 miles in either direction—and there was no sign of the bomber formation. My radio and that of my wingman had the crystals of the bomber stand-by frequency. We both tried repeatedly—desperately—to raise someone on that channel. No luck. I began to sweat now. I was quite sure the bombers were behind rather than ahead, but that meant having to kill at least twenty-five minutes, since they were not even in sight yet. It was also possible that the mission had been recalled and we had not gotten the word. That had happened before—several times. Wherever the hell they were, it was turning into a real mess. A formation of forty-eight airplanes is not the most maneuverable thing, but I tried my best to keep the group in the same piece of sky.

To make matters worse, a large formation of B-24s to the west of us, obviously going toward Vienna, came under fighter attack. One of my squadrons went over to check them out, saw the attack, and waded right in. I couldn't blame them; they were damned if they did and damned if they didn't. But I still believed our bombers were going to show. If I was wrong, I was sure going to look bad, stooging around while some bomb wings were getting shot up. In spite of long-standing orders to the contrary, some of the remaining flights—including one of mine, led by Claude—dropped their tanks and gave chase.

Almost forty minutes later, the bombers finally showed up, victims of some very strong headwinds. What was left of my group, no more than six flights, picked up station and resumed course northward, zigzagging above the plodding bombers. But there was no way we could carry out the mission as planned.

Before we were across Czechoslovakia, flight leaders began calling in a low-fuel state and starting for home. Contrails ahead, which probably meant that our approach had not gone unnoticed by the Luftwaffe, provided an incentive to stay with the big friends as long as possible. I was down to one flight in the 308th, my own, and I suspected that the other squadron flights were in similar straits. Then my element leader called out some bogies at three o'clock, slightly high. I felt a flood of relief; our relieving group had arrived to take over. But the planes were coming from the east rather than from the south. Also, although there was the right number of them, the formation just did not look right. I kept a jaundiced eye on them. As the aircraft got close enough for me to make out their features, my suspicions were confirmed. They were 109s.

I called them out, let go the tanks, went to full power, and got the gun switch on in one continuous motion. They didn't attack immediately; perhaps they were looking for a chance at the bombers, or maybe their surprise at finding fighters that far into Central Europe caused them to hesitate. Then I took a quick look around and saw why they hesitated. The P-51s of the 52d Group were coming up behind us from the south, not more than three or four miles away.

I figured there wasn't much point in sticking close to the bombers anymore; my job was done. I was going to have to leave in a few minutes anyway. The best help I could give was to disrupt the enemy formation, and maybe even get one or two in the process. If the fight took us down to lower altitude and we succeeded in scattering them, well and good. After we left, the 109s would take a while to climb back up, and that would give everyone a little breather. It would be better than nothing. The 109s were bound to be short on fuel by then, and the 52d would make short work of them.

Numerically, we were on the short end of 6:1 odds. But by this time we had gained a height advantage, and I was counting on the 52d, which was coming hard. A quick glance back showed that the other three members of my flight were still with me.

"Well, enough of this dancing and romancing, Robert. Let's get to it," I thought half aloud. Pulling up steeply, I rolled to the left, hauling the nose through the horizon, and came hurtling down like a bat out of hell. I lined up on the nearest 109 and let fly. A few strikes flashed on his fuselage. Instantly, he pushed over and disappeared under my nose. That was a new one on me, and it caught me absolutely flat-footed. I cocked my Mustang up on a wingtip to see where he'd gone and caught sight of him below in a steep dive. I went over in a near split S after him. Out of the corner of my eye, I caught sight of aircraft going in all directions. I almost caught my quarry, but then he did a wingover and started another dive. This time he didn't put much distance between us, but we had come down so fast that my canopy and part of the windscreen were fogged up. I could see through only a small space, which the hot, defogger air had kept clear.

We were down now, so there was no more room for him to dive, and my machine was faster than his. Closing in to point-blank range from dead astern, I gave him a long burst that lit him up pretty good, flashes dancing around the fuselage and wing roots. But I overran and again lost him under the nose.

Breaking sharply, I looked back and saw another aircraft coming at me. The deep central scoop told me that it was another Mustang. I throttled back and kept turning so he could catch up and join on me. Sure enough, it was my wingman. I called him on the R/T and told him to move out a couple of hundred yards and forward into a line-abreast position, from which we could see behind each other properly.

A black plume of smoke was rising off in the distance, about where I thought the 109 would have gone in, but I couldn't be sure.

My element leader called and said he was on course for home with his wingman. I told him to press on; I didn't see much point in flogging around trying to join up when we were so low on fuel. We all made it back to base without further incident. At the debriefing, my wingman said he saw the 109 crash in a great ball of fire in a wooded area. My wingman was a fairly new replacement, and I thought he had done a hell of a fine job staying with me through all the aerobatics. I told him so.

I found out afterward from Lam that Little Henry had gone through the usual trauma of waiting and hoping on my behalf. Claude's flight was one of the first to return, since he had dropped his tanks early. A half hour later, when I was not back yet, Henry was really worried and finally confronted Claude. He berated him openly for getting sucked into a fight before rendezvous and told him that if I didn't make it back, it would be his fault. When I showed up minutes later, the confrontation ended but the damage was done. An irreparable strain developed in their relationship. It might not have happened that way two months earlier, but I think we were all a bit edgy from the grind of going out almost every day.

No one in Group Headquarters ever said anything to me about the job I had done as group lead, but I heard via the grapevine that there was a certain amount of tongue wagging and head shaking—by people who had not been on the flight, of course. Also, I sensed a certain restraint, almost a frostiness, toward me from several senior group officers who were going to a critique of the mission at Fifteenth Air Force Headquarters. I was not asked to attend, even though I had led the mission. I suppose they were girding themselves for a verbal drubbing from the bomber group commanders whose units had sustained heavy losses, and I'm sure they didn't want any callow first lieutenants underfoot to possibly contradict their version of what happened. What the senior group officers quickly discovered, however, was that almost all the bomber losses were due to fuel exhaustion. The high-velocity headwinds aloft that had caused their late arrival at rendezvous had continued to plague them the rest of the way to the target. They were quite complimentary about any of the 31st fighters having made it to the target, considering the bombers' tardiness and slow progress. Some of the bomber pilots had reported seeing my flight and some of the 52d breaking up the enemy fighter formation and the ensuing fight with the Me-109s.

After the 31st delegation returned, I sensed a change in the wind. Although no one said anything to me directly, the substance of what transpired at Fifteenth Air Force Headquarters got back to me. No one was exactly patting me on the back, but the frostiness was gone and the matter soon forgotten. Except by me. I lost all respect for one of the officers involved, and never regained it. And, if anyone had asked my opinion, I would have told them that the entire post-flight episode had been mishandled. But, then, no one asked me. *Sic transit gloria mundi.*

26

C.D., one of the older pilots on the group headquarters staff, had been with the 31st for a long time, going all the way back to North Africa. He was now nearing the end of his tour of duty in the theater. Although he had flown a respectable number of missions in both the Spit and the Mustang, he had no confirmed victories, only a damage, which he had gotten in the Spitfire. In fairness to C.D., flying occasional combat missions was a duty additional to his administrative job. And such flying was not the greatest way in the world to maintain proficiency; it was more like an invitation to a POW camp or a pine box.

But C.D. was made of different stuff than one of his colleagues of like circumstance, who held the record for mission aborts. Whenever this chap was scheduled to such interesting places as Ploesti or Wiener Neustadt, his aircraft began to act up before he had gotten halfway to the target; he always had to return to base before any unpleasantness started. To no one's surprise, the malfunction could never be duplicated on the ground afterward, which caused a considerable amount of talk among the maintenance personnel about "phantom" engine problems. He was a standing joke among the rest of us pilots. Whenever he was on the schedule, we speculated among ourselves where the inevitable malfunction would occur.

I was scheduled to lead the squadron to Vienna on August 28, 1944, and I told Tommy Molland that I would like to take C.D. as my element leader. I didn't know anything about his flying ability, but I gave him an A+ for gameness and I wanted to give him the opportunity to do his thing. If it was a fight C.D. wanted, I was reasonably sure I could oblige him. I had acquired a nose for enemy fighters, and it almost seemed that I could make them appear at will. Nonsense, of course, but I had that feeling. Tommy agreed to my suggestion.

The bomber rendezvous was on time, and we picked up our B-17s and started our covering maneuvers. I split the squadron into two sections of eight aircraft, each taking a different part of the bomber wings and ranging out to the sides to watch for enemy fighters.

We got into some flak on the outskirts of Vienna. The flak seemed to be the tracking type rather than the barrage type, and it was heavy enough to cause us to take evasive action. No one was hit, but and a certain amount of confusion ensued as we scattered.

As I took stock of my flight, I spotted some bogies at eleven o'clock, slightly low, going toward five o'clock. They were 109s. I called them out, got the aircraft cleaned up, and gave C.D. a hand signal that we were going in.

The 109s passed almost beneath us. I noted that there were five of them and that they were flying in a vee formation, something I had not seen before. Just as they passed, I wheeled around and went tearing down, picking on the tail-end Charlie on the right side. He grew rapidly in my sight. Just as I opened up on him, the formation broke sharply left. Too late. The first burst went into the 109's fuselage and wing root—since I had about 10 degrees angle-off, I could see the strikes in the cockpit area and forward on the engine cowling. The German fighter immediately belched coolant, oil, and smoke. I turned my attention to another coming at me from eight o'clock.

We went at each other in a plain old-fashioned dogfight for a minute or two, but neither of us could get a shot at the other. This was no green new guy; he knew his business. We finally got into a turning duel. After a couple of circles, I began to gain a little on him. Then I did something that I didn't like to do: I put down 10 degrees of flaps. Putting the flaps down enabled me to turn tighter, but it reduced my speed. This was not my kind of action; I preferred to keep my speed up and get it done in one pass, if possible. I pressed on, hoping I wouldn't attract any attention, and was gradually getting a lead on him. Then, out of the corner of my eye, I thought I saw something. When I looked around, I saw white puffs, like snowballs. They were 20mm cannon shells self-detonating in midair! I continued turning as hard as I could and sneaked a look back.

Son of a bitch! Two of the nastiest, meanest-looking FW-190s imaginable were closing on me. Their ugly blunt noses pointed squarely at me, and little orange flames flicked from their 20mm cannon. Flaps up! Throttle through the gate! Keep turning! I steepened the bank past the vertical and pulled the nose through the horizon until I was in a spiral, going straight down. That kept the 190s off long enough for me to open some distance on them. I leveled off on the treetops, and the chase became a flat-ass race. The 190s were just barely out of range. The 109, my intended victim moments earlier, joined in, a distant fourth.

I concentrated on staying as low as I could, keeping the prop tips a few feet off the ground, making sure the ball was centered, and repeatedly pushing on the prop- and throttle-control levers—even though I knew they were against the stops. I was through the gate, in War Emergency—67 inches of mercury. Although the tech orders limited use of this power setting to five minutes, I wasn't about to pull anything back. I hoped the Packard people had done a good job, because that engine was going to have to pull me out of there or blow up trying.

The late-summer Austrian countryside looked strangely peaceful and verdant. Under other circumstances, watching the scenery rushing swiftly beneath my wings would have been a pleasure. I went down a short stretch of narrow dirt road and passed a moustachioed old man driving a horse and wagon. He looked up in startled disbelief as I flashed by, a scant 50 feet away, at 400 miles per hour. My passing was so quick that the horse never even reared; he just stared over at me.

I was holding my own, even gaining a little, but ever so slowly. Each time I looked back, it seemed, the 190s greeted me with a couple of bursts that fell short and scattered a few ricochets around me.

Looming ahead were some hills just high enough to screen me momentarily. I decided to make a move. As soon as I was over the ridge, I made a max turn to the left and immediately went back hard to the right, to my original heading. All the while I watched over my right shoulder for my pursuers. Nothing. For a better look, I started a turn and climbed cautiously a couple of hundred feet. Still nothing. There was no doubt about it, they had broken off the chase. Good show!

But I was alone, and no one was within sight or hearing—not C.D., not my wingman, not anyone. Where was I? Somewhere southeast of Vienna. As I gained altitude, I was just able to make out Lake Balaton in the distance. Finally, I raised Little Henry on the R/T. We rendezvoused. Since he had heard all the commotion on the air and his flight was still intact, he was spoiling for a fight. He looked over my machine as carefully as possible in the air and pronounced it to be in good

health, so off the five of us went, back to where I had last seen my
tormentors. While we searched unsuccessfully for fifteen minutes, I
managed to contact the rest of my flight and we rejoined. Little Henry
wasn't through yet though; he was going back up toward Vienna to see
what he could stir up. I wished him luck and turned back to the
bombers, which were homeward bound.

At the post-flight interrogation, I found out that C.D. had indeed
gotten his long-sought victory. Apparently he had fired almost all his
ammo in one continuous burst, tenaciously hanging on to his quarry
and hosing away. The next day one of his gun barrels was on display
in the operations hut—as an example of how *not* to treat your guns.
The inside of the barrel had to be seen to be believed. Very little rifling
was left, and there were gouges here and there the full length of the
barrel. It was junk.

C.D.'s film of the encounter was no less spectacular. By the time
the tracers started coming out, the guns must have been very hot. The
tiny bright dots traced graceful arcs as they sprayed the sky in all
directions. I think some tracers went end over end because they
appeared to stop in midair. However, none of these details could dim
his triumph; he had pulled it off, he had gotten his victory. All his
colleagues in group headquarters, pilots and ground officers alike,
were as happy for him as if they had downed the German themselves.
Besides being a courageous pilot, he was well liked. Shortly afterward,
when he got orders sending him home, we were all sorry to see him go.

★

Six days before the August 28 mission, two new pilots had been
assigned to the 308th. They were an unlikely pair, in age, rank, and
temperament. The older was a captain; the younger, a second lieutenant named Jones.

We first lieutenants who had forty to fifty missions under our belts
and were doing all the combat leading resented a newcomer senior in
rank to us. Of course it wasn't the captain's fault that he had been
promoted while doing Stateside duty. But, as far as we were concerned, a new guy was a new guy. Both of them were ignored, socially.
Afloat in this great sea of indifference, the captain and Jones gravitated toward each other and became inseparable. The captain obviously had been around and probably had a lot more flying time than
Jones did, so he looked out for the lieutenant whenever he could.

On August 28, Jones was scheduled on the mission to Vienna.
After the mission, I walked into ops, made my report, and talked to my

flight. Jones wasn't back yet. His only friend, the captain, sat on a bench outside the ops hut and waited. He had a worried frown across his brow.

Had it been only four months since I had sat there watching the eastern sky for Johnson to show up? It seemed like a year, but I remembered it well. I knew the captain was waiting in vain, as I had. Lieutenant Jones certainly was down somewhere and was not coming back. Almost everyone had left, and it was quiet now. I waited another twenty minutes inside the hut. Then I went out and put my hand on the captain's shoulder. When he looked up, the tears were streaming down his cheeks.

"I'm sorry," I said. "There's always a chance that he's a POW. But there's nothing you can do for him here."

He got into the jeep with me, and I left him with his own thoughts as we drove back to the housing area. On August 31, Lieutenant Jones was dropped from the squadron roll.

27

During the first week in September 1944, the Germans began pulling out of Greece and the Balkans and up through Yugoslavia, generally along the route of the famous Orient Express train. The Fifteenth Air Force was given the job of interdicting the road traffic and rolling stock carrying out the move. We struck with the B-17s and B-24s from altitude and with fighters from low level.

Our group's assignment was to beat up the area roughly between Nis and Belgrade; we were to attack anything that moved. For us, this type of work was new on two counts. First, we were going to work down low instead of at the usual 25,000 feet. Second, we were being given a blank check, the freedom to write our own ticket, to range about within the assigned area and to improvise our attacks. It was certainly a welcome change from the inflexible confinement of close cover during bomber escort.

As soon as we crossed the coastal mountain range, we broke into squadrons. As we began the hunt, we broke into four-ship flights. I started down a narrow valley through which a two-lane road meandered, but it was empty. Somewhere near Kraljevo I pulled up a couple of thousand feet to have a look around. I spotted a railroad engine, with a few cars behind it, standing on a track that angled across an adjacent valley.

My element leader slid under to the other side with his wingman, thus opening the way for me to make a run at the train and also positioning himself to follow in a firing pass of his own. A last quick check around told me that there was no one else, friend or enemy, in the neighborhood. I dropped the nose on the broad side of that engine. As it grew larger in the orange-lit reticle, I concentrated on holding the pipper steady on the boiler, just forward of the engineer's cab. Bouncing around in the midday turbulence was one thing we did not have to contend with at altitude. As I opened fire, the dirt kicked up short. Then, as the impacts walked upward onto the steel structure, the API flashes began to dance along its length. White jets of steam shot outward and upward. As I passed over, I thought I saw some figures crouching behind the engine. Then the first strikes from the rest of the flight began.

When the other P-51s finished their pass, the train was pretty well shot up. We just kept going. We spent another forty-five minutes thrashing around, looking for targets of opportunity, but we found nothing worth shooting at. Then farther north, near Kragujevac, I saw a large number of men, perhaps a hundred, scattered over a steep hillside. They must have heard us a second before we came into view, because some were already leaping to their feet, staring at us, as we roared past. They all appeared to be dressed alike, but the uniforms were not those of the Wehrmacht. As quickly as I could, I pulled up, made a 180-degree turn, and came back to take a closer look. Nothing. Not one soul was to be seen anywhere. I couldn't believe it. This was the place; it had taken only a minute to backtrack. But several more passes failed to yield a clue to the troops' whereabouts. They must have been somewhere near, but that was the best and quickest disappearing act I have ever seen. It was as if someone had hidden a herd of elephants in a flower garden. My guess was that they were Partisans or Chetniks and, though they probably recognized our aircraft as being American, they were not taking any chances on exposing themselves to a mistaken strafing.

The rest of the mission was uneventful. At the debriefing back at the field, we compared notes and found that everyone had had some modest success finding targets. The final tally was enlightening but hardly a war-ending success:

Item	Number Destroyed	Number Damaged
Ju-52s	2	0
Locomotives	49	17
Motor transports	35	25
Boxcars	2	68
Oil tank cars	6	0

Small boats	1	0
Barges	0	2
Gasoline trucks	5	0
Staff cars	1	2
Motorcycle	1	0
Passenger coaches	0	2

In addition, our group left two buildings burning in Knjazevac Marshaling Yard and had set a garage in the Kraljevo area on fire. Judging from the tally, it looked as though the pounding by the bombers throughout the morning had driven almost everything else to cover.

★

Lieutenant Colonel Bill Daniel, from group headquarters, and Little Henry were gone on temporary duty (TDY) for a couple of days. When they returned, Little Henry had a very interesting story to tell. He and Colonel Daniel had gone down to Fifteenth Air Force Headquarters, at Bari. There, in a very hush-hush meeting, they were told about plans to rescue American prisoners of war being held in Rumania.

The plan had been initiated by a Rumanian pilot, Captain Cantacuzino. The Rumanian had taken the ranking American prisoner, a Colonel Gunn, from a POW camp near Bucharest and had flown him to Italy in an Me-109. Exactly how they managed to get four additional arms and legs into the tiny cockpit was a mystery—the 109 had barely enough room for the pilot. Their flight also caused some embarrassment in high places, since their approach and landing went undetected by whatever air-defense system was supposed to be functioning.

Captain Cantacuzino proposed to arrange for the release and repatriation of all the American airmen who had been shot down over Ploesti—in return, I suppose, for favorable treatment for himself and his associates. They didn't have much choice or much time, either; the Russian Bear was fast approaching Rumania from the east.

Colonel Daniel and Little Henry, flying Mustangs, were to accompany the Rumanian, also in a Mustang, back to Bucharest. Cantacuzino was to land while the two American pilots circled overhead. After he had verified that all was in readiness, he was to give a coded message to the airborne pair. The message was their cue to hightail it back at max cruise and relay the message to the ground station in Italy as soon as they were within radio earshot. Receipt of the proper message at Fifteenth Air Force Headquarters would trigger the launching of an armada of aircraft to Bucharest. The armada would pick up the American POWs, who would be waiting at the airfield.

In due time Henry was introduced to the Rumanian captain. Even to someone from Missouri, the Show-me State, Cantacuzino had to be considered an exceptional man. He was older than his American counterparts, perhaps thirty years of age, and he had a swarthy, handsome face and piercing dark eyes. He carried himself with a military bearing, but with a certain aristocratic ease. He spoke excellent English and was mentally keen. In short, he was, by any measuring stick, a gentleman of the old school. The task of checking Cantacuzino out in the Mustang fell to Little Henry, but this amounted to little more than pointing out the various switches and controls and reciting the critical airspeeds.

"One hundred twenty miles per hour? Hmm, that is one ninety kilometers," Cantacuzino said, making the conversion in his head. He took off, wrung it out briefly, and then landed the Mustang as if he had flown it all his life. In the course of several conversations with him, Little Henry learned that he was the leading ace in the Rumanian Air Force, with sixty victories. Although most of his victims were Russians on the Eastern Front, he did have several B-17s and B-24s to his credit as well as a P-38.

At the final briefing, a very senior staff officer drew Little Henry aside and told him to watch Cantacuzino carefully, in case the whole setup was a trick.

"If he tries anything funny, shoot him down," he ordered. It was a simple, straightforward instruction, but it must have caused Henry to do some mental head scratching, trying to figure out not only if and when, but *how!*

At last the Mustangs were off the ground and on their way, with Lieutenant Colonel Daniel leading, Cantacuzino on his wing, and Little Henry outside the Rumanian—in echelon. Somewhere over Yugoslavia, the Rumanian ace moved out to a wider position, until he was about a hundred yards away from Daniel. Immediately, Henry got his gun switch on and slid in behind him, not quite sure of what was going on but determined to be ready for whatever it was. Captain Cantacuzino fired a short burst from his machine guns and then, as if satisfied, pulled back into his former slot. Much to Henry's relief, Cantacuzino stayed there for the rest of the flight.

What Cantacuzino was trying to do with his guns will remain a mystery, since neither Daniel nor Little Henry ever saw him again. The most likely explanation is that he considered the possibility of being jumped by German fighters and he wanted to know if his aircraft had loaded guns. It did. Whether this was an oversight or intentional is anybody's guess.

The air armada—B-17s, B-24s, and even some C-47s—shuttled between Italy and Rumania for three days, bringing POWs home. There must have been thousands of POWs held in and around Bucharest, and we wanted them out before the Russians arrived.

Tommy scheduled me to lead the squadron on one escort mission for a small group of C-47s to the POW camp near Bucharest. We normally put up four flights of four, plus two spares. The spares would return to base if no one aborted by the time we reached the Yugoslavian coast. None of the pilots liked to fly spare for two reasons. First, if you did fill in and fly the mission, you'd probably wind up flying a wing position. More important, after going through all the mission preparations with the squadron, you might have to turn back, getting a nice early-morning flight for your trouble but no mission credit.

On this day, September 5, even though there were no aborts, I let the spares go along on the mission as a short, two-ship flight. The weather deteriorated as we penetrated farther and farther into the Balkans. Finally, the 47s had to turn back; the solid, 10/10 cloud cover beneath us would prevent them from making any pickups. The poor guys in Rumania were going to have to wait another day.

In the operations hut, later, I gave Tommy a quick rundown on what had happened. When I mentioned that I had let the spares come along, he looked at me squarely and said, "You shouldn't have done that." No harsh words, no raised voice—just a simple, quiet "You shouldn't have done that."

It was the first rebuke I had ever received from him, if you could even call it that, but I felt as if I'd been hit in the face. As I thought about it for the next half hour, a realization gradually emerged. A change had taken place in my status, but, in the press of daily flying, I had failed to acknowledge it with my actions.

All through cadets and in my early months as a new second lieutenant, my attitude and that of my fellows was one of Us against Them. "They" were some nameless, unknown entity beyond our vision or understanding who controlled our destiny—how we lived, loved, and flew. To thwart Them, we found every means we could of cutting corners and getting around the letter of their regulations which we minions considered senseless.

It was in this spirit that I had allowed the spares to go along and notch another mission. We didn't need them on the mission, but it was a chance for two pilots to get credit for an unearned mission, to beat the system.

What Tommy was trying to tell me was that I was a minion no longer; I was one of Them now, part of the system. I should have turned the spares back because turning them back was in the best interests of the group. Tommy, as squadron CO, needed experienced pilots on operations as long as possible; he could not permit any cheap or unearned missions to shorten the combat tours of any pilots. Tommy saw the situation clearly, and I should have. Now I understood his response, "You shouldn't have done that." His rebuke. It woke me up to the nature of my responsibility, and I never forgot it again.

28

One afternoon in early September, Tommy Molland and I were dawdling in the tiny officers' mess when Tommy abruptly asked me how I was getting along. "Great," I replied. But Tommy stared at me a while longer, as if he was seeking a different response. "Well," I finally admitted, "I guess I could stand a couple of days off. Couldn't we all?"

"Yeah," Tommy responded after a brief pause, "that's what I was thinking. We got a couple of slots for Rome, so I put you, me, George, and Joe Sheehan on the list to go."

We were provided with rooms in one of the Eternal City's nicer hotels. Though we were doubled up, the rooms were large and could easily accommodate two. The food in the hotel dining room was excellent, a welcome change from our mess. We soon found a lively night spot somewhere near the Piazza di Spagna. A flight of steps led down below street level and brought us into a dimly lit, smoky series of rooms with vaulted arches. The waiter assured us conspiratorially that, in other times, this was a favorite watering hole of King Farouk of Egypt. We were not at all impressed by this tidbit of history but did enjoy the dash and gaiety of the place. We tried to make up for the austere weeks at San Severo; we had to grope our way back to the hotel.

George and I were interested in visiting the Vatican, and we were not disappointed. We wandered through St. Peter's, gawking at Michelangelo's Pietà, the Bernini columns, and everything else that was so old and so elegant. We also got into the Sistine Chapel and marveled at the feat of Michelangelo, who must have been a gymnast as well as a gifted artist to have done the ceiling mural work the way he did. Imagine our chagrin, when, fresh from experiencing such spirit-lifting art treasures, we were assailed by the hordes of hawkers on the street as we left the Piazza San Pietro and started down the Via della Conciliazione toward the Tiber.

"Hey, Joe, you wanna buy beads justa blessed by the Pope?"

"No, *grazie.*"

"Dirty pictures, Joe? *Bella bella.*"

"No!" More emphatically this time.

Then one, a little bolder than the rest, sidled up alongside and asked, "You wanna buy a Beretta?" and he showed a half-hidden pistol beneath his partially opened coat.

I stopped, turned, and looked at him evenly, without speaking. He started backing up, arms outstretched with palms down, gently patting the air. "Okay, okay." Then he was lost in the crowd.

George and I walked along, irritated at having our uplifted mood so rudely dashed. They were certainly different, these Romans. I guess it didn't matter whether they were governed by Italian Fascists, the *Tedeschi*—Germans—or the Yanks. They were survivors.

A PX in the city center was large and impressive, the biggest I'd seen in a long, long time. A good-sized section of it was devoted to the sale of Roman antiquities and memorabilia, which I surmised were being sold by once-wealthy families that had been impoverished by the war. I bought two coins, a small silver one dating from about 100 B.C. and a larger thick bronze one that had been struck about A.D. 300. When I showed my booty to Molland and Sheehan, I became the butt of some good-natured ribbing. "Boy, did they see you coming," they said. "Where do you plan to spend those things?" But I have both coins to this day—long after our pocketfuls of lira were gone.

★

The first news we heard when we returned to San Severo was that one of the new guys, Fitzpatrick, had crashed that morning. He had been killed on his first flight in the Mustang. This news cast a pall over our return. His was the second such death in two weeks. A couple of months earlier, replacement pilots had been like hen's teeth; now they were coming by the boatload. Most new guys had fifty hours or less of fighter time, some had none. What a bugger-up.

The veterans were such skilled fighter pilots, they could do anything with the airplane. It was easy to lose sight of what a daunting prospect it was for these newcomers, fresh from the States, to take the Mustang up for the first time. But there was no helping it. We had no two-place P-51s with which to give instruction in the air. Like our instructors at Moore Field, when we were being checked out in the P-40, all we could do for the new guys was to crouch on the wing beside them, advise and caution, and pat them on the shoulder reassuringly. It wasn't much.

★

A few days after I returned from the Rome trip, I bumped into the flight surgeon, Doc Roth. He asked me to stop in and see him. He had a small office in the same building as the officers' mess. So, after I finished my coffee, I walked down to his office and let myself in. He looked up, smiled without speaking, and handed me a typed sheet of paper. Dated September 16, 1944, it was a certificate prepared by him, and I read it carefully.

C E R T I F I C A T E

Captain Robert J. Goebel, O-681645, has been examined by me on September 15, 1944 and observed during the past six months of his tour of combat duty and it is my opinion he should be returned to the Zone of Interior for a prolonged rest. During the past six weeks Capt. Goebel has not been as eager to fly combat missions as previously. He has 61 combat missions. He has previously been a very eager pilot, destroying 11 enemy aircraft, and has expended considerable energy as a Flight Commander. It is felt that this individual is so reduced in operational efficiency that the efficiency of the squadron is affected. It is felt that following a prolonged rest in the Zone of Interior, Capt. Goebel will be capable and desirous of serving another tour of foreign duty.

signed   John B. Roth
Capt. Medical Corps
Sqdn. Flt. Surgeon

When I looked up from the paper, Doc had a puzzled expression on his face. He looked a little disappointed, too, as if he had expected me to show some enthusiasm, and perhaps gratitude.

I handed it back to him with a curt thanks and went out into the bright afternoon sun. I was happy at the prospect of going home, but I felt some strange countercurrents of emotion, too. What the hell did he mean by "not as eager to fly combat?" Maybe a little more irritable than before, but I still wanted more combat. I didn't like the idea that others would be flying my missions, carrying on in my place—that I was dispensable. In fact, I just plain resented the notion that the squadron could get along without me.

"What the hell does Doc know?" I argued silently. "The squadron is full of greenhorns who can't fly a kite or hit the broad side of a barn. Besides, Tommy needs me." After I got back to my room and cooled off, I admitted to myself that the other pilots in the squadron were pretty damn good and would do just fine without me.

The more I thought about it, the more convinced I became that Doc would never have taken me off flight status without Tommy Molland's approval. That led me to think that Tommy might have seen something in me that I was not able to see in myself—a certain brittleness around the edges, perhaps. Maybe that's why Tommy had arranged to take me on the trip to Rome; maybe he had wanted to watch me closely for a few days. When I thought about it that way, I realized that Tommy was looking out for me—and for the squadron. Anyway, I knew there was no arguing against Doc Roth's medical finding, so I decided to bow out gracefully.

I gave myself one more chore to perform before leaving. Although I had been promoted to captain a few days earlier, my self-imposed assignment represented no burst of newfound responsibility. I had survived and learned, and I wanted the new pilots to do the same— that was all. Remembering my first days in the group, recalling my personal inexperience in combat and the inexperience of the group in long-range escort, I was determined to ease the way for the newer pilots. Although *we* had had to learn the hard way, there was no reason why they should have to reinvent the wheel. I posted a list of the newer pilots in the squadron to whom I wanted to talk. We met in the briefing room for an hour and a half, with no one else around.

I tried to recall all the things I had learned—the mistakes I had made, the things I had discovered by chance, anything that would be of value to them on their future flights. I gave them an opportunity to ask questions in an atmosphere free of fear of ridicule or embarrassment. One of them asked me why I always went to full power immediately when an engagement was imminent, and I had to stop and think for a minute.

"With power," I answered, "you can get altitude, or speed, or both; it doesn't matter 'cause they're really the same thing—at least you can trade one for the other in a flash. You can lose them pretty quick, too, but it might take you a while to build them up. You know the old saying about there being only two kinds of people in the world. Well, you might say the same thing about combat: There are bouncers and bouncees. If you want to be a bouncer, it's a good idea to get the power on early. You can always throttle back."

I talked about flak and the different patterns made by the barrage type versus the tracking type. I recalled leading a flight over Vienna, when I tried to cut across the target area and got caught in barrage flak. I started to jink around, changing altitude and heading. Then I realized that it was a complete waste of time and effort; they weren't aiming at us. The only thing that made sense was to get out of that box as quickly as possible. No one was hit on that occasion, but I hadn't done a very good job.

"Why do you always start cussing on the radio when you are going into a fight?" another asked.

He had me there. I hadn't even realized I did that. When I admitted as much, I joined in the general laughter. On that note, the session ended. As we left the room, no one spoke. Yet I sensed appreciation on their part, and I was satisfied.

On September 19, Brooks, Little Henry, Sheehan, and I received orders to report to the Replacement Depot at Naples for transshipment to the States.

The night before our scheduled departure, there was a party at the Officers' Club. I couldn't seem to get into the spirit. No matter how much I drank, the liquor didn't seem to affect me. Everyone else was having a glorious time. I finally gave it up as a bad job and wandered off. Outside, I paused for a moment in the darkness. There was no moon, but the black canopy overhead was covered with millions of stars. I was startled by their brilliance—everywhere I looked the winking and twinkling made the whole sky seem alive and almost touchable. I couldn't remember ever seeing a sky like this before, but then, maybe I had never looked. I started down the road past the enlisted men's tents, the gravel crunching under my feet. At the steps of my building, I paused for one last look upward and drank in the sky. Through the stillness of the night, I could hear faintly some ragged singing coming from the direction of the Officers' Club. As I climbed the three steps, they were starting another chorus of "The Three Old Maids From Canada."

Sheehan was off somewhere. I undressed in the darkness and lay on my cot, feeling a vague sense of unease. It was over for me, the war. It was continuing on, passing me by. The close, tight-knit group I had been with since flying school was breaking apart. How could I start over again with strangers? Even talking to friends and relatives back home was going to be difficult. They wouldn't understand. How could they? I remembered a conversation that had taken place during my brief visit home in December.

"Well, how many men do you have in the plane with you?"

"None."

"Who shoots the guns?"

"I do."

"How do you find your way without a navigator?"

"Just lucky, I guess."

Only this time the chasm between me and others was going to be much wider. It would have nothing to do with facts about airplanes and crews. The chasm was loss. I would be adrift from my comrades, severed from companionship so intense it was practically an interpenetration of each personality. With my friends and fellow pilots—Brooks and Little Henry, Tommy Byrnes and Tommy Molland—understanding and trust had grown so intimate that verbal communication was hardly necessary.

Our companionship had to do with outrageous living and dying—sudden, violent dying.

What I most feared about going home was being alone among people.

Finally, I dropped off and slept.

The next morning, I started on my final round of farewells, shaking hands and saying good-bye to the people who were really close to me—my Panama buddies who were staying on a while longer; Lam; and Tommy Molland. When we shook hands for the last time, Tommy said, "I wish we had flown another Black Flight together." I sensed that he had thought hard about something meaningful to say. Coming from him, that sentence was a full-blown speech. I choked up and could only mumble an incoherent reply.

As I sat in the recon car waiting for the others, I reflected on the time I had spent at San Severo and on my successes and failures. It seemed incredible to me that I had come here to San Severo less than six months before. In that time I had flown 303 hours of combat—sixty-one missions. I had ranged across Europe to Milan, Munich, Vienna, Budapest, Bucharest, and even to Russia. I had shot down eleven enemy aircraft and been awarded the Silver Star, the Distinguished Flying Cross with one oak-leaf cluster, and the Air Medal with seventeen oak-leaf clusters. The group had earned two Presidential Unit Citations during my stay. I had achieved a position of responsibility here. This was my place, where I was respected, where I belonged.

I thought of Johnson and Ricks and Reynolds, of Boyd, Jackson, Mansberger, Twig Byrnes, and Harry—all killed in action. I thought of Jones, who was lost on his first mission, and of Lockwood and Fitzpatrick, who were killed before they even got to fly a mission. None of them would be leaving San Severo.

Finally, the car started to roll. As we went past the stone pillars that served as a gate, I leaned out for one last look. There were the buildings, the tents, the dusty street, and the familiar figures moving to and from their daily tasks.

I felt like an old man.

I was twenty-one years old.

Epilogue

The 31st Fighter Group continued to fly missions from San Severo through October and November 1944. Enemy contacts were becoming less frequent, but they still occurred. In December, two 308th pilots shared an Me-262, the first victory over a jet in the Mediterranean Theater.

The last week in February 1945, the 31st Group left San Severo and moved to Mondolfo, north of Ancona and about two miles south of Fano. By April, one year after entering the strategic bombing fray, the 31st was reduced to flying tactical missions in support of the U.S. Fifth and the British Eighth armies.

The war in Europe ended on May 7, 1945. On July 15, the 31st left Mondolfo by ship and docked in Boston in August.

★

The 31st Fighter Group had joined the Fifteenth Air Force in the spring of 1944. At that time, the 82d Group was leading the theater in victories, with more than twice the 194 counted by the 31st. By war's end, a little more than a year later, the 31st had climbed to the top, with 571 air-combat victories. The group produced thirty-three aces including the top ace in the theater, Captain John Voll, who had twenty-one victories.

Of the eighteen pilots who had come out of Panama together, five became aces. Two of my closest friends were double aces: Jim Brooks got thirteen victories and Walter (Little Henry) Goehausen had ten. Five of my friends were shot down.

James "Stick" Thorsen was killed shortly after the war, while on a cross-country flight over Arizona.

Leland "Tommy" Molland was killed in Korea while riding in the rear seat of a T-33. What a terrible waste!

May their souls and those of all departed fighter pilots, of all countries and creeds, rest in peace.

And though they fell, they fell like stars,
Streaming splendor down the skies.

And After

In the process of preparing this manuscript, dusting off old pictures, going back through old records, and talking to friends who shared these times and events related herein, I often experienced the strange feeling of being back at San Severo. I heard a few bars of an Andrews Sisters song or the distinctive drone of the Mustang's Merlin engine just as it sounded then. The leap through the years was more than remembering; it was being there again with those young, eager faces and being one of them.

Once, while I was reading a passage to my wife, June, my voice broke and I could not continue. She waited silently while I—head down, tears welling up—fought for control. I think I was as surprised as she was. In forty-seven years, I had talked of those times often, without the slightest trace of grief.

It had its sobering moments, this research. At one point I located the telephone number of a fellow pilot whom I had not seen or spoken to since the war. But when I called him on the telephone, his widow told me that he had died three years before. I felt worse, when, after asking my name, she said, "Oh yes, he spoke of you often."

I still see Brooks regularly, Goehausen and Lam less frequently but no less enthusiastically. We often ponder the questions of success in aerial combat and escaping death, then and since.

On the subject of combat success and from the vantage point of half a century, I feel qualified to make some observations regarding flyers.

Not all pilots who flew fighter-type aircraft were fighter pilots.

A few learned that combat flying was not at all what they expected or wanted. Of these some adopted subtle ways of avoiding operational flying whenever possible.

Some were more interested in trying to live up to the fighter-pilot image than in being a fighter pilot. It is true that the typical fighter pilot drank too much and often expressed his individuality by outrageous behavior. But these characteristics were external symptoms, certainly not defining characteristics of the fighter pilot.

I believe that the proper fighter pilot, regardless of his off-duty antics, was first and foremost a fighter who happened also to be a pilot.

I consider it a myth that all World War II aces were superb pilots in the sense of being able to do precision aerobatics or other commonly accepted measures of airmanship. Perhaps they all could have been exceptional pilots, had they had the necessary time to develop those skills. But there were other, more important weapons to be brought to the combat arena. The aces had the confident air of the hunter, the steely eye. All knew instinctively the right moves to make in a combat situation, anticipating the actions and reactions of their adversaries. All were cool and decisive in action. They had lightning-quick reflexes and aggressively sought out the enemy wherever he could be found. Having these attributes wasn't an act, nor did they come out of a bottle. The aces' instinct and attitude were what General Adolph Galland of the Luftwaffe so eloquently described as the "spirit of attack." And, of course, luck played a small part, too. Luck took the ace where the action was and assigned him to a good machine.

I have never fully understood the nature of luck, random occurrence, or the will of God. Several times after the war I was involved in accidents or incidents where I thought, for a second or two, that I had had it. I don't know why I survived those incidents any more than I know why I survived the war.

★

We gather with our old mates at American Fighter Aces Association meetings or 31st Fighter Group reunions, and it is impossible to ignore the fact that the ranks are thinning. Contrary to what we all believed so long ago, we are not immortal. The words I wrote in the Foreword several years ago are truer today than they were then, and they will be truer still tomorrow: We are a dying breed, the World War II aviator, and soon we will all be gone.

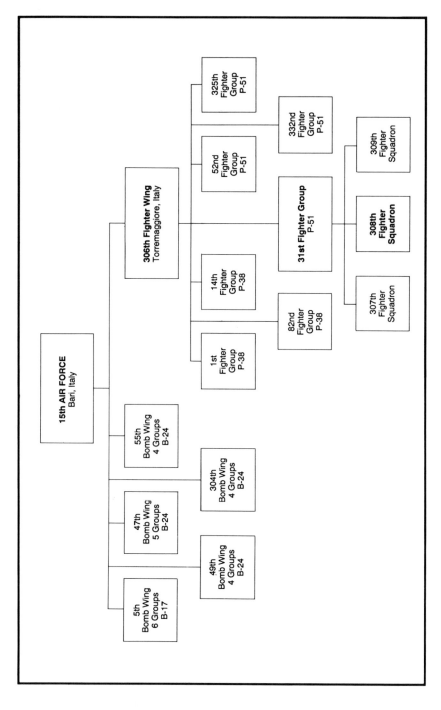

Mission List

Mission	Date	Duration (Hours)	Position	Target
1.	16 Apr. '44	4:20		Turnul Severin, Rumania
2.	18 Apr. '44	3:15		Udine, Italy
3.	20 Apr. '44	3:20		Trieste, Yugoslavia
4.	21 Apr. '44	5:05		Ploesti, Rumania
5.	23 Apr. '44	5:10		Wiener Neustadt, Austria
6.	24 Apr. '44	5:00		Ploesti, Rumania
7.	28 Apr. '44	3:50		Piombino, Italy
8.	29 Apr. '44	5:35		Toulon, France
9.	2 May '44	3:00		Castel Maggiore, Italy
10.	5 May '44	5:30		Ploesti, Rumania
11.	6 May '44	4:45		Brasov, Rumania
12.	10 May '44	4:50		Wiener Neustadt, Austria
13.	12 May '44	4:25		Piacenza, Italy
14.	13 May '44	4:00		Bolzano, Italy
15.	14 May '44	3:45		Piacenza, Italy
16.	17 May '44	4:15		Piombino, Italy
17.	19 May '44	4:00		Livorno, Italy
18.	22 May '44	3:10		Latisana, Italy

Duration

Mission	Date	(Hours)	Position	Target
19.	25 May '44	6:30		Toulon, France
20.	26 May '44	6:40	Flight Leader	Saint Etienne, France
21.	27 May '44	6:10	Flight Leader	Montpellier, France
22.	29 May '44	4:15	Flight Leader	Wiener Neustadt, Austria
23.	31 May '44	5:45	Flight Leader	Ploesti, Rumania
24.	2 June '44	5:00	Flight Leader	Oradea, Hungary
25.	4 June '44	3:00		Turin, Italy
26.	5 June '44	3:30		Bologna, Italy
27.	9 June '44	5:15		Munich, Germany
28.	10 June '44	4:00	Flight Leader	Trieste, Yugoslavia
29.	11 June '44	5:20		Constanza, Rumania
30.	13 June '44	5:15		Oberpfoffenhofen, Germany
31.	14 June '44	4:45	Flight Leader	Budapest, Hungary
32.	15 June '44	6:15		La Jasse, France
33.	16 June '44	5:15		Vienna, Austria
34.	23 June '44	5:00	Flight Leader	Ploesti, Rumania
35.	24 June '44	4:45		Bucharest, Rumania
36.	25 June '44	5:30	Flight Leader	Avignon, France
37.	26 June '44	4:30	Flight Leader	Vienna, Austria
38.	27 June '44	4:15		Budapest, Hungary
39.	28 June '44	4:45	Flight Leader	Bucharest, Rumania
40.	30 June '44	5:00		Blechhammer, Germany
41.	2 July '44	4:45	Flight Leader	Budapest, Hungary
42.	3 July '44	5:15		Bucharest, Rumania
43.	4 July '44	5:15	Flight Leader	Pitesti, Rumania
44.	20 July '44	5:00	Flight Leader	Friedrichshafen, Germany
45.	21 July '44	5:15	Flight Leader	Brux, Czechoslovakia
46.	22 July '44	5:15		Zilestia, Rumania (landed in Russia)
47.	25 July '44	5:15		Mielec, Poland (from Russia)
48.	26 July '44	4:45		Ploesti, Rumania (return from Russia)
49.	31 July '44	5:15	Squadron Leader	Bucharest, Rumania

		Duration		
Mission	**Date**	**(Hours)**	**Position**	**Target**
50.	3 Aug. '44	5:15	Flight Leader	Friedrichshafen, Germany
51.	7 Aug. '44	5:15	Squadron Leader	Blechhammer, Germany
52.	13 Aug. '44	5:00	Flight Leader	Toulon, France
53.	15 Aug. '44	3:30		Toulon, France
54.	16 Aug. '44	5:15	Flight Leader	Toulon, France
55.	18 Aug. '44	5:30		Ploesti, Rumania (Black Flight)
56.	20 Aug. '44	5:15	Squadron Leader	Oswiecim, Poland
57.	22 Aug. '44	5:30	Group Leader	Blechhammer, Germany
58.	26 Aug. '44	5:00	Squadron Leader	Bucharest, Rumania
59.	28 Aug. '44	4:30	Group Leader	Vienna, Austria
60.	2 Sept. '44	3:40	Flight Leader	Nis and Belgrade, Yugoslavia
61.	5 Sept. '44	4:30	Squadron Leader	Bucharest, Rumania

308th FIGHTER SQUADRON
31st FIGHTER GROUP
APO 520, U S ARMY

15 SEPTEMBER 1944

SUBJECT : COMBAT CLAIMS
TO   : WHOM IT MAY CONCERN

1. I CERTIFY THAT CAPTAIN ROBERT J. GOEBEL,
S/N 0-681645, HAS TO HIS CREDIT THE FOLLOWING
ENEMY AIRCRAFT ON THE DATES INDICATED.

29 MAY 1944	DESTROYED	1 ME-109
23 JUNE 1944	DESTROYED	1 ME-109
27 JUNE 1944	DESTROYED	1 ME-110
2 JULY 1944	PROBABLY DESTROYED	1 ME-109
3 JULY 1944	DESTROYED	1 ME-109
20 JULY 1944	DESTROYED	1 ME-109
3 AUGUST 1944	DESTROYED	1 ME-109
18 AUGUST 1944	DESTROYED	3 ME-109
22 AUGUST 1944	DESTROYED	1 ME-109
28 AUGUST 1944	DESTROYED	1 ME-109

2. ALL OF THE ABOVE LISTED AIRCRAFT WERE DE-
STROYED IN AERIAL COMBAT.

Jack D. Edge
Captain, Air Corps
Operations Officer

Acknowledgements

John Donne wrote, in one of his devotions, that no man is an island. He might have added that no author is, either. Any printed page has been influenced by many known and unknown contributors in subtle and, oftentimes, not-so-subtle ways. In this case the first contributors were my wife and children, who consistently encouraged, almost badgered, me to write down the stories of my youth and military experiences.

After I began to put pen to paper, I discovered ruefully that time had taken its toll; I often had to consult records and others' recollections to supplement my memory. The staff at the USAF Historical Research Center and the USAF Visual Information Library were especially helpful. Jack Edge; Charley Bushick; and, of course, Jim Brooks and Walt Goehausen were very generous in sharing their recollections, information, and photos. Ray Toliver provided untold encouragement and assistance.

But the one who really turned out to be indispensable was the well-known author-historian, Eric Hammel. When I look now at the manuscript I originally sent him, I am surprised that he even bothered to finish reading it, let alone to guide me in improving it. Through his criticism and encouragement, I finally managed to complete this work. I know I would never have been able to do it without him, and I will always be grateful for his help.

For the superb rendering of my eleventh victory that adorns this volume's dust jacket, I would also like to thank David Howarth, a fine aviation artist who deserves—and I am certain will attain—widespread renown.

So to all who aided in some degree, large or small, I proffer a heartfelt thank-you.